Martyn Whittock is half-Welsh (on his mother's side) and he was raised on stories of Wales. He graduated in Politics from Bristol University, has taught history for over thirty years and is currently the curriculum leader for Spiritual, Moral, Social and Cultural Development at a Wiltshire secondary school. He is the author of thirty-nine books, his most recent being *A Brief History of Life in the Middle Ages* (2009), *A Brief History of the Third Reich* (2011) and *The Viking Blitzkrieg* (2013), the last co-written with his eldest daughter. His specialist area of interest is early medieval British history, the period in which most of the early Celtic myths were first recorded in written form. As well as being a teacher, he is also a Lay Minister in the Church of England. He lives in Wiltshire, in a family where things Celtic and spiritual are high profile, with his eldest daughter working for the devolved Welsh government, his youngest daughter reading Theology at Cambridge and his wife being the daughter of the one-time Methodist minister of Tonypandy, south Wales.

Recent titles in the series

A BRIEF GUIDE TO

Celtic Myths & Legends

Martyn Whittock

RUNNING PRESS
PHILADELPHIA · LONDON

ROBINSON

First published in Great Britain in 2013 by Robinson

3 5 7 9 10 8 6 4

Copyright © Martyn Whittock, 2013

A CIP catalogue record for this book
is available from the British Library.

ISBN 978-1-78033-892-7

Robinson
An imprint of
Little, Brown Book Group
Carmelite House
50 Victoria Embankment
London EC4Y 0DZ

An Hachette UK Company

www.hachette.co.uk
www.littlebrown.co.uk

First Published in the United States in 2013 by Running Press Book Publishers
A member of the Perseus Books Group

Books published by Running Press are available at special discounts for bulk purchases
in the United States by corporations, institutions and other organizations. For more
information, please contact the Special Markets Department at the Perseus Books Group,
2300 Chestnut Street, Suite 200, Philadelphia, PA 19103, or call
(800) 810-4145, ext. 5000, or email special.markets@perseusbooks.com.

US ISBN: 978-0-7624-4807-4
US Library of Congress Control Number: 2013931826

10 9 8 7 6 5 4 3 2

Digit on the right indicates the number of this printing

Running Press Book Publishers
2300 Chestnut Street
Philadelphia, PA 19103-4371

Visit us on the web!
www.runningpress.com

Typeset by TW Typesetting, Plymouth, Devon
Printed and bound in Great Britain by CPI Group (UK) Ltd, Croydon CR0 4YY

Papers used by Robinson are from well-managed forests and other responsible sources

MIX
Paper from
responsible sources
FSC® C104740

CONTENTS

To the memory of my mother, Margaret Whittock, née Jones, and John Haydn 'Dee' Jones, my *tad-cu*, with love.

And to the Shields and Gibbons families, with thanks for their friendship and support.

ACKNOWLEDGEMENTS

I am grateful for assistance from Wiltshire County Library Service and was especially grateful to Bradford on Avon Library while carrying out research for this book. I wish to thank my agent, Robert Dudley, and Duncan Proudfoot, my editor at Constable & Robinson, for all their encouragement and support.

As always, my wife, Christine, and our daughters, Hannah and Esther, supported me with their interest and encouragement. I am also grateful to Hannah and Esther for reading sections of this book in manuscript form, to Jayne Gibbons for reading the Welsh chapters and to Patrice McConnell, the Head of Irish at St Columb's College, Derry, for checking my Irish. It goes without saying that all errors are my own.

Martyn Whittock

INTRODUCTION

This book examines the surviving evidence regarding the mythology of the 'Celtic world'. We will explore later exactly what is meant by both 'Celtic' and 'mythology', but at this point it may help to briefly explain that the focus of this book is on the evidence for pre-Christian beliefs that later appeared in a number of written and oral medieval and later sources. The structure of the book is designed in order to achieve this. Having identified what is meant by the key terms referred to above, the book next explores what evidence exists regarding the pre-Christian religious beliefs of 'Celtic' communities. The nature of this evidence means that much of it derives from Roman-period inscriptions and writings. The bridge between this and the surviving (later) medieval evidence is provided by an outline of the seasonal festivals that derived from these earlier beliefs and continued (albeit heavily adapted) into the medieval period. These chapters are followed by examination of the evidence for mythologies and myth-related legends that have survived in Ireland (where the medieval sources are most detailed), Wales (where they are less developed but still substantial) and finally Scotland, Cornwall, the Isle of Man and Brittany, where the medieval written evidence is less substantial (or non-existent) but where earlier mythology can be deduced from later folklore and written records from neighbouring communities.

What needs emphasizing here is that none of these medieval (and later folklore) records of Celtic myths were written or communicated by people who subscribed to the earlier pre-Christian religious beliefs. It is sometimes asserted that paganism lingered for centuries, despite the Christian conversions of the Late Roman period or the Early Middle Ages and that these recorded mythologies are evidence of that. In fact, nothing could be further from the truth and the Christian recorders of these earlier belief systems would have been horrified at the suggestion. Indeed, it has convincingly been demonstrated that there was no hidden substratum of active pagan belief beneath the surface of medieval Christianity.[1] What survived were memories of old beliefs, tribal traditions, 'heroic stories', supernatural characters and themes that were no longer the focus of active belief. Or, if they were still believed in, they had been awkwardly bolted onto a framework of dominant Christian belief. In short, a medieval Irish traveller might still believe in a being called 'the Washer at the Ford'; a Hebridean farmer's wife might leave out an offering to the *gruagach*, a form of brownie; a Breton might think that a being called Ankou ferried the souls of the dead; a Cornish fisherman might believe in mermaids; but all were practising Christians who maintained these reworked and downgraded old beliefs and superstitions without for a moment considering these beings as gods or goddesses. They were not pagans who had simply fallen in line with Christian officialdom; rather, they were devoted Christians who still carried remnants of old beliefs that had long since been stripped of their devotion and potency. This was a rather compromised Christianity, not a continuation of paganism. And when Irish monks recorded community traditions it was traditional identity that was being preserved, not pagan beliefs. This is particularly apparent when the former deities appeared in these accounts as ancient heroes or heroines and were not accorded any divine status (particularly apparent in the Welsh sources); or, if they were, they were represented as defeated old deities who had given way to the Overlordship of Christ; or were reconstructed as Christian saints, as in the cases of St Brigid (Brigit) and St Gobnet (based on the god of smiths, Goibhniu), although this may have been further complicated in the case of the former by the existence of a real woman of this name in the early Irish Church; and in the case of Arthur there may have been a conflation of semi-historical and mythical figures.

Since none of these myths were written down by pagan believers and therefore all were recorded, reworked or adapted by later (sometimes much later) medieval Christian writers, it is helpful to know when they were recorded and the nature of the sources. Consequently, alongside the retelling of the myths, readers will also find references to the sources in which they were recorded, along with some assessment of the way in which these later myths connected with evidence for earlier beliefs and evidence from other Celtic areas. To make matters more accessible the titles of written sources are given in modern English and their original titles (Latin, Irish, Welsh, Breton, etc.) follow in brackets.

I

WHO ARE AND WERE THE CELTS?

In this book we shall be exploring the myths and legends of the Celts. However, before this can be attempted, a number of issues need clarification. The first is the question of who are and were the 'Celts'? The second is what do we mean by the terms *myth/mythology* and *legend*? This second issue is far from simple but it is straightforward compared with the first.

Who are the 'Celts' today?

Today there is a generally accepted popular understanding of who we mean by 'Celtic' peoples and communities. The term has become a standard one to describe the communities of the Atlantic coastlines of Europe, who are distinct from the historically dominant populations of England, France and Spain. When the *Festival Interceltique de Lorient* (in Breton: *Goulelioù Etrekeltiek an Oriant*) takes place annually at Lorient in Brittany, France, it draws together musicians, singers, painters, dancers and other artists from across the 'Celtic world'. Principally represented are those from Brittany, Cornwall, Cumbria, Ireland, the Isle of Man, Scotland and Wales. Together these make up the most obvious modern communities who claim a 'Celtic' identity. Less obviously Celtic to non-attendees at such festivals are the visitors from Asturias and Galicia, in northern Spain, and from Cape Breton Island, Nova Scotia, Canada. In addition, there are those from the worldwide Celtic diaspora. What all these disparate groups perhaps have in common is a sense of being different from the majority populations of the countries within which they reside, alongside a sense of a harder-to-define set of common characteristics expressed in a love of traditional music, poetry and use of instruments such as the harp and bagpipes.

Those from Ireland, western Scotland and the Isle of Man share a linguistic heritage, speaking (or, in the case of the Isle of Man, reviving) languages – Irish, Scottish-Gaelic, Manx – that form part of a language group described as *Gaelic* or *Goidelic*. Each of these languages derives from Middle Irish and originally from Old or Primitive Irish. A dialect of Scottish-Gaelic is still spoken on Cape Breton and in other areas of Nova Scotia and is known as Canadian-Gaelic.

Gaelic or *Goidelic* is one of the two branches of Insular Celtic (Celtic languages originating in the British Isles). The other branch is *Brittonic* or *Brythonic* and includes Breton, Cornish, Welsh and the extinct Cumbric language that was once spoken in what is now north-west England. Pictish – the language of eastern and northern Scotland until it became extinct *c.*900 – was probably also a Brittonic language. For the modern populations of Wales and Brittany their Brittonic language is still a living and active one. Even away from the Gaelic-speaking western parts of Scotland there are many people whose roots go back to a

British heritage (which once included a Brittonic language) that was distinct from that of the Anglo-Saxons, even if they do not now speak Scottish-Gaelic.

In contrast, those from Cornwall and the Isle of Man at the *Festival Interceltique*, and at similar events, represent communities whose languages – Brittonic Cornish and Gaelic Manx – have died out in the recent past (the first in the eighteenth century, the second in the 1970s) but have since been revived.

The Anglo-Saxons frequently referred to the Cornish as the 'West Welsh' and so identified a common sense of identity that united those in the extreme west of the areas experiencing Anglo-Saxon inroads. And whether they are now speaking Gaelic or Brittonic languages or not, many of these communities have a history that sets them apart from the English-speaking culture that has dominated the British Isles for over a millennium. This conflict and competition, both military and cultural, gives them a shared sense of identity and also of vulnerability. Even when English has become the dominant language, it has not extinguished a sense of separate identity. Those from Cape Breton share a double 'Celtic' connection. The name of the place links it to Brittany via French colonization in the seventeenth century, while its living Celtic link is to the Gaelic-speaking Highland Scots who settled there in the early nineteenth century and among whose descendants a dialect of Scottish-Gaelic still survives. In Brittany, as in Britain, many modern Celtic speakers too may well feel that their linguistic heritage is under pressure from a rival and more dominant language; in this case, French. Consequently, in all these modern 'Celtic' communities there is a distinct and growing sense of self-awareness that is as much fuelled by defining themselves by what they are *not* as by what they are. The threat of the loss of cultural identity has accelerated attempts to preserve that identity and, indeed, to revive it where it has declined.

Other identities, though, are a little more complex. Among the Scots of central and southern Scotland there is an identity that is deeply influenced by English culture. Indeed, Anglo-Saxon settlers heavily infiltrated southern Scotland in the sixth and seventh centuries and so many Scots 'Celtic pipers' may, in fact, have Anglo-Saxon DNA, as well as coming from a community that speaks English. It is interesting that the rising profile of Scottish nationalism in the twenty-first century has led to an increase in the use of the label 'Celtic' to describe Scots, despite the complexity of Scotland's linguistic, historical and cultural past.[1] Those from Cumbria are a population who have no living or revived 'Celtic language' and whose origins actually combine influences from a British (non-English) past – the name Cumbria derives from a term indicating a Welsh-speaking area – and the effect of Anglo-Saxon and Norse Viking settlement. In Galicia there is no survival of any language related to the other 'Celtic' languages of the Atlantic fringe, and the Galician language is, in fact, a Romance language (i.e. derived from Latin) that is related to Portuguese and originated in medieval Galician-Portuguese and Castilian. Similarly, in Asturias, the Asturian and Eonavian languages derive from Romance languages of the Western Iberian language group. As a result, there is some controversy over whether Galicia and Asturias should be regarded as part of the 'Celtic' culture zone and they are not included in this study.

What is clear is that the so-called Insular Celtic Languages that still form a vital part of Breton, Irish, Welsh and western Scottish identity are the survivals of a once much more extensive set of related languages known today as Continental Celtic. Until the Late Roman period these languages connected people living in a great arc of central and western Europe, including Britain and Ireland, modern Spain and Portugal, France and northern Italy.[2] It extended into the Balkans and Asia Minor and had outliers in eastern Europe. Of these languages, perhaps the most famous was Gaulish or Gallic, which was spoken until the sixth century in what is now France. All these languages are now extinct but they demonstrate the wide-ranging interconnectedness of what was once a huge number of ancient communities.

What this brief survey demonstrates is that there are sufficient threads of interconnected language, culture and historical experiences for it to make sense to regard many of these areas as linked. As a result, we can identify a set of modern communities that, for all their differences, we can conveniently group under the umbrella term 'Celtic'. In reality, though, the modern diversity among these groups is arguably as great as their common linguistic and historical characteristics. Nevertheless, at least the term helps to define the area of study and challenges us to explore whether there is a similarly common mythological heritage that connects these different areas.

Historically, though, the matter gets more complex still. This is because almost none of the communities whose descendants are today described as 'Celts' ever originally used the term (or anything like it) to describe themselves. The umbrella term is itself a relatively modern invention, and this is hard to accept by communities for whom its modern usage has become very meaningful.

The historic 'Celts'

The term 'Celt' is ancient – it is just not one used in the past by those who today are often described as 'Celtic'. The Greeks used the word *'Keltoí'* to describe Gaulish people who lived near the Mediterranean coast from the sixth century BC onwards, and it is found in the writings of Hecataeus and Herodotus. In time the term came to be applied to all those speaking related languages in an area stretching from Galatia (in modern Turkey) to what is now the Iberian Peninsula; this included large swathes of central and western Europe, along with areas further east. By the first century BC, Roman accounts used a Latinized form, '*Celtae*', to refer to the people of Gaul and surrounding areas. Julius Caesar referred to inhabitants of Gaul who in their own language were called '*Celtae*' but to the Romans were known as '*Galli*'. The first-century Roman poet Martial claimed to be 'half-Celtic' and 'half-Iberian'. Consequently, there does seem to have been a cultural group that we can call the Celts and there appears to be good reason to assume that this recognizable cultural group existed from at least the later Bronze Age. It seems that loose bands of nomads, first identifiable on the Hungarian Plain *c*.1300 BC, had by the time of the Roman Empire influenced huge areas of Europe north of the river Po and become famous as warriors, metal workers and traders. Such was their power that, as well as trading with the empires of first Greece and then Rome, they also raided and threatened these empires.[3] By this time they had drawn into their cultural orbit a large number of different peoples who had probably at one time exhibited different cultural characteristics but over time came to share features of a more common culture that we now tend to call 'Celtic'. These included related languages and social and political institutions.[4]

In many modern accounts those groups living east of the Rhine in the Roman period are identified as 'Germans' and so are distinct from the 'Celts'. This is a misunderstanding caused by Caesar's efforts to impose labels of difference on closely related ancient tribal groups. In contrast, the Roman geographer Strabo insisted that Gauls west of the Rhine and Germans living east of the river were in fact closely related. The question is: can we identify 'Celts' in terms of their art and archaeology?[5]

The answer to this question is frequently 'yes' and the evidence that is presented in support of this idea is often described by archaeologists as Urnfield Culture, Hallstatt Culture and La Tène Culture. Each one of these terms is a modern label used to describe common features of material culture found by archaeologists across a wide area of central Europe. Urnfield Culture is associated with burying the bones of the cremated dead in urns in cemeteries of flat graves (i.e. not burial mounds). It was found in eastern and central Europe and northern Italy from the twelfth century BC and eventually spread as far as the Ukraine, western Europe and Scandinavia. Hallstatt Culture is named after a site in the Upper Austrian region of Salzkammergut and has been used to describe the period in the Early Iron Age in central Europe extending from the eighth to the sixth centuries BC. It is associated with iron swords and daggers, iron axes, armour and chariot burials. The distribution of these finds falls into various sub-groups. La Tène Culture describes the successor to Hallstatt and occupies the period from the fifth to the first centuries BC. It takes its name from the archaeological site of La Tène on the north side of Lake Neuchâtel, in Switzerland. A Late Iron Age culture, it influenced art and other aspects of society from France to Romania. It is associated with fine metalwork, in iron, bronze and gold, that is decorated with spirals and interlaced patterns, along with stylized curvilinear designs that represent animals and foliage, and triskeles (three interlocked spirals or three curved lines radiating from a centre). The geometric patterns found in Hallstatt Culture also continued. These are found on elite objects such as bronze vessels, shields, horse harness and jewellery.[6]

It is true to say that these recognizable archaeological characteristics do generally fall within the areas where Celtic languages were probably spoken. Therefore we may well conclude that 'there is likely to have been some feeling of common identity across Europe, at the level of a shared language'[7] and that this was reflected in some aspects of art and culture too. But we should not exaggerate the unity of this ancient 'Celtica'. In northern and western Britain, in southern Ireland, in western France and in Spain and Portugal Urnfield, Hallstatt and La Tène Culture 'made minimal impact'.[8] It seems that not all Celtic speakers shared equally in the demonstration of what we now tend to call 'Celtic culture' as measured by archaeology. And, conversely, it is likely that not everyone who wore a La Tène-style brooch spoke Celtic. History is likely to have been less tidy than some modern museum labels and the neat maps of artefact distribution found in many modern studies. What is certainly clear is that the ancient 'Celts' were composed of competing and conflicting tribes; and most probably had little awareness of any pan-Celtic identity. Celtic unity is found more in the eye of the modern beholder than in the reality of ancient competing tribal politics and alliances. People living in central Europe may have shared a language that was related to that spoken in the Atlantic zone but there is good reason to think that this did *not* make them culturally the same. And it is highly unlikely that they ever described themselves as 'Celtic'.

Furthermore, what is particularly fascinating is that the term was never used of the people living in the British Isles or those communities derived from there (for example, the Bretons). In other words, the ancestors of not one of the modern communities we now call 'Celtic' were called this by Greek or Roman writers and they never used the word to describe themselves. There is, in contrast, a strong case to be made that insular Celtic identity was really a product of nineteenth-century nationalism and was further developed by the politics of the twentieth century.[9] Today all the surviving 'Celtic' languages, literature, traditions, mythology and legends are part of the identity of people whose ancestors never once called themselves 'Celtic' and were never called this by others. The sole and partial exception is that of the Asturians and Galicians, who may have been described as '*Celtae*' and whose descendants have some cultural characteristics that connect them to the modern

'Celtic world'. However, their Celtic language is now extinct and so that vital thread of continuity is broken.

Nevertheless, 'Celtic' is still a useful word. As we shall see there are clues that suggest that there were some common religious beliefs among these disparate groups of people as they were recorded by Roman writers and are discovered by modern archaeologists. As a result, it is reasonable to suggest that some of these beliefs may have influenced the mythology that survived to be recorded in the medieval period and that we are aware of today. In addition, there are real common features and connections in related languages, features of archaeology and history that link the so-called modern Celtic peoples of Brittany, Cornwall, Ireland, the Isle of Man, Wales, western Scotland, and even Asturias and Galicia. This is true even if they never historically called themselves 'Celts'. If we did not have the term, we would probably have to invent one in order to describe this cultural unity. The term 'Celtic' will serve the purpose, because it has meaning even if not antiquity. When attempting to sum up the early medieval peoples who inhabited the British Isles and Brittany the relevant University of Cambridge department chose to call itself 'Anglo-Saxon, Norse and *Celtic*' because the latter word is still a useful tool. We just have to accept its limitations and not attempt to make it carry too great a weight of expectations.

Mythology and legend

As we shall see, the people who are the focus of this exploration of Celtic mythology and legend have left us a varied body of evidence about their beliefs. Some of these may be the remnants of very old belief systems that pre-date the medieval conversion to Christianity. Others are probably local variations of Roman and Greek ideas but with a local appearance and form. There are many common themes that crop up in the mythologies of the various Celtic peoples and a number of these may reflect similar religious ideas that were once found across the 'Celtic world'. Others are peculiar to particular Celtic communities. We should not expect uniformity and – for all the common features – we will not find it. This is because there is no evidence to suggest that there ever was a uniform ancient Celtic religion. But there were similarities, and some common gods and goddesses (see Chapters 2 and 3), and the evidence reflects this.

When we use the term '*mythology*' we are using a word that has several meanings. Some use it to describe stories associated with religious rites and rituals, which they seek to explain and give meaning to. Others see myths as accounts that, to those who retell them, explain the events of an ancient past when the world was not as it is today. Usually these myths take the form of narratives: they are stories that illustrate significant beliefs. They tend to have religious content and intentions.

On the other hand, the term '*legend*' tends to be used of accounts that are thought to be true by the person retelling the story but the story itself is set in a more recent world, one like that in which it is being told. In contrast, a '*folk tale*' is not necessarily considered to be true by the person communicating it.[10]

As these terms are used in this book, their general meaning is:

'*Myth*'/'*mythology*': stories, usually religious, that explain origins, why things are as they are, and the nature of the spiritual. In these we will find stories of gods, goddesses, other supernatural beings, creation stories, and the like. In this book the term refers to beliefs derived from pre-Christian Celtic religions.

'*Legends*': stories that attempt to explain historical events and that may involve historical characters but that are told in a non-historical way. They may include supernatural events but tend to attempt an account of more recent times (from the perspective of the storyteller). In these we will find heroes whose exploits include both the mundane and the semi-supernatural, protagonists whose lives are adapted in order to make a particular point, the simplified or construed origins of dynasties and kingdoms, and the representation of heroes and villains in order to teach moral lessons. At times, characters from older mythologies also appear in these accounts and these are primarily the kind of Celtic legend that is explored in this book.

'*Folk tales*': accounts such as cautionary tales or stories which attempt to explain aspects of society or ritual. However, they lack the religious focus of a myth and the semi-historical focus of a legend. As such, they are fictional stories intended to entertain or instruct. The folk tales referred to in this book are those that contain references to Celtic mythological characters and themes.

2

THE GODS AND RELIGION OF THE CELTS: THE EUROPEAN PICTURE

Celtic mythology arose from the religious beliefs of the people we now commonly call 'Celts'. Using the evidence of archaeology and the written records of Greek and Roman writers, we can explore something of the religious outlook of the pre-Christian Celtic peoples of Europe.

However, it is important to remember that, while the people we today describe as the ancient Celts shared certain features of language, belief and culture, they did not constitute a unified group. As a result, any examination of the evidence produces both unifying features and significant differences. This has to be kept in mind when attempting to identify the religious beliefs and practices of pre-Christian Celtic peoples. As a consequence, it is not possible to set out a comprehensive picture of Celtic religious beliefs and practices. Nevertheless, we can still identify the main outline of pre-Christian 'Celtic religion'; or rather the beliefs that were held by a number of different groups across the so-called 'Celtic' areas of Europe. However, this is not the same as being able to describe a single Celtic religious system.[1]

The gods of the Gauls

Of all the Celtic peoples, we know most about the Gauls (of, roughly speaking, modern France) as they interacted with the Roman Empire. Julius Caesar, writing in the first century BC about the religious beliefs of the tribes of Gaul, commented that Mercury was the chief god, followed by Apollo, Mars, Jupiter and Minerva. He went on to expand this by explaining what the Gauls believed about these gods: Mercury invented the arts and was also god of journeys and of commerce; Apollo was a healer god; Mars a god of war; Jupiter was thought to rule the heavens and presumably had oversight of weather; Minerva was goddess of arts and crafts. This all sounds straightforward. Caesar also referred to Celtic religious practices being overseen by a triumvirate of druids (acting as priests and judges), ovates (who acted as prophets) and bards (responsible for keeping track of ancestry and of community lore). A similar account can also be found in the first-century BC writings of Poseidonius.[2] However, Caesar's account of Celtic deities is very problematic. First, it used Roman names and gives us no idea of what the Gaulish Celts actually called their deities. Secondly, it assumed that the divine attributes of Gaulish deities were easily translatable into terms familiar to a Roman readership. Thirdly, and most significantly, it was too simplistic. As we will see, while there were some parallels between Celtic and Roman deities, the two sets of beliefs were very different in many areas and, furthermore, there was no simple formula that described the deities worshipped and the religious practices followed throughout Gaul. The situation was, as we shall see, much more complex than this in Gaul and even more so across the 'Celtic world', where there existed a great diversity of belief and practice.[3]

Indeed, one of the most striking characteristics of Gaulish religion is how locally focused it was. With the coming of Roman literacy those dedicating altars and temples soon adopted the Roman pattern of setting up carved dedications that revealed the names of the gods and goddesses being honoured. Studies of these inscriptions reveal that many names of divinities appeared only once. There was also a tendency for names to cluster in certain geographical areas when they appeared a number of times. This is highly significant since it indicates, first, that there were many more gods and goddesses than Caesar alluded to and, secondly, that many of them were very localized. Far from being general gods of the Celtic pantheon, they were the local gods and goddesses of individual tribes and clans. In a number of inscriptions this tribal nature was explicitly stated. So, *dea Tricoria* was the goddess of the *Tricorii*, who were a people living between the river Rhone and the Alps. One Gallic deity, Teutates or Toutatis, actually had a name derived from the word *teuta/touta/tota*, meaning 'tribe'.[4] This suggests that there were, in fact, a huge number of deities who were thought to have very local areas of responsibility and who were closely connected with a particular community. Later Irish mythology referred to deities who married the local goddess of the land and who were clearly regarded as tribal protectors.

Yet things may not have been quite so anarchic and lacking in cohesion. There is plenty of evidence that certain gods had similar functions but were known by different names in different locations. This may suggest different gods performing a limited range of essential functions. However, it may also indicate the belief in a related set of deities that were called by different names in different areas. Consequently, one god or goddess may have been represented by different names that were appropriated by different communities. As we will see with regard to Irish mythology, while a goddess such as Boann might have been particularly associated with the area of the river Boyne, a god such as the Daghda was widely accepted across Irish communities. Similar examples of deities with obviously widespread acceptance could be cited for Wales, in the form of gods such as Manawyddan son of Llŷr and brother of the god Brân; or the sun-god Lleu. And when an example such as the latter was known in Ireland as Lugh Lámh-fada (Lugh of the Long Arm, or, literally, the Long Hand), in Wales as Lleu, and in Gaul as Lugus or Lug,[5] there is strong evidence that the worship of certain Celtic deities was a common feature of a number of communities separated by very great distances. This needs to be set alongside the evidence suggesting scattered and localized deities.

It is possible to make sense of this apparent contradiction between local tribal gods and gods who were worshipped over large distances by suggesting that there was a hierarchy of divinities in which sky gods, sun gods and mother goddesses were worshipped across tribal boundaries and had similar characteristics and names; while below this layer of high gods localized deities were venerated in particular areas.[6] Some may have started as localized gods or goddesses and then become more popular owing to socio-economic factors that led to the expansion of their cult across a wide geographical area. An example of this would be Nehalennia, who appeared originally to have been a maritime goddess of the coastal Netherlands (her name means 'steerswoman') and whose cult spread with the enhanced trade of the Roman Empire until it could be found as far away as Rouen (France) and the vicinity of Freising (Germany). A complex goddess, Nehalennia was associated with both seafaring and fertility. The dog, so frequently depicted as her companion, suggests that it – and she – had a role as guardian-protector and possibly healer.[7]

The sky and sun gods

Sky gods were depicted in different, though related, guises across the 'Celtic world'. Sometimes the depiction was of a warrior horseman, and sometimes the god was associated with a disc or sun wheel; at other times the dominant symbol was the swastika. Incidentally, this symbol was later associated in Germanic pagan religion with Thunor/Thor, who was a weather god – hence 'thunder' – and may once have been the chief god until displaced by the cult of Woden/Odin. A Celtic god whose name meant 'thunder' was Taranis; in Welsh and Breton the word for thunder is *taran*. In a number of Roman-era inscriptions Taranis was explicitly identified as the equivalent of Roman Jupiter. In these cases he was clearly considered an important deity with authority over weather and the sky in general. The first-century Roman poet Lucan thought that Taranis was a dominant Celtic deity. It is difficult to decide whether he was correct since the evidence is contradictory; the surviving inscriptions are both geographically widespread and few in number for a divinity whose importance was allegedly widely recognized. So it is uncertain whether Lucan was right, particularly as he himself never visited Gaul and probably drew his information from other Classical sources. At Tours and Orgon (both France) dedications to 'Thunder' were probably intended as references to this deity. The same probably applied to dedications to the 'Thunderer' at Böckingen and Godramstein (western Germany) and also at Scardona (Croatia).[8] This last inscription, along with another from Thauron (France), explicitly equated Taranis with Jupiter, which lends support to the interpretation of Lucan mentioned earlier. Taranis may also have had connections with the Underworld since a medieval monastic commentator on Lucan (living in Berne, Switzerland) equated Taranis with Dis Pater (or Pluto), the god of the Underworld.

The sun god Lugh (Ireland), Lleu (Wales), Lugus or

Lug (Gaul) was also clearly a significant deity. Apparent in the Latin place name Lugudunum, the name also gave rise to surviving place names such as Laon and Lyon (both France), Leiden (the Netherlands), Legnica (Poland) and Luguvalium, the Roman name for Carlisle (England). A similar concern with solar imagery can be discerned in depictions of those gods who were regarded as equivalents of Roman Apollo. One such was Belenus (whose worship was found in southern Gaul, in the eastern Alps and in northern Italy). Another god whose name was substituted for Apollo was Grannus (who was often paired with a goddess named Sirona, or 'star'). This deity was also credited with healing powers (see below). However, despite the prevalence of solar imagery and deities associated with the sun, there is little evidence for sun worship among Celtic peoples and no real evidence for this in later Irish and Welsh mythology either.[9]

The gods of the mountains
Inscriptions at Roman-era shrines in a number of mountain locations reveal the names of deities that were clearly associated with these commanding geographical features. In some cases the Celtic names are unknown, since the inscriptions simply refer to Jupiter (the Roman god) alongside a tribal name (implying 'Jupiter of the ... tribe'). Examples include Jupiter Brixianus in the Italian alps, Jupiter Ladicus in north-west Spain, and Jupiter Poeninus in the vicinity of the Great St Bernard Pass, Switzerland. Others, though, are more specifically named, such as Latobius in southern Austria, and Uxellinus, also in Austria.[10]

The mother goddesses
Mother goddesses occurred prominently in Celtic religious iconography. They often appeared in threes as the *deae matres* (this threefold form being a feature of a number of Celtic female deities) and were often depicted nursing or

bathing babies. Sometimes the mother goddesses appeared more matronly and were associated with baskets of fruit (*cornuacopiae*). In this form they were portrayed in the Rhineland (Germany) and clearly had attributes of fertility that were also generally associated with fertility gods and goddesses of farming and horticulture. In Burgundy the goddess Epona – worshipped across a wide area – was also identified as having maternal characteristics via a horse suckling a foal. The threefold *deae matres* were named the *matronae* in northern Italy and parts of Germany; they were often associated with a particular area or people. At Nîmes (France) goddesses named the Nemausicae were venerated, as were the Treverae at Trier (Germany), the Matronis Assingenehis in the Rhineland and the Matres Glanicae in Provence (France).

Sometimes a mother goddess was depicted singly, as at Crozant and Naix (both France); a similar statue of a single mother has been found at Trier and, as at Naix, was depicted with a dog and fruit.

The gods of fertility and the natural world
A number of cult statues from Gaul show divinities whose attributes seem connected with fertility and abundance. At Entrains, in Burgundy, a god was carved holding a goblet of wine along with a purse and a platter of fruit. The same site also produced a similar image holding two large loaves of bread. Also in Burgundy, at St Aubin des Chaumes, a god was depicted holding a pot, an amphora and a cornucopia filled with fruit. On a table were set three cakes, one large and two smaller.[11] A number of such gods were also accompanied by a ram-horned snake that appears to have combined attributes of fertility, regeneration and Underworld connections.

Some of these gods were associated with the Roman god Mercury, who was associated with commercial success. In Gaulish religion this association made Mercury a fertility god as well as one overseeing commerce. At Glanum, south of Avignon (France), he was partnered with a fertility goddess called Rosmerta, whose name meant 'great provider'. This pairing may be based on a Celtic association of sun god with tribal fertility deity such as is found in later Irish mythology, in which the god Lugh was married to a female deity described as the sovereignty of Ireland. At Le Donon, in the Vosges mountains (France), a deity interpreted as the equivalent of Mercury was worshipped as a mountain god, which probably suggests that he was believed to have authority over nature. At Bonn (Germany) the composite god worshipped was named Mercury-Gebrinius, and was clearly linked to a local deity. A similarly partnered god was named Mercury-Cissonius, a deity worshipped in places as far apart as Köln (Germany) and Saintes, in south-west France. Cissonius on his own was worshipped at Metz, in north-east France. Occasionally, this god was depicted as three-headed or three-phallused; the number three being frequently found as a special number in Celtic religious beliefs. In southern France a god named Sucellus (depicted with a hammer atop a long shaft) appears to have had mixed attributes. These included connections with woodland and fertility since he was sometimes given emblems otherwise associated with Silvanus (the Roman god of the woods) and he was, in some areas, depicted as protector of the wine trade.

The antlered Gaulish god Cernunnos was also sometimes associated with Mercury, as at Lyon and Reims (both France). Cernunnos was often depicted as sitting cross-legged and feeding serpents; in a similar way Mercury was depicted as sitting cross-legged at Puy-de-Touges (France), and at Néris-les-Bains (France) Mercury was depicted with a ram-horned serpent across his knees.[12]

The horse goddess Epona (whose name meant 'horse') clearly had some attributes associated with warfare, or at least appreciated by the military (see below), but she also had characteristics associated with mother goddesses and with fertility. She was often depicted in association with a cornucopia, corn and fruits of various kinds. In these characteristics her depiction may be compared with that of mother goddesses. Like these, she was sometimes represented in multiple form, as in a threefold form at Hogondange (France) and as 'the Eponas' (plural) at Varhély (Hungary).[13] Her iconography shows how complex the attributes associated with particular Celtic deities could be and this complexity is found in a large number of cases.

Clearly, a number of the fertility gods and goddesses were considered to have had a close association with the natural world. Some, however, were particularly associated with specific animals. Epona, whose name was linked to the word for 'horse', was usually depicted riding side-saddle, occasionally astride a horse and sometimes in the company of foals. Given the importance of horses in a warrior society and as a source of transportation generally, it is not surprising that they had goddesses specifically associated with them. Another goddess apparently closely associated with a particular animal was Sequana, venerated at an Iron Age shrine in the Loire Valley (France) that was later developed into a Roman temple. Here the particular association was with waterfowl, and the connection of ducks with a ritual site has recently also been suggested regarding possible votive offerings in the shape of ducks at a spring near the famous British site of Stonehenge.[14]

There also survives inscriptional evidence in connection with gods and goddesses associated with a cult of the bear. These included divinities with names such as Dea Artio (bear goddess), Andarta (powerful bear), Artaios (bear-like) and Artgenos (bear's son). Given the possibility that the later Welsh mythological figure Arthur had a name that may have derived from the Welsh word for 'bear' (*arth*), this earlier evidence may be significant and may suggest that the myth of Arthur originated (in part at least) from a bear cult associated with a pagan god. Alternatively, Arthur's name may have come from a non-Celtic origin such as the Latin name Artorius (see Chapter 13).[15]

The gods of war

Warfare played a major part in Celtic society and a number of pre-Roman carvings show deities that were clearly associated with fighting and death. Before the Roman conquest, however, these particular deities were not named. A large carved stone at St-Michel-de-Valbonne, in southern France, depicts a figure riding over five severed heads. A similar carving from Entremont (France) includes a severed head hanging from the neck of a rider's mount. It is hard to be sure whether all such depictions represented divinities but some probably did.[16]

What is more certain is the evidence for local tribal defender gods becoming associated and partnered with Mars during the literate years of Roman rule. The god Teutates was equated with Mars and this partnership appeared as far apart as Switzerland and Barkway (Hertfordshire) and the East Midlands of England; in southern France, Mars was partnered with Albiorix; in the form Mars-Vesontius the same linking with a Celtic tribal deity occurred at Besançon (France). The warrior nature of Celtic society may have ensured that war gods (as well as the imported Roman worship of Mars) were accorded high status in the pantheon of deities worshipped. This is revealed in a number of the titles Mars was given in European dedications, and these include Mars-Rigisamus ('king of kings') and Mars-Belatucadrus ('bright one').

There is some suggestion that the deity presiding over a man being plunged headfirst into a vat, as depicted on the Gundestrup cauldron found in Denmark, may represent Teutates. This is because Teutates was associated with such a style of sacrifice in later written accounts. However, the link between this tradition and this particular cauldron is

open to question, since the deity is not named on the cauldron. Incidentally, there appears to be an etymological link
between this god's name (meaning 'tribe' or 'people') and
the Irish word *'tuatha'* (from *'tuath'*, Old Irish for people/
tribe/nation), which appeared in the name of a race of Irish
deities, the *Tuatha Dé Danann*. The first-century Roman
writer Lucan mentioned Teutates alongside two other
prominent deities: Esus ('lord') and Taranis ('thunderer').
Taranis has already been considered here. Of Esus we
know very little. A stone relief from Paris (France) named
him and depicted him cutting branches from a tree, alongside a bull and three cranes. At Trier (Germany) a similarly
dressed figure was shown hacking at a tree that contained
a bull and three birds.[17] Clearly, there was a well-known
mythological tradition involving Esus that has since been
completely lost. This reminds us how little we know of
pre-Christian Celtic belief systems.

The horse goddess Epona may also have had associations
with warfare since dedications to her were popular among
soldiers (as well as civilians). Her worship was particularly prevalent in north-east Gaul and along the German
military frontier. This association of horses with war gods
and goddesses was understandable given the high status of
horses among warrior elites. In a feature rare in Celtic deities, Epona appeared in Roman literature, being referred
to by two writers: Juvenal (late first/early second century)
and Marcus Minucius Felix (died *c.*250).

In Burgundy – at a site where archaeologists have
unearthed a number of pipe-clay models of horses and
horsemen – a bronze model was dedicated to a god named
Segomo (probably meaning 'victorious'). A dedication to
Mars-Segomo has been discovered at a separate site in the
vicinity. As far apart as Reims (France), Rindern (Germany) and Bar Hill (Scotland) a god named Camulus was
worshipped, and in the example at Reims was explicitly
called Mars-Camulus in a dedication made by a Roman

cavalryman. In this way a tribal deity came to be represented as the local manifestation of the Roman god.[18]

The gods of healing

The god Lenus was worshipped at Trier (Germany), as well as in Britain, and was associated with Mars in a mixture of warfare (probably in the sense of 'defender') and healing. In 215 the Emperor Caracalla invoked a Celtic deity – Grannus – alongside Aesculapius and Serapis, according to the Roman writer Dio Cassius. The context and the mention of Aesculapius indicate the healing power apparently attributed to Grannus. The cult of this deity was widespread, leaving inscriptional evidence in locations as far apart as Brittany in the west and the Hungarian Danube Basin in eastern Europe. At a cult centre at Grand (France) epigraphic evidence attests to the practice of so-called religious healing sleep, in which it was thought that Grannus would reveal himself to the sleeper in a vision in order to heal. This phenomenon was also a feature of healing centres dedicated to the Greek deity Aesculapius and so it is difficult to decide whether it was originally an element of the cult of Grannus, or whether it was imported into the Celtic cult from the Mediterranean healing centres of Aesculapius as a result of an association between the two healing cults during the period of Roman rule.

Another god associated with healing was Belenus, referred to above as a solar deity. Often linked to the Classical god Apollo, he was referred to as being worshipped in Gaul, by the fourth-century writer Ausonius, and inscriptions indicate that this god was venerated in what is now France, in northern Italy and in Austria.

Springs in Gaul reputed to have healing properties were associated with a number of deities, including gods named Borvo (or Bormanus), Maponos (also well attested in northern Britain) and goddesses such as Damona ('divine cow'). In continental Arthurian romances Maponos became known as Mabon (as in Wales) and also as Mabuz. At Luxeuil-les-Bains, in eastern France, the local god Luxovius combined attributes of light and healing at this thermal spring. There are echoes here of the solar/healing cult found at the British Romano-British temple complex at Aquae Sulis (Bath).

The mother goddesses were sometimes also linked to healing. An inscription from Aix-les-Bains (France) referred to them having healing powers. Similar references associated mother goddesses with healing practised at sites as widely dispersed as places in France, Hungary and Germany.

The gods of the dead

The second-century Roman writer Lucian named a Gaulish god called Ogmios who seemed to have been a counterpart of Hercules and was associated with both eloquence and death. A deity whose cult is often interpreted as being connected with the Underworld (as well as with fertility) was the antlered god Cernunnos, referred to earlier. A number of carvings show this god, although only one (from Paris) actually names him; nevertheless, it is commonly assumed that all such representations of this deity refer to Cernunnos. Another deity, Sucellus, also may have combined the characteristics of a god of the Underworld and a god of fertility. A representation of him from Hungary portrayed him with a raven and a three-headed dog. The raven was often associated with death in later Celtic mythology and the three-headed dog was reminiscent of Cerberus, the dog belonging to Hades in Classical tradition. Both Cernunnos and Sucellus have been taken by some writers to have been the gods that Julius Caesar had in mind when he stated that the druids claimed a god as a common ancestor, who was equated by Caesar with the Roman god of the dead, Dis Pater.[19] This connection is far from clear, however, and a closer parallel can perhaps be drawn between the attributes of Dis Pater and the Irish Donn, god of the Underworld.[20]

3

THE GODS AND RELIGION OF THE CELTS: THE BRITISH PICTURE

A number of the gods and goddesses discernible from the European evidence can also be identified in Britain. In fact, it is often the more explicit European evidence that can help us understand some of the British examples. Such evidence includes references to Celtic deities recorded by Roman writers and epigraphic evidence from inscriptions on altars and similar items. For example, British archaeologists and students of Celtic religious beliefs refer to the worship of Cernunnos – and this is clearly justified – but we would not even know the name of this antlered god were it not for rare inscriptional evidence from France. In the sole example, from Paris, the name was not quite complete: '-ernunnos'. However, the addition of a capital 'C' gives the name Cernunnos ('the horned one') and it seems clear that this was the name/title of this particular god. From this, it is surmised that all such antlered deities were known as Cernunnos, including those found carved on stone in Britain. This is a reasonable assumption and one followed here, though it must be borne in mind that it is just that, an assumption. It is also possible that the word was a more general title that may have been applied to a number of different Celtic deities.[1] The example of Cernunnos reminds us both of the common features of Celtic religion that can be discerned from evidence across a wide geographical area and of how much we do not know for certain.

Even so, it is possible to draw conclusions about aspects of the pre-Christian beliefs of the Celtic inhabitants of Britain before the conversion to Christianity and the later Anglo-Saxon conquests of what would become England. As we explore some of this evidence, it is also possible to suggest ways in which some of these pagan beliefs fed into later mythology that was finally written down by Irish and Welsh Christian monks in the medieval period. By this time many beliefs had changed considerably from their original form, or had been consciously revised in order to reduce gods and goddesses to more acceptable heroic figures from the ancient past or fairies. Despite this process of transformation of pagan belief system into later mythology, some of the origins of these later figures can be identified.

However, before any such identifications can be made, it is necessary to consider what evidence survives of these earlier Celtic beliefs and the names of deities. Most of this evidence comes from the Roman era as a result of the introduction of written dedications; these allow us to put names to carved figures and to identify aspects of the Celtic pantheon.

The gods of war
Although lacking names, a number of probable deities were depicted brandishing a sword and shield. These include an example at Yardhope (Northumberland) in which a figure

was carved into rock near a Roman military camp. This may have been Cocidius, a god who appears to have been associated with both woodland (he was at times linked with the Roman deity Silvanus) and warfare (he was also associated with the Roman god Mars). Archaeologists have unearthed evidence for a similar figure at Tre Owen (Powys), at Wall (Staffordshire) and at Stow-on-the-Wold (Gloucestershire).[2]

In a number of cases these warrior gods were depicted as horsemen. In Suffolk a bronze figure of a god named Corotiacus was partnered with Mars. At Peterborough (Cambridgeshire) and at Brigstock (Northamptonshire) statues of warriors probably indicate the worship of a similar deity – but are unnamed. Most are found in eastern England and may suggest a survival of a horse cult as well as the worship of a mounted war god. There is, however, an exception to this geographical bias, in a western example discovered at Bisley (Gloucestershire) that depicted a horseman armed with a shield and an axe.[3]

A recent find near Hallaton, in Leicestershire, added to the existing evidence for a cult dedicated to Teutates or Toutatis. A silver ring found by a metal-detector carried the inscription 'TOT' and – from similar finds in Gaul – was clearly dedicated to this deity. This corroborates other evidence from the East Midlands suggesting a cult here of this Gaulish god in association with the Roman god Mars.[4]

The Roman writer Dio mentioned a war goddess of the Britons named Andraste; however, we know little else about this particular British deity, apart from the claim that hares were sacrificed to her.

The sky and sun gods
A dedication to 'Thunder' on an altar discovered at Chester was probably made as a reference to the god Taranis, whose name meant 'thunder' (*taran* in Welsh).[5] The inscription from Chester equated Taranis with Jupiter and this same

equation has been noted on a small number of continental dedications.

The sun god known as Lugh (Ireland), Lleu (Wales), Lugus or Lug (Gaul) was probably venerated at Luguvalium (Carlisle), where his name may appear in the Romano-British name of the settlement, meaning 'the wall of [the Celtic god] Lugus'.[6] This suggestion, though, is not without controversy and a strong argument insists that the name actually came from a British personal name such as *Luguualos*.[7] Consequently, this evidence remains open to interpretation. The river Lea, famous for its course through the 2012 Olympic Park in east London, takes its name from a British river name derived from 'lug' (light). It may even have meant 'the river of the god Lugus'.[8]

The mother goddesses

Mother goddesses appear prominently in Celtic religious iconography in Britain, as in continental Europe. In later Welsh mythology such a figure was Modron, who clearly derived from earlier pre-Christian beliefs. Tangled into later literature, this originally pagan divinity may have given rise to the figure of Morgan le Fay in medieval Arthurian tales. As these stories were written in a Christian milieu, the old belief in this figure's divinity was downgraded to a skill in sorcery and magic. Revision of this kind was a common feature of the way in which once-pagan beliefs were restructured and re-presented in the literature of medieval Ireland and Wales.

It may be the mother goddesses known as the *deae matres*, mentioned above, that lay behind cults popular in the Cotswolds and along Hadrian's Wall in the form of the *genii cucullati* (hooded spirits), which were also represented in groups of three. These mother goddesses were often identified as having oversight of named communities or nations. An inscription at Winchester referred to the Mothers of Italy, Germany, Gaul and Britain. One at York referred to those of Africa, Italy and Gaul. Other dedications referred to the *matres domesticae*. This reminds us of the goddesses of the sovereignty of Ireland who featured in a number of later Irish myths. This suggests that the concept was common across the Celtic world.

In Britain and Ireland a number of these triple goddesses – when they were recorded in later, medieval traditions – combined aspects of fertility, territorial sovereignty and war. Ériu, Banbha and Fódla were later associated with the sovereignty of Ireland; the goddess Macha had a threefold association with fertility, war and horses; the war goddesses the Morrígan and the Badbh used shape-shifting to move between different forms and in the case of the Morrígan this could include forms indicative of sexuality and fertility. These goddesses may all have derived from earlier traditions that linked fertility and war across the beliefs of many Celtic peoples.

In later Irish tradition this significance of a goddess of the land was apparent in the mythology that the chief god, the Daghda, was considered to have married Boann, goddess of the river Boyne, who was also stated as being the wife of the river god Nechtan or Echmar. While there is no etymological link between Boann and the fertility goddesses that were carved on Roman-era inscriptions, the religious concept was similar but given an Irish setting. There is every likelihood that similar – though unrecorded – mythologies once existed across the Celtic world, from Asia Minor to Ireland, that recounted the beliefs surrounding goddesses, many of whom are known only from inscriptions.

The gods and goddesses of fertility

At Bath (Somerset) the goddess Rosmerta (whose name meant 'good provider') was coupled with the Roman god Mercury and with three *genii cucullati* and a ram. In the Roman world Mercury's role included one connected with fertility. A number of similar representations of

Mercury and Rosmerta have been discovered at Gloucester (Gloucestershire) and another was discovered at Nettleton Shrub (Wiltshire). The juxtaposition of Rosmerta and the *genii cucullati* reveals that there was a clear (and not surprising) overlap between goddesses of fertility and mother goddesses who often had a role as regional sovereigns.

A goddess whose attributes included fertility and possibly warfare, alongside the more obvious role as the deity of horses, was Epona. There survives more evidence for this deity from the continent than from Britain, but there are some clues that indicate that her cult was also found here. The evidence includes, most famously, a bronze figurine found in Wiltshire that portrayed Epona sitting between two diminutive horses, while a dish on her lap overflowed with corn. In later Welsh mythology, as evidenced in the *Mabinogi*, Rhiannon the wife of Pwyll was associated with horses and may have represented a reworking of echoes of the earlier figure of Epona. This, though, is speculation.

The association of Iron Age Celtic ritual sites with specific animals has recently been suggested regarding the discovery of two objects possibly representing ducks at the spring-site of Blick Mead, near Stonehenge (Amesbury). Here they seem to represent part of a tradition of offerings at the site dating back to the Mesolithic (*c.*9000 BC). While they are not associated here with any named Celtic deity, they are reminiscent of evidence found in the Loire valley (France) and there linked to the worship of a goddess named Sequana.[9] This association of mythological beings with waterfowl is found in a number of (much later recorded) Celtic traditions. It is noteworthy that waterfowl, for example, were strongly associated with the Irish story of Oengus Óg and Cáer, the swan princess; in addition, four swans circled over Angus's head while he was travelling; the swan children of Lír were made to have only flocks of wildfowl as their family after their transformation.[10] Again in Irish mythology, the minor Irish agricultural deity Mac

Cécht (who was one of the three kings of the *Tuatha Dé Danann* at the time of the invasion of the Milesians), was led to a spring by a duck when he was searching for water with which to revive the dying king of the *Tuatha Dé Danann*.[11]

The gods of the forest, of the wild and of the mountains
A Welsh tale tells of Owain, a herdsman god who subdued animals. This story may have been a later survival of traditions once associated with the antlered god Cernunnos,[12] who was often depicted in association with animals, but this is uncertain. Another god depicted with a stag was Cocidius in northern Britain, as was Callirius ('woodland king'), who was linking to Silvanus on a bronze plaque discovered at Colchester (Essex). The stag played a significant role in later Irish mythology, being one of the animal forms taken on by the Morrígan. In the case of Cernunnos, the stag image also appeared with that of ram-horned snakes. On a stone plaque from Cirencester (Gloucestershire), Cernunnos's legs were replaced by two ram-horned snakes. That the snakes' heads were beside two purses suggests that Cernunnos was considered a god of prosperity. But it should be noted that the British evidence for the cult of Cernunnos is rare compared with continental examples. Nevertheless, the depiction of an antlered god on a pre-Roman Iron Age silver coin from Petersfield (Hampshire) shows that the cult certainly existed in Britain and must have been of some importance to cause it to be shown on this coin.

Later Irish mythology included a figure named Furbaide Ferbend, which means Furbaide 'the horned'. This character was the son of one of the associates of the mythical Irish warrior Cú Chulainn and was responsible for the death of the equally mythical Queen Medb of Connacht (Connaught). According to the Irish tradition, Furbaide Ferbend killed Medb with hard cheese hurled from his sling while she was bathing in Lough Ree (County Roscommon). His killing of her featured in the story known as *The Violent Death of Medb* (*Aided Meidbe*), which survives in a manuscript of the mid-twelfth century, the *Book of Leinster* (*Lebor Laignech*).[13] Furbaide Ferbend was described as having bull's horns; according to the twelfth-century Irish *History of Places* (*Dinnshenchas*) he had two horns, which gave rise to the epithet 'the horned'. The glossary, known as *Fitness of Names* (*Cóir Anmann*) and found in a number of manuscripts (some fragmentary) dating from the fourteenth to the sixteenth century,[14] claimed that the horns (in this case, two made from silver and the third made from gold) were actually placed on his helmet. The horned appearance of Furbaide Ferbend was an attribute he shared with another mythical figure in Irish mythology, Feradach Fechtnach. In the same medieval Irish account of the origins of place names, the *History of Places* (*Dinnshenchas*), this latter figure was also described as having three horns.

Another, later Irish mythical figure was Conall Cernach, whose name may have had a linguistic connection to that of Cernunnos. An even more distinctive similarity lay in a reference in one Irish story to a snake wrapping itself around the waist of Conall in a way reminiscent of carvings of the antlered god usually assumed to portray Cernunnos.[15] None of this later evidence proves that these Irish figures derived from Cernunnos, or even were this god in a later guise. The horned appearance may simply have alluded to the potent symbolism of horns, implying strength and vitality and so, coincidentally, linking the figure of Cernunnos and these figures from later Irish mythology. As part of this note of caution it should be remembered that Cernunnos was deer-antlered, whereas these Irish figures were bull-horned. Nevertheless, the similarity may have been more than a coincidence.

It is also worth noting that two representations of an antler-horned figure found in Britain were of a female form. The name of this antlered goddess is unknown and it reminds us that the worship of the antlered god, named as Cernunnos, may have been more complex than is sometimes assumed, and it seems that both male and female deities could have attributes usually associated with this one, male, god.[16] Whether this meant that they were similar figures, with similar areas of authority, is not possible to determine.

It is interesting that one form of horned deity was more common in Britain than on the continent and this was the bull-horned figure. A number of figures representing deities, usually in stone, had bull's horns added to them. This occurred in many instances and seems to have applied to a number of gods and goddesses.[17]

A mountain god mentioned on continental inscriptions was Uxellinus (the name means 'high'). The name of this god may have given rise to the Roman-period name of the fort on Hadrian's Wall, now called Stanwix (Cumbria), or perhaps the large fort at Netherby (North Yorkshire). This name was Axeloduno in the *Notitia Dignitatum*, an official Roman administrative document of the early fifth century that listed every military and governmental post in the Late Roman Empire. The name also appeared – in the form Uxelludamo – in the seventh-century list of all the towns and road-stations throughout the Roman Empire known as the *Ravenna Cosmography*; and as Uxelodum on the Rudge Cup and Uxelodunum on the Amiens Patera and on the Staffordshire Patera.[18] The name probably meant: 'The fortress of Uxellinus', although there is a possibility that it derived from a Celtic word for water that lies behind the river names Exe, Axe, Usk and Esk.[19]

The god Sucellus – associated in France with the woodland god Silvanus and with the wine trade – also appeared in inscriptions in Britain at East Stoke (Nottinghamshire) and in York. An example from Bath provided the name of a goddess of woodland, Nemetona ('goddess of the grove').

A similar god, with the title/name Rigonemetis ('king of the grove'), was paired with Mars in Lincolnshire.

There have been suggestions that the later early medieval hero Arthur derived from a bear deity. However, while there is evidence for such a deity on the continent (for example, the cult of Artio in Switzerland), this latter deity was female and there is very limited evidence for such a cult in Britain. Bear amulets have been discovered but without epigraphic evidence to indicate the name of any bear god.

The gods of healing

A British counterpart to the Gaulish god of healing, Maponos, was Mabon son of Modron (clearly a mother goddess), who appeared in Welsh literature. In the Welsh story *Culhwch and Olwen* (*Culhwch ac Olwen*), which probably dates from the eleventh century, Mabon was credited with seizing the magical razor held between the ears of the great boar Twrch Trwyth. In this later tradition Mabon had become a heroic hunter with mythical powers; powers sufficient to seize the razor from the fearsome boar. However, the story suggested that he had once been venerated as a hunter, and another aspect of the Welsh tradition preserved in *Culhwch and Olwen* indicated that he was probably associated with the Underworld too, since the hero Culhwch freed him from captivity in the fortress of Caer Loyw (Gloucester). While Gloucester may seem a rather surprising location for the Underworld, it seems that the place had been seized on in the writing of this tradition, without any intended reference to geography.

That a god associated on the continent with healing should have become a god of the Underworld in Welsh mythology is not really surprising since a role connected with death may have also been considered compatible with the role of healer (who saves devotees from illness and death). In the same way, the Roman god Mars was transformed in Britain (as in Gaul) into a god of healing. In this case the attributes that were associated with victory in battle were probably reinvented as providing victory over disease. A distinctive example was that of Mars Nodens, worshipped at Lydney (Gloucestershire). Here, in the Forest of Dean, a healing centre grew up around the temple dedicated to this paired deity. The god worshipped here – Nodens – was one of the relatively small number of Celtic deities whose actual names can be directly traced from the Romano-British epigraphic evidence to the later, medieval survival of memories of cults such as this within Irish and Welsh mythology. In this case the later written references were to Nuada Airgedlámh (Nuada of the Silver Hand) in Ireland. The Welsh equivalent of Nuada was written as either Nudd Llaw Ereint or Lludd Llaw Ereint (Nudd/Lludd of the Silver Hand). At Lydney, the discovery of a number of dog figurines suggests that this was an animal closely linked to the cult of Nodens. Interestingly, there is also evidence from the site that links Nodens to both the sun and sea. That this latter was indeed the case is revealed by an inscription from Chesterholm (Northumberland), where, at the Roman fort of Vindolanda, Nodens was equated with Neptune. The reason for a connection between healing and a sea god is unclear, but the solar/healing focus is more readily understood and is found in a number of Roman and Celtic religious cults.

Worship of Lenus Mars (this is the word order common on inscriptions) revealed another pairing of the Roman god with a Celtic deity of healing. This linkage has left evidence at Caerwent (Monmouthshire) and Chedworth (Gloucestershire). The same pairing of Lenus with Mars left evidence at Trier (Germany). At the villa site of Chedworth there is a real possibility that the whole complex was a healing shrine that accommodated devotees of the god. The villa's function, though, remains a matter of some contention among archaeologists.

Another famous instance of a healing deity was that of
Sulis-Minerva at Aquae Sulis (Bath). Here, as in a number
of examples in the Roman period, a native Celtic deity of
healing (Sulis) was paired with the Classical goddess Minerva. In Ireland the association of St Brigid (Brigit) with
fire supports the interpretation that St Brigid was probably
a Christianized form of an earlier pagan goddess and, in
this case, one with attributes similar to those of both Minerva and Sulis. The third-century Roman writer Solinus
indicated that the shrine of Minerva in Britain contained a
perpetual fire. It is also highly possible that the tribal goddess of the north British tribe of the Brigantes – Brigantia
– had a name related to the goddess who gave rise to the
legends of ('St') Brigid. In which case, this, alongside continental evidence, suggests the widespread cult of a healer,
and tribal goddess, who was associated by Caesar on the
continent with Minerva. Brigantia's name was placed on a
number of altar dedications, such as that to 'Victoria Brigantia and the Deities of the two Emperors', by Titus Aurelius Aurelianus 'when master of the sacred rites' (c.205),
from Bank Top (Yorkshire).[20] However, the interpretation
of the evidence for the existence of a cult of Brigantia is
not straightforward. All the datable evidence for the cult
comes from one particular period, the reigns of the emperors Severus and Caracalla, and there is only one stone relief
that certainly shows this goddess. This comes from Bir-
rens, in southern Scotland. It has been argued that there
is nothing on this stone figure to indicate that Brigantia
was a Celtic deity; instead, it is postulated that the cult of
Brigantia was actually invented as a personification of the
province of Lower (northern) Britain that occurred during
the reign of the Emperor Severus (193–211), when the government of Britain was split into two parts.[21]

Some mother goddesses were also associated with healing. The Suleviae – recorded at Bath, Cirencester and
Colchester – appear to have been considered goddesses of

healing, and this suggests that Sulis too was considered to have had healing powers, given her association with the hot spring. At Castleford (West Yorkshire) an inscription linked three nymphs to the supposed healing quality of the local water. This connection between water and deities associated with healing can be discerned in a number of places from various forms of evidence. The northern British goddess Coventina was worshipped at the spring at Carrawburgh (Northumberland); Verbeia was worshipped beside the river Wharfe in Teesdale; Latis ('goddess of the water') was venerated at a number of north British sites. A similar activity clearly occurred at Buxton (Derbyshire) in the Roman period, since the Roman name for the place was Aquae Arnemetiae ('waters of the goddess of the sacred grove'). This is comparable with the evidence already cited regarding Aquae Sulis (Bath). At Nettleton Shrub (Wiltshire) the main god of this shrine appears to have been Apollo Cunomaglus ('hound lord'). While the obvious interpretation is that Cunomaglus was a hunter deity, it is also likely, from other evidence found at this site and from associations of Apollo and healing found elsewhere, that this was a healing shrine and that Cunomaglus was considered to be a god of both hunting and healing.

What is clear is that later Celtic mythology derived from these earlier traditions and some of these connections can be identified, as we have seen.

4

FESTIVALS AND CELEBRATIONS ACROSS THE YEAR

It is possible to outline some of the main events of the pre-Christian Celtic ritual year, since some references to them survived in medieval and later evidence in Ireland, Wales and elsewhere. A number of modern seasonal festivals still have roots that stretch back to the pre-Christian Celtic past and are associated with a number of strands of Celtic mythology. Owing to 'Celtic' culture's modern popularity, and especially the influence of Irish culture, a number of these festivities are known on either side of the North Atlantic, both within the Irish diaspora and among others who take an interest in 'Celtic' culture. The 1990 play *Dancing at Lughnasa*, by Brian Friel, was set in the context of August 1936 in County Donegal, and the harvest festival of Lughnasa, which took its name from an ancient Irish celebration. As well as portraying a month in the lives of an impoverished Irish family, it also illustrates the longevity of Celtic seasonal celebrations that date from at least the early medieval period (and probably much earlier). As in a number of Celtic traditions, the evidence is strongest from Ireland, since the surviving medieval Welsh literature says much less about pre-Christian beliefs and evidence regarding these is more implied than explicitly stated, in contrast to the Irish evidence.

Midwinter celebrations

Surprisingly, we know very little about the midwinter festivities and ceremonies associated with the Celtic peoples of the British Isles. The Irish stories in the Ulster Cycle (which reached its present form between the twelfth and the fifteenth centuries) preserve no references to midwinter feasts, or other ceremonies. Neither in the Ulster Cycle nor in the *Book of Invasions* (*Leabhar Gábhala*) do we find any mention of the worship of a sun god so often associated with midwinter rites. This clearly was not in fact the case, since St Patrick (writing in the fifth century) was very much aware of Irish pagan sun worship and an early tenth-century work known as *Cormac's Glossary* (*Sanas Chormaic*), referred to sun symbols carved on some altars. What were probably sun gods were referred to in the later mythology and it would be surprising if these had not been venerated in festivities that included midwinter ones. Notable sun gods or deities associated with the sun were Lugh or Lugh Lámhfada (Lugh of the Long Arm, or, literally the Long Hand) in Ireland, and Lleu in Wales. Another was the Irish god of the sun and of lightning, Eochaid.

Some later writers have suggested that a midwinter festivity accompanied the gathering of mistletoe by druids.[1] In fact, the only source for this gathering of mistletoe is the Roman writer Pliny the Elder and he simply claimed that mistletoe was sacred to the Gauls and especially when found growing on oak. It was then cut on the sixth day of the moon. Pliny made no mention of this occurring at a particular time of the year.[2]

Nevertheless, there was clearly a concentration on New Year feasts in the Welsh literature (in contrast to the Irish). The poem *The Gododdin* (*Y Gododdin*), dating from sometime between the seventh and the tenth century, refers to a Welsh warrior singing at the New Year feast. Similarly the ninth- or tenth-century poem *The Praise of Tenby* (*Etmich Dinbych*) suggests that New Year was a significant time of male bonding in the royal hall of a Welsh prince. It is also significant that the Arthurian adventure *Culhwch and Olwen* (*Culhwch ac Olwen*), probably eleventh-century, began at a midwinter New Year feast. This suggests that modern claims that the Celtic New Year began at Samhain, on 31 October, are not supported by the medieval evidence; certainly not by the Welsh evidence.[3] Despite this, it has become customary among some living in modern 'Celtic nations' to identify Samhain as the traditional 'Celtic New Year'.[4]

Earlier Celtic rituals may have left echoes on Shetland and in the Scottish traditions of burning juniper in houses and cattle pens around New Year. Burning torches were also sometimes carried through the fields.[5] The association of juniper and fire with this time of midwinter darkness may suggest a dual role of driving out evil and – in the case of the fire – celebrating the light.

While it seems clear now that Mummers plays – traditionally celebrated in England around the Christmas period – do not have roots that go further back than the seventeenth century, one character designated as a devil and carrying a club and a pan, it has been noted, bore a clear resemblance to both the figure of the Irish Daghda, chief god of the *Tuatha Dé Danann*, and the earlier (in terms of when recorded) Romano-Gallic deity Sucellus,[6] who appears to have had connections with woodland and fertility. This similarity may suggest a surviving folk memory of this pagan deity, though a memory much changed over the years until it influenced the characterization of this figure in the later plays.

Another midwinter custom involved killing wrens and parading with their tiny corpses and was found across the British Isles in the nineteenth century but was particularly well evidenced in some of the Celtic areas (Ireland, Wales, the Isle of Man). This may well have had its roots in a Celtic attribution of special powers to this tiniest of birds. Cormac of Cashel (died 908), an Irish bishop and King of Munster and the writer credited with the compilation of *Cormac's Glossary*,[7] stated that its Irish name – *dreean* – originated from *drui-én*, meaning druid-bird,[8] and suggested that the bird was thought capable of prophetic announcements. A similar tradition was recorded in the tenth-century Irish manuscript the *Birth and Life of St Moling* (*Geinemain Moiling ocus a Bhetae*), where it was stated that some people claimed to tell the future from the behaviour of the bird. The modern English word 'wren' derives from Old English '*wrenna*' or '*wrænna*',[9] which it has been suggested comes from the Irish *dreean*. The Welsh name – *dryw* – and the Manx name – *dreain* – also appear to be connected to the word 'druid'.[10] The bird appears in Welsh mythology in what is today termed 'The Fourth Branch' of the *Mabinogi* or *Mabinogion*. The wren was the reason for the naming of Lleu Llaw Gyffes ('the fair-haired one with the skilful hand').When a wren landed on the deck of the ship on which he was travelling, 'The boy aims at it and hits it in the leg, between the tendon and the bone.'[11] This may suggest that the wren was considered a significant bird; but it is more likely that it was chosen simply because its diminutive size emphasized the skill of the boy's aim.

Imbolc and the start of spring

An Irish feast that was held to mark the end of winter and the beginning of spring was called Imbolc. Other forms of the name include Imbolg and Óimelc. The feast was mentioned in the tenth- or eleventh-century story of the relationship between Cú Chulainn and a woman known as *The Wooing of Emer* (*Tochmarc Emire*). It was, in this account, one of the events associated with the beginning of the four seasons. In the story these four seasonal feasts that opened periods in the annual calendar were: Imbolc (1 February), Beltane (1 May), Lughnasa (1 August) and Samhain (31 October). Within the story, Emer explained that Imbolc was when the milking of ewes started. The same association with sheep's milk is found in *Cormac's Glossary* and it does seem that part, at least, of the word derived from the word for milking.[12]

Beyond this we know virtually nothing about the activities associated with this festivity. In the Christian calendar it was placed on 1 February and became associated with St Brigid (Brigit). There is reason to think that a goddess of this name lay behind this allegedly historical figure, or perhaps was conflated with a real woman of this name.[13] Probably beginning as a tribal deity of Leinster (though her cult centre was in the town of Kildare), she was regarded as both a battle goddess and a fertility deity and associated with metalworking, prophecy and poetry. Therefore it is not surprising that she was linked to a festival associated with spring and the birth of the new season of lambs. Her name meant 'fiery arrow' and Irish legends also claimed that she had been Christ's wet nurse. This may have been a Christian version of her original connection with lambs and milking. By the eighteenth century the eve of this saint's day was marked by family meals and the displaying of crosses made from plaited rushes or straw, placed at doors or windows to welcome the saint. In a further connection with animal fertility, the crosses were put up in stables.[14] These were the so-called St Brigid's cross (*críosog Bridghe*). The lateness of surviving references to these activities is largely due to the general lack of evidence for popular Irish customs before the seventeenth and eighteenth centuries. Along with the crosses, a garment or piece of cloth (the *bratog Bride*), was often hung outside a cottage for the saint to bless as she passed. It was thought that these could then be used to cure headaches. This notion probably derived from an original healing role associated with this strangely conflated goddess/saint. The overall effects of these celebrations was to create a Mother Saint for Ireland, whose cult almost certainly represented a Christianization of an earlier pagan set of beliefs and communal activities.[15] In this, Brigid stands in sharp contrast to the very historical St Patrick.

While the cult of St Brigid was strongest in Ireland, there is evidence that it was also celebrated in other western areas of Britain that formed part of the Irish-Gaelic culture zone around the Irish Sea. On the Isle of Man, Brigid's Festival (*Laa'l Breeshey*) was celebrated with rushes laid on the floor of a house to provide a bed for the saint, or a bed was made up in a barn.[16] This Manx tradition was similar to the Irish ones in that it involved invitations to Brigid to bless the home and family.

Similar traditions were noted in the Scottish-Gaelic areas of the Hebrides and on the west coast of mainland Scotland and indicate the widespread nature of the cult of Brigid among the communities either side of the northern Irish Sea. In the Hebrides, according to a late seventeenth-century account, a sheaf of wheat was dressed as a woman and laid in a basket called 'Brüd's bed'.[17] Another, and slightly later account, stated that the bed was made to the recitation of '*a Bhrid, a Bhrid, thig a sligh as gabh do hea-baidh*' ('Bridget, Bridget, come in; thy bed is ready').[18] As late as the end of the nineteenth century, girls in the Gaelic-speaking communities of the Outer Hebrides dressed a sheaf of corn as St Brigid (termed St Bride) and placed over the 'heart' a bright shell that they called 'the guiding star of Bride' (*reul-iuil Bride*) and that was thought to represent the star over the stable door at Bethlehem. The image was then carried from door to door and food was collected that was then eaten in a females-only feast. Afterwards, young men were admitted and dancing took place until dawn, when a song was sung: '*Bride bhoidheach muime chorr Chriosda*' ('Beauteous Bride, foster mother of Christ').[19] This was a reference to the myth, found also in Ireland, that St Brigid had been Christ's wet nurse.

Clearly, the cult of St Brigid was an amalgamation of activities associated with a pre-Christian mythical being and Christian themes. Veneration, usually associated with the Virgin Mary in Catholic communities, was extended to some extent to Brigid, and themes associated with Christmas and Epiphany were likewise adapted to incorporate her. However, while it is impossible to definitively state what was the original nature of the pre-Christian cult and its rituals, it seems safe to assume that Brigid was probably a Celtic fertility deity, closely associated with farming communities in Ireland and in those parts of mainland Britain most influenced by Irish culture. In this capacity she seems to have been particularly venerated in early spring. Anything beyond this is speculation.

Beltane and the beginning of summer

The earliest reference to this seasonal event is found in the Irish manuscript *Cormac's Glossary*. Beltane in this text was described as being associated with 'lucky fire'. The name itself derived from 'fire of Bel'. The event occurred on 1 May. The writer of one of the two surviving manuscripts noted that cattle were driven between two fires (presumably because this was considered a way of driving off impurities, including disease). The compiler of *The Wooing of Emer* specifically stated that Beltane occurred at the beginning of summer. This start-of-summer fire ritual may originally have had an earlier Irish name of *Cetsoman*, since *Cormac's Glossary* associated this name with May Day events. The god Bel may have been a reference to the Old Testament Baal, used in this context because Baal was a pagan Canaanite deity whose worship was condemned in the Bible and whose name would have been familiar to the Christian compiler of *Cormac's Glossary*. Since this document specifically referred to the 'idol god' Bel, this is a real possibility. Alternatively, the name may have represented the survival of the worship of the Celtic god Belenus (Belenos, Belinos) into the early medieval period, when the name of the festival was first recorded. From as late as the early nineteenth century there are records of Irish farmers driving their cattle between two fires on May Eve.

Most of the European inscriptions relating to this god have been found in Aquileia (modern north-east Italy). However, from other – albeit limited evidence – it seems likely that his cult was fairly widespread in western Europe, being evidenced as far apart as Noricum (modern Austria and part of Slovenia) and Bayeux (France). The god's name may have meant 'the bright one' and this would be consistent with fire festivities. We know very little about the cult of Belenus in Britain but it probably occurred here since, in the twelfth-century writings of Geoffrey of Monmouth, 'Belinus' was remembered as a Welsh mythical ruler famous for a peaceful reign, building roads and restoring devastated towns. In his *History of the Kings of Britain* (*Historia Regum Britanniae*) Geoffrey even went so far as to claim that Billingsgate in London was named after him. The name of the first-century, pre-Roman, British king Cunobelinos (referred to by the Roman historians Suetonius and Dio Cassius) contained a reference to the name of this god.[20] The royal name meant something like 'hound of Belenus'. What this indicates is that the cult of Belenus was a fairly widespread phenomenon and it is likely that so was Beltane or something similar. While the evidence is very limited, it seems reasonable to assume that this event was not just an Irish one.

Not surprisingly, given the spread of Irish cultural influence, there is evidence of Beltane activities from a number of places in Scotland. These range from eighteenth-century records of Highland feasts and ceremonies designed to protect flocks and herds from threatening animals such as foxes and eagles, to sixteenth-century festivities in the Scottish Lowlands. Many of these events were associated with the lighting of fires. In the Western Isles a striking ceremony involved the drawing of lots until one man was designated the *cailleach bealtine* and was ceremonially threatened with being thrown into the fire. Only by leaping through the flames was the ceremony concluded.[21] There may be a hint here that earlier celebrations might have involved the sacrifice of a person, but this is speculation.

Similarly, a huge number of fires were lit on the Isle of Man although the nineteenth-century records indicate that these were caused by setting fire to gorse. While there is little evidence for such events occurring in England there were two notable exceptions. Fires on May Eve or May Day were recorded in Cumbria in the late eighteenth century and were also noted in Cornwall and Devon. On Dartmoor the association of the fires with the purification of cattle is consistent with the Irish traditions. Nineteenth-century accounts record May Day fires in Glamorgan and Montgomeryshire.[22] These cases were probably the last survival of Celtic celebrations that were once found across Britain. In a number of these cases rowan, or mountain ash, was sometimes employed in the ceremonies and sometimes formed into crosses (indicating a Christianization of the rites). This was a common use of this tree and the name 'rowan' came from a Germanic root word connected with divination.[23] These rites marked the beginning of summer and the attempted protection of the herds from danger as they were set loose in the fields. Other 'Celtic' areas of Europe, though, have few of these ceremonies[24] and this reminds us once again of how cautious we must be in making generalizations about 'pan-Celtic customs' and Europe-wide 'Celtic culture'.

Midsummer fires

While Beltane – like a number of 'Celtic' events – celebrated the start of a season, there is evidence that fire was also associated with the high point of summer. Eighteenth-century records tell of Irish traditions of fires lit on the edges of corn fields and carried around cattle pens, particularly in the west of the country. There is little evidence of this in the Hebrides and Wales, although there are records of fires lit at this time on Orkney and Shetland but these latter ones were probably due to Viking influence. It is another example of why we have to be cautious when talking about widespread 'Celtic' customs, since the Celtic nature of this one seems limited mainly to Ireland.

Lughnasa: harvest and the beginning of autumn

Traditionally celebrated in early medieval Ireland on 1 August, this seasonal event seems to have taken its name from the Irish sun god Lugh Lámhfada (Lugh of the Long Arm). Curiously, while this was the name found in many early medieval Irish sources, *The Wooing of Emer* – uniquely – named it as *Bron Trogain* ('the wrath of Trogain'). The identity of Trogain is unknown, so the mythology behind this alternative name remains a mystery, although the event was clearly viewed as a time of sorrow, as the season turned to autumn. In eighteenth- and nineteenth-century Ireland, however, the event was associated with the corn harvest, celebrations on hilltops and communal meals.[25] On the Isle of Man the festival was called *Laa'l Lhuanys* and again was associated with communal events on hills. In Wales villagers climbed the Brecon Beacons for festivities. In the Hebrides a ceremony occurred at the same time but the Hebridean making of bannocks from newly cut corn and ceremonies held by the hearth were not features of the celebration in Ireland, Wales and on the Isle of Man. Consequently, it is difficult to say how far Lughnasa was once widespread among Celtic communities and how far it was a ceremony peculiar to Ireland – and also to the Isle of Man and parts of Wales. In Wales the phrase used to describe 1 August was *gwyl aust* (Feast of August) and this may have been prompted by a memory of this earlier harvest event.

Samhain and the beginning of winter

The Irish festival of Samhain occurred from 31 October–1 November and marked the beginning of winter. In *The Wooing of Emer* it was named as the first of the seasonal events, 'when the summer goes to its rest'. It was at this time that many tribal gatherings (the *feis*) took place and these were times of feasting, sports and amusements. What is surprising is that none of the stories that feature a *feis* of Samhain gives us any insight into religious rites associated with this event. It seems that, by the time Christian writers recorded traditions connected with Samhain, all memory of the pagan mythology connected to it had been forgotten. It is possible that the time was associated with a particular closeness between the human and the Otherworld and that this explains why this time of the year featured in stories of the deaths of legendary kings and contacts between Otherworld beings and people.[26] However, this may simply have been because the feast was traditionally a time of gatherings and not because it was regarded as being a time when the barriers between the earth and the Otherworld were thin.[27] What is clear is that by the fourteenth century it was thought that at Samhain there were (as well as human gatherings) assemblies of fairy-folk, who feasted on nuts at the great passage graves of Newgrange, Knowth and Dowth at the *Bru na Bóinne* (the bend of the river Boyne).

Similarly, in Wales there is evidence of a significant seasonal event occurring at this point of the year, with the day called *Calan Gaeaf* ('start of winter') and the previous evening being termed *Nos Galan Gaea* ('eve of winter'), but there is no medieval record of this being regarded as having any spiritual significance. In contrast, the equivalent event in May, *Nos Galan Mai* (May Day Eve), was, in medieval Welsh literature, associated with unearthly screams in the story *Lludd and Llefelys* (*Lludd a Llefelys*) and Otherworldly annual conflicts in *Culhwch and Olwen*.[28] However, in later folklore *Nos Galan Gaea* did become identified as an *ysbrydnos* ('spirit night'), when spirits walked the earth. In short, despite many modern claims to the contrary, there is very little early (i.e. medieval) evidence that Samhain was regarded as a major mythological and Otherworld-connected time of the year. It was during the nineteenth century that the idea was first promoted, by some folklorists, that Samhain was a kind of Celtic New Year. However, except for the fact that it headed the four seasonal feasts in *The Wooing of Emer*, there is little evidence to support this and that which is sometimes quoted seems to be no older than the nineteenth century. From this starting point (and with even less support), it was then argued by some other students of folklore that Samhain was the Celtic day of the dead. This was (and is) largely done by arguing that the Christian feast of All Saints or All Hallows (1 November) and All Souls (2 November) represent a Christianization of a previous pagan celebration. This is possible, but lacks evidence from medieval sources to prove it. On the contrary, it seems that the early Irish Church originally kept its All Saints' Day on 20 April and the relocation of the event to early November may simply have been due to the turning of the year towards shorter days and longer nights, which seemed a suitable time for a Christian celebration and then – later – this day also became focused on celebrating those whose faith had carried them through death.[29] Despite this, the interpretation of Samhain as originally a Celtic day of the dead has become widely accepted in the twenty-first century.

This said, there is evidence from much later folklore that it had, by the nineteenth century, become associated with anxieties about spirits affecting human events and in this it was a wintry counterpart to May Eve, when there was also concern that fairies, witches and Otherworldly beings had to be especially guarded against. How much of this was rooted in ancient Celtic mythology and seasonal practices and how much derived from folklore reinterpretations of the official Christian events of All Saints and All Souls is difficult to say. What is clear is that in a number of areas this event – like Beltane – was associated with bonfires across large parts of Ireland, Wales, the Isle of Man and Scotland and this has led to its being described in some folklore studies as another fire festival. To what extent this derived from original pre-Christian practices is difficult to say in the absence of the crucial medieval evidence. Similarly, attempts to link these activities with mythological beings is fraught with difficulty. Across Wales there was a belief in *yr Hwrch Ddu Gwta* ('the tail-less black sow'), who hunted for victims on this night. It is tempting to make a connection with boars that appeared in a number of medieval mythological tales such as that of Torc Triath, the great boar belonging to Brigid in Irish mythology. In Welsh mythology a similar boar was called Twrch Trwyth and was connected to Arthurian adventures. This connection is possible, although the names were totally different, as was the gender, and the supposed activities of these latter pigs bore no resemblance to the threat attributed to *yr Hwrch Ddu Gwta* on *Nos Galan Gaea*.

5

IRISH ORIGIN MYTHS: IRISH GODS BEFORE THE GODS

In Irish mythology the *Fomoire* or *Fomorii* (also often anglicized as Fomorians) were a race of sea gods of misshapen and hideous appearance. They were presented as semi-divine beings who were said to have lived in Ireland in very ancient times. They were sometimes said to have had the body of a man and the head of a goat or to have had one eye, one arm and one leg. They were beings of chaos. They may also have been considered to represent untamed nature before its harnessing by farmers and settlers. In these characteristics they stood in contrast to the *Tuatha Dé Danann* (see Chapter 6), who appeared to represent the gods of human activity and civilization. Given the negative way in which the Fomorians were portrayed in Irish mythology, it is possible that they were survivals from a belief system dating from before the culture of the Gaelic, or Goidelic, language speakers became dominant in Ireland. This may have led to their being shorn of any positive features they had possessed in earlier times. This is, of course, speculation, but it would explain something of their nature and the way in which they represented a stratum of gods earlier than the *Tuatha Dé Danann*. In the myths of the conflicts between these two groups of mythological beings we may see echoes of an actual conflict between competing sets of religious ideas in which one system superseded the other. We may even be seeing – through the lens of one layer of beliefs replacing another – the actual aftermath of violent invasion and cultural conquest. This, though, is harder to decide, as twenty-first century historians, archaeologists and students of mythology are far less willing than previous generations to associate changes of culture and language with the actual physical movement of peoples. In short, what are termed models of 'acculturation' (by which people adopt and adapt new ways of expressing their identities) have replaced theories of invasion. As a result, it is now less certain why belief in the Fomorians gave way to belief in the *Tuatha Dé Danann*.

However, the battles between the Fomorians and the *Tuatha Dé Danann* were simply one aspect of a series of mythological traditions of ancient invasions that attempted to explain the origins of Ireland and that culminated in the invasion of the *Tuatha Dé Danann* – who constituted a pantheon of gods whose attributes appeared in a number of forms across the 'Celtic world'. Since the *Tuatha Dé Danann* were the gods and goddesses of pre-Christian Ireland, these earlier invasions were, in effect, the doings of heroes and gods before the time of the gods. These accounts of the origins of Ireland are found in the *Book of Invasions* (*Leabhar Gábhala*) also known as the *Book of Invasions of Ireland* (*Lebor Gabála Érenn*). These two works form the major part of what modern students of Irish mythology call the Mythological Cycle. The *Book of Invasions*, which claims to tell the story of the early history of Ireland, is found in a manuscript of the twelfth century called the *Book of Leinster* (*Leabhar Laignech*) and was based on earlier traditions.[1] In these accounts we hear of the exploits of successive waves of invaders. These included the Cesair, the Partholonians, the Fomorians, the Nemedians and their descendants the *Firbolg*, the *Tuatha Dé Danann* and the Milesians, who were the final invaders and became the ancestors of the modern Gaelic-speaking Irish. The exploits of the *Tuatha Dé Danann* tended to dominate the mythology and so these will be explored in later chapters, along with the adventures of the Milesians. In this chapter, though, we will explore what evidence there is for the earlier stratum of Irish mythology, as recorded in the *Book of Invasions*.

Cesair, the granddaughter of Noah

This earliest invasion of Ireland was led by Cesair, the granddaughter of Noah. In this connection we see the activities of early Christian Irish writers attempting to connect their myths into biblical accounts by the creation of Bible-linked personalities who were then given Irish adventures. In some cases these may have been mythological beings who had had an independent existence in Irish mythology before being given their biblical pedigree. In other cases they may have been manufactured no earlier than the compilation of the first written sources in order to provide Ireland with a biblical connection. This was not at all unusual in the early medieval period and the same connections can be seen in Old English accounts that linked once-pagan Anglo-Saxon genealogies to Noah, through Sceaf, an invented son of Noah (said to have been born to Noah's wife in the ark in order to explain why he does not exist in the Genesis account that lists the sons of Noah who went into the ark!).[2] Cesair was not allowed into the ark and left before the Flood, travelling to Ireland. As he arrived with fifty women but only three men, the survival of the settlement was in jeopardy. Cesair married one of these: Fintan Mac Bochra. However, the settlement failed because the other two men died and Fintan left Ireland in the form of a salmon. Cesair died of a broken heart and the whole settlement came to nothing.

The Partholonians

These were the first to arrive in Ireland *after* the biblical Flood. According to the *Book of Invasions* they arrived some 312 years after Cesair. Coming from the West their origins were rather obscure even by the standards of mythology since they were also said to have originated in Greece. Their leader, Partholon, was in exile after murdering his own parents. After seven years of wandering they reached Ireland. Here, they battled the Fomorians, who were already in Ireland, and drove them from that country. However, the Partholonians' settlement foundered because a plague killed them all except for Tuan, a nephew of Partholon. In turn, Tuan witnessed the arrival of a new group of settlers, the Nemedians. He survived this invasion by taking on the appearance of a number of animals: stag, boar, eagle, salmon. Finally – while in this final transformation – he was caught and eaten by the wife of a man named Cairill. Having eaten him, the woman became pregnant and gave birth to a son named Tuan mac Cairill. Tuan went on to write a history of the early settlement of Ireland. This shape-shifting is a feature of Celtic mythology and will be explored in more detail later (see Chapter 9).

The Nemedians and their descendants

In Irish mythology the Fomorians fought three other competitors for control of the island of Ireland: the Partholonians, the Nemedians and the descendants of the latter, the *Firbolg* (or *Fir Bholg*) and the *Tuatha Dé Danann.*

After the Partholonians, the Nemedians, as we have seen, invaded Ireland. Coming variously from the West and from Spain, they are the first hint of a recurring theme in Irish mythology: a connection between Ireland and the Iberian peninsula.[3] They wandered the sea for eighteen months in a fleet of thirty-two ships, only one of which made it to Ireland. This ship carried Nemed, his four sons and their followers. Nemed was descended from Japheth, a son of Noah. Like the Partholonians before them, the Nemedians battled the fearsome Fomorians. Despite four great victories over the Fomorians, the Nemedians were devastated by plague (like the Partholonians before them) and so succumbed to the power of the Fomorians. Forced to pay huge tribute to their overlords, the Nemedians eventually rose in revolt and besieged the Fomorians on their stronghold of Tory Island. Despite killing a Fomorian king, only thirty Nemedians survived the battle and they fled from Ireland. Fergus Lethderg, their leader, went with his son Britán Máel to Alba (i.e. Scotland) and from this son the island of 'Britain' took its name.[4] Other surviving Nemedians reached Greece, where they were enslaved and became known as the *Firbolg*, which means 'bag men'. In an attempt to link Irish mythology to the Classical world their name was said to derive from the time when they were enslaved in Greece, in Thrace.[5] At that time they were forced to carry bags of fertile soil up the rocky Thracian hillsides to prepare the terrain for cultivation. This rather curious tradition may itself indicate that the *Firbolg* were associated with fertility cults of early Irish communities. Eventually the *Firbolg* revolted against their slave status, turned their bags into hide boats and set sail for Ireland. In this way descendants of the Nemedians returned to that land. In reality the *Firbolg* may have taken their name from an otherwise unknown god, Builg.[6] Other members of the Nemedians were said to have reached the far north of the known world. Here they became known as the '*Tuatha Dé*'. They too would later return to Ireland and would be remembered as the *Tuatha Dé Danann*.[7]

This connection between Ireland and the European mainland is present in a number of Irish myths and may represent two main outlooks. One was an attempt to reflect a tradition of successive invasions of Ireland in pre-history. This may have arisen from real movements of peoples or elites, or may have been influenced by Christian accounts of Old Testament movements of peoples. Such an Old Testament influence is now thought to have impacted on Anglo-Saxon traditions of invasion and settlement that are found in Old English sources such as *The Anglo-Saxon Chronicle* and Bede.[8] In these Old English accounts the protagonists were always described as fully human but they often reveal mythological elements such as genealogies descending from Germanic gods and have names such as Hengest and Horsa (Stallion and Mare) that may indicate originally mythological characters. In the Anglo-Saxon accounts the style of their conquest owed a great deal to models drawn from the Old Testament and the Israelite conquest of Canaan. The Irish accounts, by contrast, clearly portrayed the protagonists as god-like but still provided them with a semi-historical setting as if they really were actual invaders. Here we see an example of how real peoples and their culture were later presented as divine. In this process, known as 'euhemerism', myths are interpreted as traditional accounts of historical persons and events that have been given mythological attributes and status. Also, although seeming thoroughly pagan, these Irish accounts too may have been influenced by Old Testament models of conquest, along with Greek and Roman traditions about their own civilizations having been founded by the arrival of their ancestors. The second reason for the reference to Thrace may simply have been that classically literate Church writers wished to link Irish origins to the Ancient Greeks and the world of the Mediterranean. A connection with the Greeks or Romans conferred a civilized legitimacy to the concepts of many early medieval writers.

In the Irish accounts the *Firbolg* were defeated by the Fomorians, although they were actually vanquished by the incoming *Tuatha Dé Danann*. This victory, though, came at a heavy price for the leader of the *Tuatha Dé Danann*, Nuada, who lost a hand in the battle. The defeated *Firbolg* retreated to the Aran Islands (County Galway) where they constructed the stone-built fort of Dún Aonghasa on the island of Inishmore. This spectacular fortification still stands on the edge of a 100-metre high cliff. It is actually an Iron Age fort that may date from the second century BC, but its impressive ramparts and dramatic setting have caused it to be woven into folklore and mythology. Its name means the 'Fort of Aonghus', which may be a reference to one of the *Tuatha Dé Danann*, named Oengus in Old Irish. In Middle Irish this name became Áengus, and in Modern Irish Aengus, Aonghus or Angus. Alternatively, the fort may take its name from Aonghus mac Úmhór (Aengus mac Umor), a king of the *Firbolg*, whose people – the *Tuath mhac nUmhoir* – moved here after their defeat at the first battle of Magh Tuireadh (see below). Despite their defeat at the hands of the *Tuatha Dé Danann*, the *Firbolg* were allowed to retain control of the province of Connacht.

The continuing connection between the *Firbolg* and the *Tuatha Dé Danann* was reinforced by the marriage of Tailtiu – the widow of the last *Firbolg* king, Eochaid mac Eirc – to a warrior of the *Tuatha Dé Danann*, Eochaid Garb mac Dúach. Tailtiu was the daughter of the King of the Mag Mor ('the Great Plain'), from the Land of the Dead. This was probably another reference to Spain. As the foster mother of Lugh, the sun god, Tailtiu was honoured by the *Tuatha Dé Danann* at the religious festival of Lughnasa on 1 August. This event was established by Lugh as a funeral feast and commemorative games in memory of his foster mother, who had died from exhaustion after preparing the plains of Ireland for farming. Traditionally, the first day of

August marked the start of the harvest festival and was a popular time for making marriage contracts.

Despite the fact that in the mythology of invasions the *Firbolg* appeared as inferior to both the later *Tuatha Dé Danann* and the Milesians, a *Firbolg* warrior, named Fer Díad, appeared as a childhood companion of Cú Chulainn, the so-called Hound of Ulster in the Ulster Heroic Cycle. He was eventually forced into combat with Cú Chulainn and was killed by him.

The Fomorians

After the *Tuatha Dé Danann* defeated the *Firbolg* at the first battle of Magh Tuireadh (County Sligo) they then had to repeat this conflict, at the same place, in order to defeat the Fomorians. In this battle the Fomorians appeared as a menacing and evil force. This is well represented in John Duncan's painting of 1912 *The Fomors or the Power of Evil abroad in the World*. In this the violent and misshapen Fomorians appear in a range of ugly forms, including: a Gollum-like creature advancing on all fours, a fish walking on two legs, a hobgoblin-like figure, a club-wielding dog-faced creature, a red baby-like dwarf and a white-veiled being riding on a broken-down white horse. Their ugliness and threat are major elements of the painting and for Duncan they had clearly become a metaphor for all that was violent and ill-formed in the world. The Fomorians are made to communicate frenzy and menace, so it is not surprising that their eventual defeat at the second battle of Magh Tuireadh was largely due to the courage of the sun god Lugh. Here we can see a clear contrast between the forces of darkness and light, in which the forces of light triumphed.

The Fomorians featured in the traditions associated with a number of the invaders of Ireland but were never themselves depicted as arriving there. They were portrayed as raiders and destroyers rather than settlers. Nor were they depicted as ancestors of the later Irish peoples, and they appeared at the edges of other traditions as a negative and destructive force that overshadowed Ireland. At various times they oppressed both the Nemedians and the *Tuatha Dé Danann* before being finally overthrown at the second battle of Magh Tuireadh. In accounts of this battle their total untrustworthiness is paramount to the story. The most detailed of these accounts is found in the *Battle of Mag Tuired* (*Cath Maige Tuired*), which, while surviving in only two manuscripts, from the sixteenth and seventeenth centuries, clearly contained much older traditions.[9] After defeating the *Firbolg* at the first battle of Magh Tuireadh the *Tuatha Dé Danann* found themselves leaderless since Nuada lost his right hand in single combat. Even though he was given a replacement silver hand,[10] his maimed status rendered him ineligible for leadership. In order to repair relations with the Fomorians, the *Tuatha Dé Danann* chose as their leader a Fomorian named Bres son of Elatha. In addition, a warrior of the *Tuatha Dé Danann* – Dian Cécht (or Céc) – married Ethne, the daughter of the leading Fomorian warrior Balor of the One Eye or Balor of the Evil Eye. Almost immediately the error of choosing Bres was revealed as he showed himself a tyrannical king, who reduced the *Tuatha Dé Danann* to slavery. This was therefore a period in which darkness and evil dominated Ireland and oppressed its non-Fomorian settlers. It was only when a new hand of flesh and bone was fashioned for Nuada that the tyranny of Bres was challenged. Even then it was only after Fomorian deceit and treachery came close to defeating the *Tuatha Dé Danann*. Disguised as one of the *Tuatha Dé Danann*, Ruadan son of Bres killed the god of smiths, Goibhniu, who was repairing the broken weapons of the *Tuatha Dé Danann*. That night another Fomorian, Octriallach son of Indech, along with other Fomorians, destroyed the healing spring that was being used to revive the wounded warriors of the *Tuatha Dé Danann*. It was only then – confident that the *Tuatha Dé Danann* were now mortal – that Bres launched into a pitched battle.

During this battle the Fomorians came close to victory when the Fomorian champion, Balor of the Evil Eye, killed both Nuada of the Silver Hand and Nuada's beautiful wife, Macha, the goddess of warriors. The evil of Balor was so pronounced that he killed with his one-eyed stare. So terrible and large was this killing-eye that it took nine attendants with hooks to lift the lid. The hideous nature and appearance of the Fomorians was clearly revealed in the descriptions of Balor of the Evil Eye. It is also significant that the concept of the curse of the evil eye, which is found in many cultures,[11] was explicitly associated with the Fomorians. It was only the late arrival of Lugh Lámhfada (Lugh of the Long Arm, or, literally, the Long Hand) – previously kept from battle by the *Tuatha Dé Danann* for his own safety – that saved the *Tuatha Dé Danann* from destruction and led to the death of Balor of the Evil Eye. Lugh's slingshot knocked out Balor's eye, but even as it lay on the ground, its evil was so potent that it killed twenty-seven of his own Fomorian warriors who looked at it. Lugh then spared the life of Bres, in return for Bres teaching the skills of knowing when to plough, sow and reap. After this the Fomorians were driven back to their underwater fortress and forced to accept the dominance of the *Tuatha Dé Danann* over Ireland.

The strangely disconnected status of the Fomorians as a result of never being directly described as settlers, along with the explicit association of their influence with evil, may suggest, as was mentioned earlier, either that they were always regarded as the embodiment of evil or that they were reduced to this status because of the success of later pagan religious ideologies in prehistoric Ireland. It is now impossible to decide between these two possibilities. It is significant, though, that the mythological traditions concerning their eventual defeat at the second battle of

Magh Tuireadh stated that the battle lines were drawn up on the evening of the Feast of Samhain (31 October). This association of the battle with Samhain is surely important since this end-of-harvest event also marked the end of the light half of the year and the start of the dark half. As such it also became associated, in historic times, with a festival of the dead. That the defeat of the Fomorians was thought to have occurred at this time, and that this defeat was finally brought about by the sun god Lugh, further emphasized the mythological association of the Fomorians with darkness and their defeat with the victory of light at a darkening time of the year.

Other strands within Irish mythology also picked up this connection between the Fomorians and darkness and winter. In the tales of Colgáin Mac Teine (found within the collection of stories called the Fenian Cycle, or Ossianic Cycle) this warrior was made King of Lochlann and was a descendant of the Fomorians. Lochlann was described as a land of fjords and lakes, cold, snowy and dark; from it came sea pirates who pillaged Ireland. This was not the only connection made between the Fomorians, Scandinavia and what are clearly the historic Viking enemies of Ireland. Lochlann was described as the home of the Fomorians in the *Book of Invasions* (*Leabhar Gábhala*). The association of the mythical Fomorians with the very real Vikings of the ninth and tenth centuries was also made in the manuscript the *Book of the Dun Cow* (*Lebor na hUidre*) and in the *Book of Leinster* (*Lebor Laignech*), both compiled in the twelfth century and in both of which the Fomorians were described as pirates living in the Outer Hebrides. Clearly, by that time at least, the Fomorians had become synonymous with forces of destruction both mythical and historical.

What is also clear is that, within the cycle of Irish mythological traditions, their defeat gave rise to the triumphant settlement and dominance of the *Tuatha Dé Danann*. And

it was this group whose exploits dominated Irish mythological traditions and whose members were regarded as
gods by the pre-Christian Irish population. It is significant
that, as well as being called 'the Children of Danu', they
were also referred to as the 'Ever-Living Ones', which further emphasized the belief in their divine status.

6

IRISH ORIGIN MYTHS: THE PEOPLE OF THE GODDESS DANA

In Gaelic literature the '*Tuatha Dé Danann*' were the descendants of the goddess Dana, or Danu. The *Tuatha Dé Danann* were the race of supernatural beings who conquered the Fomorians, who previously had dominated Ireland. As has been explained in Chapter 5, this mythological 'invasion' (the fifth one of several) was described in the twelfth-century *Book of Invasions* (*Leabhar Gábhala*) also known as the *Book of Invasions of Ireland* (*Lebor Gabála Érenn*).[1] Before the compilation of the *Book of Invasions*, the fifth group of invaders were simply called the *Tuatha Dé* ('the people of the god'); it was the twelfth-century reworking of this tradition that created the name '*Tuatha Dé Danann*' ('the people of the goddess Dana'). This may have been due to the writer's attempt to differentiate this group from other mythical beings, or to an attempt to downgrade pagan beliefs by identifying Irish pagans as subject to a female divinity.[2]

In the Irish tradition of the origins of the inhabitants of Ireland, the *Tuatha Dé Danann* were the immediate pre-decessors of the final invaders: the Gaelic Sons of Mil (the Milesians). Consequently, the *Tuatha Dé Danann* were a bridge between the mythological inhabitants of Ireland and its human inhabitants who became the historic, Gael-ic-speaking Irish.

The invasion of the *Tuatha Dé Danann*

According to the *Book of Invasions of Ireland*, the *Tuatha Dé Danann* fought two great battles when they invaded Ireland. At the first battle of Magh Tuireadh they defeated the previous inhabitants of the island, the *Firbolg*. At the second battle of Magh Tuireadh they defeated the Fomo-rians, a hideous race of misshapen monsters who had oppressed Ireland before this event.

According to Irish tradition, the *Tuatha Dé Danann* brought four talismans to assist them in the conquest of Ireland. The first was the Stone of Fál. This was said to cry out when a lawful king sat on it and so proved his right to rule. The second was the Spear, or slingshot of Lugh Lámh-fada (Lugh of the Long Arm, or, literally, the Long Hand). This guaranteed victory in battle. The third was the Sword of Nuada, or Nuadu. It was such a powerful weapon that no one could escape it in battle. The fourth was the Caul-dron of the Daghda (see Chapter 7). This had the power to satisfy all who consumed its contents. The possession of talismans that reinforced authority is common to a number of mythological traditions, including those of Greece and Rome. In contrast with the Greek and Roman ones, the Irish talismans were not thought of as falling from the sky but were still considered to have had an airborne origin. In the Irish account, the *Tuatha Dé Danann* arrived – with their talismans – on dark clouds, transported to a moun-tain in western Ireland.[3]

The different areas of expertise of the
Tuatha Dé Danann

The *Tuatha Dé Danann* were skilled in the use of magic and in druidic lore and knowledge. For this reason, traditions about them formed the basis for the claims of historic early medieval Irish pagan priests that their rites and learning were directly gained from the gods.[4] Different gods were associated with different aspects of this knowledge. The chief deity, the Daghda, was thought to be the god who specialized in druidic magic. The god Ogma (see below) specialized in the skills required for the successful pursuit of warfare. He was therefore the god of warriors but also of writing. Lugh was the god of arts and crafts as well as the sun god. Dian Cécht (or Céc) knew the secrets of medicine and healing. In the war against the Fomorians he provided the healing water in which wounded members of the *Tuatha Dé Danann* bathed and were restored to health. He was, however, jealous of his healing knowledge and killed his own son when his healing powers surpassed those of his father. Goibhniu was the god of smithing and the making of weapons. He was later reinvented as 'St Gobnet' and archaeological excavation of his shrine at Ballyvourney (County Cork) revealed that it was built on the multiple forges of a pre-Christian industrial centre.[5] These skills and knowledge were said to have been gained in four cities of the north: Falias, Gorias, Finias and Murias.[6]

Irish mythology names many other gods and goddesses of the *Tuatha Dé Danann*; too many to list them all. In fact, within the two main sources that list the descendants of Dana – found in the *Book of Invasions of Ireland* and the *Battle of Magh Tuireadh* (*Cath Maige Tuired*) of the sixteenth century – the contradictions in the genealogies cannot be reconciled. However, despite this complexity, some stand out as particularly prominent in Irish myths.

Members of the *Tuatha Dé Danann*

The chief god of the *Tuatha Dé Danann* was thought to be the Daghda (see Chapter 7), who was the son of Dana, a mother goddess with powers over the earth and fertility. Like a number of the gods of the *Tuatha Dé Danann*, Dana was worshipped in a number of pagan societies, and surviving names for her include Dana, Danu and Anu among European Celts and in Ireland, and Don in Wales. Dana appears to have been the wife of Bilé and the mother of the Daghda and possibly the mother of the gods Dian Cécht (or Céc) and Nuada of the Silver Hand. The complexity and lack of clarity in the myths reveals itself in one tradition that made the Irish god of writing (Ogma or Oghma) the son of the Daghda and Dana (who in other sources was the mother of the Daghda). However, in a different source Ogma was the brother of the Daghda and both were described as the sons of Eithne. Druid tradition claimed Ogma as the originator of the early medieval linear, twiglike writing used to carve words on stone, wood and bone that became known as Ogham.[7] During the time that the Fomorian, Bres son of Elatha, was king over the *Tuatha Dé Danann*, Ogma was humiliated and forced to gather firewood. This was probably a tradition designed to signal the extent of the Fomorian opposition to the forces of civilization, as exemplified by the use of writing (i.e. Ogham). Nuada was King of Erin (Ireland) and leader of the *Tuatha Dé Danann*. The name may mean 'cloud maker'. In the first battle of Magh Tuireadh, against the *Firbolg* (see Chapter 5), Nuada lost his hand and, because he was maimed, his kingship. He regained this status, though, when a silver replacement hand was fashioned for him by Dian Cécht. Hence his new name of Nuada Airgedlámh (Nuada of the Silver Hand). Leading the *Tuatha Dé Danann* in the second battle of Magh Tuireadh, against the Fomorians, Nuada was killed. He was apparently the father of Murna of the White Neck, who was the mother of the warrior hero Finn (or Fionn) mac Cumhaill. The Welsh equivalent of Nuada was either Nudd Llaw Ereint or Lludd Llaw Ereint (Nudd/Lludd of the Silver Hand).

In the second battle of Magh Tuireadh, the *Tuatha Dé Danann* were saved from defeat by the timely arrival of Lugh. Lugh was the son of a god named Cian, who was the son of Dian Cécht. Cian was mortally wounded while on a journey in the form of a pig. His death was only briefly described in the twelfth-century *Book of Invasions of Ireland* but this tradition was later expanded in a story called the *Death of the Children of Tuireann* (*Oidheadh Chlainne Tuireann*), the earliest manuscript of which survives from the sixteenth century, with seventeenth-century additions. In this expanded account, Lugh avenged his father's death by capturing those responsible (the sons of Tuireann) and setting them tasks that eventually led to their deaths. The last task involved the gaining of a magic pig-skin that would cure all wounds. Mortally injured in obtaining it, the warriors were denied its use to heal their wounds by Lugh, who thus avenged his father's death at their hands. There is a great deal of evidence to show that the god Lugh of the Irish sources was a sun god worshipped across the Celtic world. In Ireland, Lugh was particularly associated with the feast of Lughnasa on 1 August. He was thought to own a magic sword that was one of the treasures of the *Tuatha Dé Danann*. In later Irish traditions Lugh was made the father of the great warrior hero Cú Chulainn and fought disguised as his son – as described in the twelfth-century *Cattle Raid of Cooley* (*Táin Bó Cúailnge*) – in order to allow Cú Chulainn time to recover from wounds sustained in an encounter with the war goddess the Morrígan.

A number of Irish goddesses associated with the *Tuatha Dé Danann* had a triple character that derived from the sacred nature of the number three in Celtic mythology. They also combined a sexual role with a war role. Perhaps the most famous of these was the Morrígan, a name that means something like 'phantom queen'. The Morrígan was one of the wives of the Daghda. During the festival of Samhain (1 November) it was believed that she slept with the Daghda and that this annual coupling renewed the prosperity of Ireland. Consequently, she was seen as the sovereignty of Ireland. This ritual mating with the Daghda was thought to occur with the Morrígan standing with either foot on the banks of a river. However, this was not the only role this goddess played. Like the Badbh (see below), the Morrígan could also shape-shift into a crow or a raven and affect the course of battles. Her third role was as the goddess of prophecy. The Morrígan also appeared in the forms of the goddesses the Badbh and Macha.[8] It is unclear whether these were three aspects of the same goddess or originally three separate goddesses[9] who became so closely associated that the name 'the Morrígan' became applied to all three. To complicate things further, some sources claim that 'the Morrígan' was another name for Dana/Danu. A famous story concerning the Morrígan linked her to the Ulster hero Cú Chulainn. She appeared to him in the form of a beautiful girl but, when spurned, attacked him in the form of an eel, a wolf and a red heifer. Cú Chulainn beat off her attacks but was exhausted by the contest; then the Morrígan appeared as an old woman milking a cow. She gave Cú Chulainn milk and was herself healed of the wounds inflicted on her. Traditions concerning the Morrígan also represented her as a prophetess. In this role she warned the Brown Bull of Cúailnge (Cooley) of its fate; a story found in the *Cattle Raid of Cooley* already referred to. After mating with the Daghda, she told him how to defeat the Fomorians. The Morrígan was also believed to appear as the 'Washer at the Ford' who foretold the deaths of warriors by washing their weapons and armour in a river. She was also described as a caster of spells, as when she transformed a woman named Odras into a pool of water because her bull had mated with the Morrígan's magic cows.

The Badbh ('fury', 'violence') had a role very similar to that of the Morrígan in the Ulster Cycle of tales, and sometimes appeared in a triple form. It was the Badbh who, in the form of a crow, landed on Cú Chulainn's shoulder and so signalled to his attackers that it was safe to approach him and behead him. As evidence of the similarity between the Badbh and the Morrígan, some accounts claimed that it was the Morrígan who did this. Similarly, the Badbh was also believed to show herself as the 'Washer at the Ford'. In *The Destruction of Da Derga's Hostel* (*Togail Bruidne Dá Derga*), composed c.1100 and a part of the Ulster Cycle, she appeared as a sign of impending doom.

Macha, like the Morrígan, was also thought to have combined sexual and war roles. The same characteristic was also associated with Queen Medb of Connacht, who, though represented as a queen, seems actually to have been regarded as a goddess. A ninth-century commentator described her as 'Macha the crow',[10] underlining her similarity to the Morrígan and the Badbh. Irish traditions gave Macha three functions: prophetess, warrior and mother. This triple nature is again reminiscent of the Morrígan and the Badbh. In the mother role she was made by her husband, Crunnchu, to compete in a race against horses while heavily pregnant and this cost Macha her life. Before she died she uttered the curse that, in their hour of need, the men of Ulster would become as weak as a woman in childbirth for five days and four nights.

A similar goddess who sometimes appeared as a beautiful woman but was also a war goddess was Nemain ('venomous' or 'dreadful') and she too was sometimes portrayed as a crow flying over a battlefield. She was identified as the wife of Nuada, the King of Erin (Ireland) and leader of the *Tuatha Dé Danann*; or sometimes as the wife of Neit, god of war.

Another goddess with a triple character was Ernmas. She was believed to have been the mother of the three goddesses who protected the sovereignty of Ireland.[11] These were Banbha, Fódla and Ériu. In one tradition the father of these three goddesses was Ernmas's own son, Fiachna. In the battle of Tailtiu, Ériu and her sisters, along with their husbands, were killed by the Milesians. The deaths were highly symbolic as they represented the end of the sovereignty of the *Tuatha Dé Danann* over Ireland and its transfer to the Milesians.

A very famous goddess was Brigid (Brigit), the goddess of healing and fertility and of poetry and metalworking. This deity's name was originally a title, 'exalted one'. In common with other Irish goddesses, there was a tripartite aspect to her nature and she was often associated with two sisters. She was considered to be the daughter of the Daghda and was particularly associated with the province of Leinster. The fertility aspect of her cult explains her association with the festival of Imbolc (1 February), which was one of the four main Celtic seasonal festivals (see Chapter 4) and was associated with the lactation of ewes. She is particularly notable for being reinvented as a Christian saint. St Brigid was, in hagiographical accounts, raised in the household of a druid and could supply limitless food and huge quantities of milk and malt for brewing. Her feast day was fixed on 1 February and underscores the connection with the pagan goddess.

Boann was the wife of the river god Nechtan, or Echmar, and she was particularly associated with the river Boyne. It is likely that she was a personification of the river and that the river was originally thought of as being divine. The story of Boann is found in the twelfth-century *History of Places* (*Dinnshenchas*). This account explained the origins of her association with the river Boyne by explaining that she had visited the forbidden well of her husband, Nechtan, which was located in the fairy mound of *Sídhe Nechtan*. Since she had broken a taboo, the water became a river that overwhelmed her. In this way she became synonymous with the river Boyne. In addition to this tale there is one in which, while her husband was away, Boann had an affair with the Daghda. As a result of enchantment by the Daghda, her husband thought that his journey took one day and one night, when it actually took nine months. During this time the Daghda concealed the pregnancy of Boann and the birth of a son (Oengus Óg, or Oengus mac Óg) to her.

Flidais was goddess of the hunt but also the protector of wild animals. She had a chariot pulled by deer. A fertility role for Flidais was also apparent in the tradition that she was the only woman, apart from Queen Medb of Connacht, who could sexually satisfy Ferghus mac Róich. Otherwise, Ferghus would need to bed no fewer than seven ordinary women. Ferghus mac Róich was a warrior of the Red Branch of Ulster and was one of those who found the infant hero Cú Chulainn and later trained him as a warrior.

The Irish goddess of the sky and of human love was Áine. She was the patron goddess of the province of Munster. Her annual festival was celebrated on Midsummer Eve at Knockainy (the Hill of Áine), County Limerick. In the tale the *Battle of Mag Mucrama* (*Cath Maige Mucrama*) – the earliest version of which survives in the *Book of Leinster* (*Lebor Laignech*) and dates from the middle of the twelfth century – Áine had a son by Ailill Aulom, who was named Éogan Mór and whose descendants, the Eóganachta, became the kings of Munster. This seems to have been a politically motivated story that explained why this family was so prominent and connected it to a mythic origin in the *Tuatha Dé Danann*.

The god of the sea was Lír, who appeared in Welsh mythology as Llŷr. The most famous tale about Lir was actually not about him but about his children, who were changed into swans by his third wife. This tradition can be found in a late medieval romance, the *Death of the Children of Lir* (*Oidheadh Chlainne Lír*), which is found in a

manuscript of *c.*1500 (see Chapter 9). Manannán was identified as the son of Lir and was also god of the sea. It seems
that Manannán supplanted Lir in this role and it may be
that they were originally from different traditions and were
brought together in this 'family' relationship. Manannán
was also believed to have been a god of healing and the
weather. Other traditions in the Ulster Cycle described
his wife having an affair with the warrior Cú Chulainn.
Manannán was called Manawyddan in Welsh, and was the
son of Llŷr and the brother of the god Brân. He was married to Aife (Aoífe), who was transformed into a crane, and
in this form she was killed and her skin used to create a
magical treasure bag. In the twelfth-century Fenian Cycle
of tales this skin came to belong to the warrior Finn (or
Fionn) mac Cumhaill. Manannán drove a chariot pulled
by two supernatural horses across the waves and, when
the *Tuatha Dé Danann* were defeated by the Milesians,
it was he who led them into their new Otherworld – and
underground – home. Traditionally, Manannán's home lay
on the Isle of Man. This was probably less a geographical
location and more a statement that he lived on an island in
the ocean. Another tradition named his home as being on
Emhain Abhlach ('Emhain of the apple trees'), which some
sources identified as the Isle of Arran, in the Firth of Clyde.
As with the reference to the Isle of Man, this was apparently a geographical surrogate for a place that was really of
the Otherworld.[12] The same image of an Otherworld isle of
apples appeared in the Welsh traditions relating to Avalon
(also meaning 'isle of apples') and King Arthur. Some Irish
traditions attempted to portray Manannán as a historical
figure who was later regarded as a divinity. This approach
was followed by the writer Cormac macCuilennáin in his
Glossary, written *c.*900. In this account, Manannán was
presented as a merchant and navigator who lived on the Isle
of Man and was later treated as a god by the Irish and the
British. This reworking of pagan gods as heroic ancestors

is found in a number of early medieval accounts, where Christian writers adapted the traditions of their once-pagan cultures. Manannán featured in the fabulous voyage of Bran son of Febal. As Bran and his twenty-seven kinsmen set off on their journey they met Manannán driving his chariot across the waves. The sea god then informed the travellers of the marvels awaiting them on their journey.[13]

Other gods of the *Tuatha Dé Danann* included Oengus Óg (or mac Óg), the god of love and youth; Bodb Derg, the god of poetry and wisdom, whose silver-sandalled feet did not disturb the dew on the grass; Midir son of the Daghda, who featured in the Ulster and Fenian Cycles of stories; Neit, the god of war, who may have been the consort of the Morrígan, and was also associated with both Nemain and the Badbh. Given the complex nature of the Morrígan and her association with other female war deities, it is possible that these different wives were actually regarded as one and the same goddess.

The traditions associated with Bodb Derg, Oengus Óg and Midir will be dealt with in an exploration of the beliefs associated with the family of the Daghda (see Chapter 7).

Irish mythology also contained the names of other deities who were not members of the *Tuatha Dé Danann*. One was Donn, god of the Underworld and responsible for the journey of the dead from the land of the living. There seems to have been a particular focus on the worship of this god in Munster. Another was Crom Cruach, the god of weather and fertility. His worship involved human sacrifice, especially of the first-born. In the *Book of Leinster*, once known as the *Book of Nuachongbáil* (*Lebor na Nuachongbála*) and compiled *c.*1160, it was the Milesian king Tigernmas, son of Fallach and High King of Ireland, who first introduced the worship of Crom Cruach to Ireland. In this bloody account, one Samhain night Tigernmas and a third of the worshippers destroyed themselves in the violence associated with the worship of Crom Cruach. Two other deities separate from the *Tuatha Dé Danann* were Domnu, a goddess of the Fomorians, and Eochaid, god of the sun and of lightning. His sword was described as a thunderbolt and he was depicted as a warrior on horseback. These gods were possibly deities of one of the groups later subsumed by other prehistoric movements of either tribes or elites and whose only survival in the written record is in the names of some of their gods.

7

IRISH ORIGIN MYTHS: THE DAGHDA AND HIS CHILDREN

Regarded as chief of the Celtic gods in Irish tradition and a High King of the *Tuatha Dé Danann* (see Chapter 6), the Daghda was presented as a warrior armed with a massive club, a craftsman, controller of the seasons, owner of a magical cauldron, two pigs (one was always growing and the other was always roasting) and of fruit trees that were always bearing fruit. By examining the stories that explained the attributes of the Daghda we can begin to understand the role of this chief god and his family within Irish mythology. The mythology of the Daghda was confined to Ireland and does not appear among the traditions of other Celtic peoples.

The name of the Daghda was actually a title meaning 'the good god'. Presented as a father god in the Irish myths, he was associated with magical powers and with fertility and abundance. His other titles included *Eochaidh ollathair*

('Eochaidh the great father') and *Ruadh rofhessa* ('mighty one of great knowledge').[1] Some sources named his father as Elatha, a Fomorian. Unlike the other Fomorians, Elatha was described as handsome, with long, golden hair, and wearing a golden cloak decorated with five golden wheels. He was also named as the father of Bres, the Fomorian who was, for a short time, the tyrannical ruler of the *Tuatha Dé Danann* before being overthrown. The claim that Elatha was also the father of the Daghda suggests either a confusion in the sources or an attempt by an editor to reconcile the fact that he had before him both the mythological tradition that a Fomorian once ruled the *Tuatha Dé Danann* and the separate strand of tradition that described the powerful battle skills of the Daghda. The invention of a common father to both the tyrannical Bres and the approved-of figure of the Daghda may have been regarded as explaining how such a complex situation occurred, since both would then have been half-brothers of comparable power. Alternatively, this may be assuming too great a logical motivation and it may have been due to nothing more than a compiler who was aware of two mythological figures – the handsome Elatha and the powerful Daghda – and so invented a new relationship between them in order to harmonize his sources. The sources are even more confused regarding the mother of the Daghda. She was sometimes named as Ethniu (daughter of Delbáeth), who was the wife of Nuada. However, other sources made her the daughter of the Fomorian Balor and the mother of Lugh of the *Tuatha Dé Danann*. The confusion is complete in that other texts named the goddess Danu as mother of the Daghda, while yet others named the Daghda as the father of Danu. This is an example of the genealogical confusion in the texts relating the origins of the Irish gods, and this textual confusion is irresolvable.

The Daghda was regarded as the god of druidism and its magical spells. This association of power (including power to deal death) with the provision of life was made clear in two of the objects associated with the Daghda. The first was his club, one end of which killed the living while the other revived the dead.[2] This club was so large that it was often depicted as being pulled along on wheels. It was so heavy, it was said, that as he dragged it the track left behind was as deep as the boundary ditch between two kingdoms. It was therefore similar to Thor's hammer in Norse mythology.[3] Allied to the concept of provision was the huge cauldron of the Daghda, named the Undry, which produced an inexhaustible supply of food and drink. The cauldron was from a magical city called Murias; this was one of the four great cities of the *Tuatha Dé Danann*. In a related characteristic, the Daghda was also regarded as the god of weather and crops. This responsibility also affected his magic harp of oak, Uaithne, which, when the Daghda played it, ensured that the seasons of the year fell into their correct sequence. Uaithne was once captured by the Fomorians, but when the Daghda chanted a magic spell the harp flew to him and killed nine of them as it did so.

The paradoxes of the Daghda

The paradoxical nature of the Daghda was made clear in the ambiguous death-dealing and life-giving club. When he wielded his club, it was said, the bones of his enemies were broken like hailstones under the hooves of horses. The club could kill nine men at one blow. In battle the Daghda led the *Tuatha Dé Danann* and destroyed their enemies.

The same ambiguity concerning life and death was revealed in the sexual activity of the Daghda. He was depicted as mating with Boann – the spiritual representation of the river Boyne – and this sexual act clearly represented the mother goddess mating with the tribal god in order to ensure the fertility of the land. On the other hand, the Daghda was also described as mating with the Morrígan, who was associated with war, death and destruction.

This may have been understood to have represented the Daghda ensuring the security of Ireland by being allied with the forces of war.

This complex and dual nature appeared in other aspects of the mythology associated with the Daghda, this leading god of the *Tuatha Dé Danann*. He was presented as a god of wisdom but also as crude and rough. He was portrayed as wearing a very short rustic tunic[4] that did not cover his massive penis, which dragged along the ground.[5] The shortness of the tunic was significant because it was a fashion associated with the poor peasant and it exemplified the strange way in which this father god was also considered an object of ridicule and fun.[6]

Similarly, on one occasion an encounter with the Fomorians revealed his huge capacity for overeating. On the eve of the second battle of Magh Tuireadh he was said to have visited the camp of the Fomorians. This was during a truce at the time of the New Year festival. The Fomorians made for him a massive porridge from eighty measures of milk, eighty measures of fat, eighty measures of flour, and to this they added goats and sheep and pigs. It was enough to have fed fifty men. The meal was designed to mock the Daghda because it was well known that he greatly liked porridge and could not resist it when it was offered. After it was cooked the porridge was poured into a great hole in the ground. The Daghda was ordered to eat this vast meal or be killed by his Fomorian enemies. Far from being overwhelmed by the task, he consumed it all with a ladle so large that it was said that a man and a woman could have lain together in its bowl. When the ladle could not retrieve any more, the Daghda scraped the bottom of the hole with his fingers. As a result of eating this gargantuan meal the Daghda was changed into a grossly overweight old man and fell asleep. But once again his ambiguity was apparent, for even in this state he had sex with a Fomorian woman, who then promised to use her magic on behalf of the *Tuatha Dé*

Danann. It has been suggested that this was a mythological accompaniment to a real-life union of king and priestess in prehistoric Ireland: an act that was believed to ensure the prosperity of the land.[7]

Although the Daghda was usually portrayed as victorious in battle, the narrative of the subjugation of the *Tuatha Dé Danann* during the reign of the Fomorian King Bres saw him as subject to the tyrant, like the other gods. During this time he was said to have been reduced to digging the defences and building a fortress for Bres. This was in the period before the second battle of Magh Tuireadh, which eventually led to the victory of the *Tuatha Dé Danann* over the Fomorians.

Earlier than this defeat of the Fomorians, the Daghda was described as meeting a woman who was standing astride the river Unius in Connacht, washing herself. The description indicated that she was the 'Washer at the Ford', one of the manifestations of the war goddess, the Morrígan. She and the Daghda had intercourse and she promised him assistance in the forthcoming battle against the Fomorians.

Similarly, the Daghda was described as having an affair with Boann, the personification of the river Boyne. From this union came his son Oengus Óg, or Oengus mac Óg.

The sons of the Daghda
The mention of Oengus Óg brings us to the subject of the children of the Daghda. As to Oengus Óg's parentage, there was no uniformity or consistency across all the sources but a number of children were generally accepted in most texts as children of the Daghda.

One of his sons was Bodb Derg, the god of poetry and wisdom. Bodb Derg was claimed to be lord of the *sídhe* ('fairy mound') of ar Femin and lord of the Otherworld fairy mounds of Munster. His name meant 'red raven' and he was associated with the great prehistoric passage grave of Newgrange, in the Boyne valley. He was described as having a retinue made up of 1,210 divinities. His sons included Artrach, Aed Alaind ('fair flame'), also called Aed of the poets, Oengus Ilclessach ('Oengus of the many feats'), Ferdoman and Derg ('red'). This last son was said to have resided in the *sídhe* of Dorn Buide. Bodb Derg's daughters included Findine, Scothníam, Mumain, Slat (the last two were said to have imprisoned a son of the King of Leinster in their *sídhe* for three years), Muirenn and Aillenn Fhialchorca ('Ailleen of the purple veil'), who was, it was claimed, allowed by St Patrick to marry the King of Connacht because she gave up her false druid ways. Another daughter was Dairenn, who wished to be the sole wife of Finn (or Fionn) mac Cumhaill for a year and tricked him into drinking a befuddling goblet of mead when he refused. Another was Sadhbh, who was also wife to Finn and mother of Oisín ('little deer') and was enchanted into the form of a deer by a druid. Finn had a taboo not to sleep with her on the shortest night of summer.[8] Bodb Derg's name also appeared in connection with his swineherds, who became locked into bitter conflicts and bloodshed.[9] This was referred to in, for example, the twelfth-century tale called *The Destruction of Da Derga's Hostel* (*Togail Bruidne Dá Derga*). The association with pigs was similar to that of Brigid (Brigit) and reminds us of the role of pork consumption in warrior societies of both prehistory and the early medieval period. It is instructive that the word for pig in a number of Celtic languages (*torc*) was the same as that used for the warriors' neck rings of precious metal.[10]

Cermait Milbél ('Cermait the honey-mouthed') was another son. He met his death at the hands of Lugh because he had had an affair with Lugh's wife. The three sons of Cermait Milbél were Mac Cuill, Mac Cécht and Mac Gréine. They avenged his death by spearing Lugh; they later became joint High Kings of Ireland.

Another son was Midir, the lord of the *sídhe* of Brí

Léith. One of the most famous of the traditions concerning Midir was written in *The Wooing of Étaín* (*Tochmarc Étaíne*). This was an early text of the so-called Irish Mythological Cycle. The story also involved characters from the Ulster Cycle and the Cycles of the Kings. It is partially preserved in the *Book of the Dun Cow* (*Lebor na hUidre*) of *c.*1100, and completely preserved in another manuscript, the *Yellow Book of Lecan* (*Leabhar Buidhe Leacáin*) of *c.*1400. The story was written in language that may indicate that what survives is a redaction of a story originally written perhaps as early as the eighth century. This story involved Étaín, a beautiful mortal woman of Ulster, who had once been a member of the *Tuatha Dé Danann* until a magical rebirth – following being turned into a butterfly – resulted in her becoming mortal. This transformation had occurred because Midir had brought her home as a new wife, thereby arousing the anger of his current wife, Fuamnach. In order to destroy her younger rival, Fuamnach used magic to turn Étaín into a butterfly. Midir searched for her but only found her a millennium after her original birth, reborn as a mortal and married to Eochaidh Airem, a High King of Ireland. At first Étaín did not recognize her previous husband but Midir used trickery to kiss her and then she remembered. The two escaped from the royal fortress at Tara, disguised as two swans. Eochaidh pursued them but was denied the return of his bride because, when Midir magically transformed fifty women into her likeness, Eochaidh chose the wrong one. More terribly, this turned out to be his own daughter, who had been disguised by the magic of Midir. This Eochaidh was claimed to have destroyed the *sídhe* of Bri Leith, because Étaín had been taken there by Midir. The mid twelfth-century *Book of Leinster* (*Lebor Laignech*) contains another tradition relating to Midir. In this one it was said that he owned three cranes who kept travellers away from his home and stole the courage from warriors. This association of cranes with ill omen and death was clearly a well-known feature of Celtic lore, since the twelfth-century Welsh writer Gerald of Wales (also known by the Latin form of his name, *Giraldus Cambrensis*) referred to an Irish taboo against eating the flesh of cranes in his *Conquest of Ireland* (*Expugnatio Hibernica*) of c.1188.[11] While Gerald (1146–1223) wrote some very unflattering and slanderous descriptions of the Irish, he was also acquainted with some genuine Irish traditions, having accompanied Prince John of England on an expedition to Ireland in 1185.

A possible son of the Daghda was Ogma, the Irish god of writing, although this deity was sometimes described as his brother rather than his son.

Oengus Óg and the Daghda fell out over the sharing of land between the children of the Daghda. With nothing left for him, Oengus retaliated by tricking his father. He asked the Daghda for the right to live in the Daghda's home of Brú na Bóinne (the prehistoric passage grave of Newgrange) for the duration of '*láa ogus oidhche*'. This phrase, though, was ambiguous and could mean both 'a day and a night' and 'day and night' (i.e. forever). As a result, the Daghda lost his home to his own son. This story, like a number in Irish mythology, was known in more than one form. In an alternative version, preserved in *The Wooing of Étaín*, Oengus tricked a different character out of his home. In this version the one who lost his home was Oengus's foster father, Elcmar (which may have been a pseudonym for Nuada of the Silver Hand), who had been persuaded to foster Oengus in order to hide his real parentage as the result of the affair between the Daghda and Boann. This illustrates the shifting and complex nature of Irish mythology, which often varied in key details between different manuscript traditions. A further illustration of this tendency is that even this duping of Elcmar existed in two different forms, along with a third (and Christianized) version that is found in the fifteenth-century *The Nurture of the House of the Two Milk Vessels* (*Altrom Tige Dá Medar*), which presented his loss of Brú na Bóinne as an expulsion that occurred at the same time as the casting out of the fallen angels from heaven.

The daughters of the Daghda

The Daghda was named as the father of two daughters. One was Áine, goddess of the sky and human love. Áine was raped by Ailill Aulomm and so became the mother of Eógan, who was the ancestor of the Eóganacht (a noble dynasty of Munster and Connacht). This tradition may have prompted a later legend that it was a rape that gave rise to the birth of Gerald, 3rd Earl of Desmond (died 1398). In this case, though, the man responsible was claimed to be Maurice FitzGerald, 1st Earl of Desmond. In this latter case, this new Hiberno-Norman aristocratic family were clearly staking their claim to authority by a reference to indigenous Irish mythology. In some traditions Áine was the lover of Manannán son of Lir. In these accounts Manannán took Áine with him to the Otherworldly land of Tír Tairngire (from the Irish for 'prophecy' or 'promise'). The Áine – who appeared in the twelfth-century Fenian Cycle of tales as the wife of warrior, Finn (or Fionn) – may have been a reworked version of the older mythological character, or a different female character with the same name.

The other daughter was Brigid (Brigit), the goddess of healing and fertility and of metalworking. Her name meant 'exalted one' and she was described as being the wife of Bres, who was one of the Fomorians and who subjugated and oppressed the *Tuatha Dé Danann*. With Bres she had a son, named Ruadán. In the twelfth-century *Book of Invasions of Ireland* (*Lebor Gabála Érenn*) it was stated that the Plain of Femen (which extends south from Cashel, as far as the boundary between Tipperary and Waterford) was named after her two oxen, Fe and Men. It is a common feature of a number of Irish medieval manuscripts to attempt to explain the origins of existing place names by reference to mythological events, people or animals. Some place names – as almost certainly in this case – were invented at the time of the writing of the manuscript. Brigid was also said to have owned a great boar, Torc Triath. In Welsh mythology a similar boar was called Twrch Trwyth. In addition, she was said to own Cirb, the King of Sheep. A later tradition claimed that Brigid was the wife of Senchán Torpéist, who was allegedly a candidate for authorship of the epic tale the *Cattle Raid of Cooley* (*Táin Bó Cúailnge*). She was later reinvented as the Irish St Brigid or possibly conflated with a real woman of that name (see Chapter 4).

The Daghda and the end of the rule of the
Tuatha Dé Danann

When the *Tuatha Dé Danann* were defeated by the Milesians it was the Daghda who led them underground to their new homes beneath the *sídhe*, or fairy mounds (see Chapter 8). The Daghda was credited with a reign of seventy or eighty years over the *Tuatha Dé Danann* before dying at his home of Brú na Bóinne, as a result of a wound he had earlier sustained at the second battle of Magh Tuireadh. Other accounts stated that he died in that battle. This combination of a relatively short reign and a fairly timeless one is characteristic of a number of the Irish myths. In some accounts the Daghda seems to have been thought of as permanently reigning in his *sídhe*, yet in others he appeared as mortal, with a clearly defined reign and death. It is fitting that we end this examination of traditions relating to the Daghda with a paradox.

8

IRISH ORIGIN MYTHS: THE COMING OF THE MILESIANS

In Irish mythology these were the final inhabitants of Ireland and from them were descended the Gaelic-speaking people of the island. The eight sons of Míl Espáine ('Soldier of Hispania') led an invasion force that defeated the *Tuatha Dé Danann* and conquered Ireland. Meeting with the *Tuatha Dé Danann* at the great royal site at Tara, they agreed with them a treaty that stipulated that the invaders should return to their ships and sail a distance of nine waves from Ireland and then, if they were able to land again, the island of Ireland would be theirs to settle. Having agreed to this, the *Tuatha Dé Danann* used their magical powers to call up a storm in which five of the sons of Míl Espáine were drowned, leaving only three survivors to land. Despite their reduction in numbers, this diminished force of warriors still succeeded in conquering the island. Because Míl Espáine is claimed to be their ancestor, his supposed descendants have been called Milesians. One of the earliest uses of this word – in the Latin form 'stirps Melesia', referring to the descendants of Mil – is found in the twelfth-century *Topography of Ireland* (*Topographia Hibernica*) written by Gerald of Wales.[1]

Biblical parallels with Irish origin myths

The account of the Milesians' invasion is given in the twelfth-century *Book of Invasions of Ireland* (*Lebor Gabála Érenn*). This is the source of most of the invasion origin myths of Irish mythology. According to its account, the Milesians were descended from the Scythian Niúl and from Scota, who was a daughter of the Egyptian pharaoh. In this way the tradition linked Irish origins to one of the barbarian tribes whose name early medieval monastic writers would know from Classical sources. A tradition of Scythian tribes migrating to Ireland had first appeared in Britain in the eighth century, in the writings of the Anglo-Saxon scholar Bede, who stated: 'Some Picts from Scythia put to sea in a few longships and were driven by storms around the coasts of Britain, arriving at length on the north coast of Ireland.'[2] Here Bede may have confused Scythia with Scandinavia, and, if he did, this is problematic as there is no evidence to link the northern British tribe of the Picts with Scandinavia. In this identification Bede was probably influenced by Isidore of Seville's *History of the Goths* (*Historia de regibus Gothorum*), written in the early seventh century, which derived *Scot(t)i* – the early medieval name for the Irish – from *Scythae*. This connection between Ireland and Scythia clearly encouraged the tradition that was later made explicit in the *Book of Invasions*. And this later tradition also linked this mythical invasion force to the Egyptians, whose antiquity and prominence would have been familiar from accounts in the Old Testament. This linkage gave the Irish a doubly impressive pedigree, one rooted in both Classical and biblical traditions.

Furthermore, according to the *Book of Invasions*, the son of Niúl and Scota, Goídel Glas,[3] lived in Egypt at the time of the Exodus led by Moses. The infant Goídel had earlier been saved from a snake bite by being touched by the rod of Moses. Moses then promised that Goídel's descendants would inhabit a land without snakes. This again reinforced the connection with the Old Testament and paralleled the later invasion history of the Milesians with the Israelites' wanderings in the desert and the eventual conquest of the Promised Land. This parallel was strengthened by an account of the Egyptians persecuting the descendants of Goídel in the generations after the biblical Exodus. Sources outside the *Book of Invasions* also indicate that another tradition linked the Milesians with ancient Miletus, in Asia Minor.[4] This added to the biblical connection but this time with a New Testament link, since it was at Miletus that the Apostle Paul met with the elders from the early church at Ephesus; an event recorded in the Acts of the Apostles.[5] That it was from Ephesus that Paul then departed for Jerusalem may have given it particular resonance in an account of a great journey in the *Book of Invasions*.

In this way we can see how early medieval Irish writers created their own origin myth in the pattern of biblical models.[6] In the same way, Bede drew discernible parallels between seventh-century historic Anglo-Saxon kings and Old Testament kings; and the Welsh writer Nennius modelled his account of the mythical figure of Arthur on the person of Joshua in the Old Testament (see Chapter 13).[7] This attempt by Irish monastic writers to create an origin myth that paralleled Old Testament experiences is seen in a number of aspects of the account of successive settlements in the *Book of Invasions*. Hence we have Cesair described as the granddaughter of Noah; the seaborne wandering of the Nemedians is reminiscent of the Israelites' wandering in the wilderness; the enslavement of the Nemedians by the Fomorians and the later enslavement of their descendants, the *Firbolg*, in Greece drew a clear parallel with the Israelites' time of slavery in Egypt; and the eventual exodus of the *Firbolg* from Greece and their journey to Ireland mirrored the Exodus account of the Israelites' liberation from Egypt and their journey to Canaan. It was in this context that the tradition of the Milesians reconstructed a number of these, already rehearsed, themes and once again connected Egypt with a time of wanderings and linked this with the settlement of Ireland. For, according to the *Book of Invasions*, it was only after a period of wandering and led by the hero Míl Espáine – first returning to their ancestral homeland in Scythia, then living around the Caspian Sea, and later living around the shores of the Mediterranean – that the descendants of Goídel Glas finally arrived in the Iberian Peninsula, where they fought a number of battles and eventually settled. Here one of them, Breogán, built a high tower at Brigantia (La Coruña, in Galicia, Spain). From this tower his son, Íth, first caught a glimpse of Ireland, and it was this that caused him to set sail for the land that he had seen from afar. However, this invasion by Íth was only a prelude to the final – and successful – invasion by his Milesian descendants. Even this has echoes of the Old Testament themes of Moses looking into the Promised Land and the Israelite spies entering Canaan before the full invasion led by Joshua.

These parallels are not exact and we should not expect them to be. The twelfth-century creators of these origin myths were not seeking to create an exact replica of Old Testament events. Rather, they used and adapted Old Testament themes in order to construct their accounts. And they did this in order to impose a familiar and acceptable structure and pattern on a set of pre-Christian beliefs and divinities whose original form and character are now no longer fully discernible to us. The compilers of the *Book of Invasions* may also have been influenced by aspects of another earlier Christian work, the fifth-century *Seven*

Books of History Against the Pagans (*Historiarum Adversum Paganos Libri VII*), by Orosius. However, through this overlay of medieval expectations we can still discern something of the earlier mythology, albeit one heavily influenced and restructured by Christian Irish compilers and redactors. And often the traditions that were recorded were not the creations of their twelfth-century compilers, even if some aspects were clearly freshly minted in the twelfth century.

The invasion of the Milesians

When Íth reached Ireland, landing at Derry, he was impressed by the abundance of the island. Addressing the *Tuatha Dé Danann*, he declared: 'you dwell in a good land. Abundant are its [oak] mast and honey and wheat and fish.'[8] He then became the first of the Gaels to die in Ireland, since he was treacherously killed by the *Tuatha Dé Danann* kings Mac Cuill, Mac Cécht and Mac Gréine. But this was not to be the end of the Milesian invasion of Ireland, for a consequence of Íth's death was that his nine brothers, along with the eight sons of Íth's brother, Míl Espáine, were determined to avenge his death and conquer Ireland. As a result, yet another invasion of Ireland was planned in Spain.

The Spanish connection is curious and suggests the presence of a much earlier tradition that preceded the inventiveness of twelfth-century Irish compilers of the accounts relating to the Milesians. The *Book of Invasions* had also earlier linked the Nemedians to the Iberian peninsula and this Spanish connection did not begin with the *Book of Invasions*. As early as the ninth century, the Welsh compiler of *The History of the Britons* (*Historia Brittonum*) – often named as Nennius – recounted a Welsh version of Irish origins. This told of a series of invasions of Ireland from Spain and it was this account, written in Latin, that heavily influenced the later writer(s) of the *Book of*

Invasions. For Nennius, as for later Irish writers, this may have arisen from a confusion between 'Iberia' and 'Hibernia' (the Latin name for Ireland).[9] However, this Iberian connection is intriguing and may well have been an echo of real events that were dimly remembered in oral traditions from prehistory. Once the Bronze Age became established in Ireland, from *c.*2200 BC, the country became part of a trading network that connected it with Britain, Armorica (the land between the rivers Seine and Loire, that includes Brittany) and the Iberian peninsula.[10] Similarly, there is some evidence to connect traditions of Bronze Age rock art in Ireland and Spain.[11] This archaeologically attested connection indicates that some real events may lie behind some of the traditions recorded in the *Book of Invasions*, woven into themes and divinities from Irish mythology and structured by writers seeking to exploit analogies with the Old Testament.

When the sons of Míl reached Ireland they established a beachhead in County Kerry and from there struck inland to the royal centre at Tara. In what seems to have been a prediction of the eventual Milesian victory the three wives of the Irish kings mentioned earlier – Ériu, Banbha and Fódla – each requested that their name would become that of the island. These three *Tuatha Dé Danann* members were sisters and this is another example of the tripartite nature associated with a number of Irish goddesses. These three queens/ goddesses clearly represented the sovereignty of Ireland and the transfer of their names to the island (with that of Ériu, or Éire, being the most commonly used) at the time of the Milesian invasions seems to indicate, within the account, the beginning of the transfer of control to the Milesians.

Reaching Tara, the Milesians negotiated with the three kings and agreed a deal by which the three kings would hold Ireland for only three more days if the invaders would stay just nine waves from the shore. Here again we see multiples of the number three. Once at sea the druids of the

Tuatha Dé Danann raised a storm to drive the ships further out from the shore. In response the leading spokesman of the Milesians, Amairgin, calmed the raging waves with a verse of poetry. The Milesians then sailed sunwise around Ireland until they reached the estuary of the river Boyne. Here they landed, on the feast of Beltane (May Day), the start of summer. The Milesians defeated the *Tuatha Dé Danann* in two battles. The first was fought at Tailtiu (Meath), the second at Druim Ligen (Donegal). The victorious Milesians were accompanied by Scota, after whom, the story claims, the Gaelic Irish were named the Scotti. In reality, this tribal name was the Latin word, of debatable origin, used by the Romans for Irish tribes and was first recorded in the late fourth century by Pacatus.[12]

There followed one hundred years of Milesian rule, until the subject peoples of Ireland – the *Aitheachthuatha* – revolted and set up their own ruler, Cairbre Cinn-Chait. These subject peoples were surviving members of the *Firbolg*, who had earlier been defeated by the *Tuatha Dé Danann*. However, the son of Cairbre Cinn-Chait declined to continue the dynasty and instead recognized the right to rule of the Milesians. In this way the Milesians became the ancestors of the Gaelic people of Ireland. This account, in the *Book of Invasions*, became so well known that it eclipsed any earlier myths of origins and eventually became adopted by the Irish aristocracy, who then all claimed an original ancestor in Míl Espáine.

The *Tuatha Dé Danann* after the coming of the Milesians

After the *Tuatha Dé Danann* were defeated by the invading Milesians, they were forced to give up their occupation of the upper world. Instead they set up an alternative underground kingdom that mirrored life on the earth. From this new kingdom they bargained with the Milesians by denying them milk and corn. This feature of Irish mythology clearly indicates the belief that a form of contractual relationship existed between humans and the gods that was designed to give the gods their place and, consequently, assured people of the fertility of the soil and the abundance of their crops. In pre-literate, agricultural, pagan society this contract clearly lay at the centre of religious understanding and practice.

The compromise reached ensured that – while the Milesians kept control of the upper world – the *Tuatha Dé Danann* were accorded the right to have authority within their underground realm. The places where the *Tuatha Dé Danann* lived, according to this agreement, were in the *sídhe*, the fairy mounds. This Gaelic word can also mean 'peace'[13] and the fairy mounds were probably named *sídhe* in order to emphasize the idyllic character associated with the Otherworld. The word's use may also have been related to a tendency in Irish mythology to link the gods residing in the *sídhe* with kings and heroes (themselves also mythological) ruling on earth. This may have been because actual pagan kings were thought to be spiritually connected with dead ancestors living in the *sídhe* and, in this way, they were thought to have peacefulness conferred on their reign and kingdom.[14] The word *sídhe* derived from the Gaelic phrases *aos sídhe*, and *daoine sídhe*, both meaning 'people of the fairy mound'. These mounds were, in reality, the Long Barrows and Round Barrows of Neolithic and Bronze Age Ireland. This appropriation of archaeological sites as places of the ancestors and of the gods was certainly not confined to Irish mythology. In Scottish-Gaelic the phrase is *daoine sìth* and refers to the same concept of a fairy realm (see Chapter 18); and the same association is found in many cultures.

Intriguingly, the word 'sith' appears in George Lucas's Star Wars series, in *Star Wars Episode I: The Phantom Menace*, which was the fourth film to be released. In this film the Sith are beings that use the dark side of the force.

Lucas himself appears to have borrowed the name from Edgar Rice Burroughs's 'Barsoom' stories, which featured John Carter of Mars and appeared from 1912 to 1943. In these the Sith are poisonous insect-like creatures. The name itself seems to have been originally borrowed from Irish traditions, since the Scottish-Gaelic word *sith* is a variant of *sídhe* ('fairy'). The very dark association that is reflected in Burroughs's and then Lucas's use of the name, however, probably came via the word *banshee* (first recorded in 1771), which is a phonetic spelling of the Irish *bean sídhe* and means 'woman of the elves/fairies'. The implication in the use of this term was one who called on the spirits of the dead. Clearly, this later folklore figure derived from a much older pagan religious tradition.[15] In later Irish folklore there was a fear of travellers being lured into these *sídhe* at times of the year when it was thought that the invisible door might be open (Beltane, 1 May, and Samhain, 1 November) and becoming trapped in an endless dance.[16]

According to mythological tradition, the Daghda allocated one of the *sídhe* to each of the *Tuatha Dé Danann*. In this way the god Nuada of the Silver Hand was lord of the *sídhe* of Almu and the god Midir was lord of the *sídhe* of Brí Léith. When the great heroic warrior Cú Chulainn eventually met his death it was because the death-dealing Morrígan had come out of her *sídhe* and brought death into the world of men. In the Daghda's own *sídhe* it was believed that there grew three trees that always bore fruit, along with a pig that never died and an ever-flowing quantity of alcoholic drink. In early medieval Ireland it was believed that at the festival of Samhain the earth-bound spirits were temporarily free to leave the *sídhe*, since it was believed that at this time the boundary between the natural world and the Otherworld no longer operated.

In this understanding of cosmology the *sídhe* were the entrance places to the Otherworld of *Tír na nÓg*, the Land of the Forever Young. This then was the distinct difference between the world of human beings and the world of the gods. And immortality was not the only characteristic believed to be integral to this Otherworld. In this underground land there was no pain, illness, ugliness or decay. All was thought to be beautiful there. It was, though, a mirror image of the upper world in other respects, in that there were hierarchies of rulers, love intrigues and relationships, quarrels and conflicts. In short, the Irish of late prehistory and the early medieval period had created, in their mythological construct, a world for their gods that was a divine version of their own society and political organization. This also validated and explained Irish social structures and religious ceremonies, lore and organization, since these were claimed to have arisen from this separation of spheres of influence that had been agreed between humans and the gods. Similarly, kings and druids legitimated their power and influence by reference to these divinities, who were thought to have once occupied the very same physical space but had then bequeathed it – albeit under duress – to human beings. It was thought that, from this fairy realm, the *Tuatha Dé Danann* continued to practise their magic and from there they controlled the supernatural, including its interface with human society.

The *Tuatha Dé Danann*, within their *sídhe*, had mixed relations with humans. At times the relationship could involve cooperation, but at other times there was conflict. In the same way there were occasions when members of the *Tuatha Dé Danann* would marry mortals and this usually was facilitated by the *Tuatha Dé Danann* coming into the human world; while at other times it involved mortals entering and living within the *sídhe* of the *Tuatha Dé Danann*.

The society within *Tír na nÓg*
The belief in *Tír na nÓg* was influential in a range of traditional Irish beliefs and accounts, including in the Fenian

Cycle of Irish mythology (see Chapter 11). Within *Tír na nÓg*, Oisín (or Ossian), son of Finn (or Fionn) mac Cumhaill, was thought to have lived with Niamh, the daughter of the King of the Land of Forever Young. In this tradition, Oisín was the son of the warband leader, Finn. Found in the wilderness by Finn, after his mother, Sadhbh (or Sava), was reclaimed by a mysterious magical Black Druid, Oisín grew up to be a leading warrior in Finn's warband, the *fianna*.

Oisín fell under the spell of Niamh of the Golden Hair, who was the daughter of the ruler of *Tír na nÓg*, and married her. While living with her, Oisín desired to journey back to his own land. When – against Niamh's will and advice – he did journey there he found that three centuries had passed since he left. Niamh warned Oisín that he must not step on his old land but Oisín fell from his horse and suddenly became three hundred years old. As he touched the ground his youthful appearance immediately crumpled into old age and he died.

In this account we see a number of the characteristic features of the land of the *Tuatha Dé Danann* after they had relinquished control of Ireland to the Milesians. It was a land of the beautiful, as exemplified by Niamh of the Golden Hair; its powers could enchant human beings who came into contact with it, as seen when Oisín met Niamh; it was outside of human time, as indicated by the difference between the passage of time there and in the human world; those who entered it could only exit it with difficulty, as seen in Oisín's tragic demise. In these features we see many of the characteristics associated with fairy realms that occur in a number of cultures and that will reappear in a range of very different Celtic myths and legends.

Similarly, Midir, a son of the Daghda of the *Tuatha Dé Danann* (see Chapter 7), married Étaín and brought her to his *sídhe* at Brí Léith, despite already being married to

Fúamnach. This provoked the anger of his first wife, who attempted to kill Étaín, and this led to a tangle of relationships that linked human society to the world of the gods. This situation illustrates the complex love relationships, feuds and human–god interactions that were associated with the Underworld realm of the *Tuatha Dé Danann*.

Whatever the complexity of the relationships between mortals and members of the *Tuatha Dé Danann* in the later mythological traditions, what is clear is that there is a discernible difference in the way they were treated in the various cycles of stories. In the Ulster Cycle (surviving in manuscripts dating from the twelfth to the fifteenth century) the *Tuatha Dé Danann* were still represented as deities. However, in the Fenian Cycle (dating from the twelfth century), their nature was much diminished and they appeared as fairy-folk. Showing a Christian influence that is not surprising given that they were recorded by monks, a number of these tales described members of the *Tuatha Dé Danann* dying of old age when they left the world of the *sídhe* and being baptized as Christians before they died. In this way, we see the older, pagan Irish tradition becoming assimilated to the Christian faith and outlook of medieval Ireland.

9

MAGIC AND SHAPE-SHIFTERS IN THE IRISH MYTHOLOGICAL CYCLE

A theme that runs through a number of Irish myths is that of shape-shifting. In these accounts humans became animals and could be reborn again as humans. One of the characteristics of the stories is that those involved often kept their character throughout their process of transformation and took their present experiences and knowledge into the next phase of their life. In a collection of explanations of over 1,400 Irish words known as *Cormac's Glossary* (*Sanas Chormaic*) – which may date from as early as the tenth century, though the earliest surviving manuscript is found in the so-called *Speckled Book* (*Leabhar Breac*) of *c.*1410 – there survives a definition of transmigration, which in Gaelic is *tuirigin*. This explanation includes this definition: 'a birth that passes from every nature into another . . . a transitory birth which has traversed all nature from

Adam and goes through every wonderful time down to the world's doom'.[1]

The belief in *tuirigin* implied an indistinct line between humans and animals, and this was emphasized by the fact that there were mythical beings whose characters were expressed in certain attributes of animals. In this way the battlefield activities of the Morrígan were represented in the form of crows who feasted on the bodies of the slain. However, this anthropomorphic aspect did not cover all examples and a number of other instances in the mythological tradition were based on the belief in the ability of magic to transform humans into animals. This could include instances when such a transformation occurred against the will of those affected.

Within these examples, the shape-shifting can be divided into three main kinds. When the shape-shifting involved gods, goddesses and mythological heroes, it was presented as part of their characters and was not regarded as a particular cause of fear. The second aspect of shape-shifting was that associated with magicians and witches and most examples of this belief involved the involuntary transformation of a human being (or a god or goddess) as the result of a curse or magic spell. The third kind involved later reworking of this belief within folklore. When this last form of shape-shifting involved fairies and lesser supernatural figures, it appeared as a threat to ordinary people. In this way the folklore traditions about the Irish *fir dhearga* (shape-shifting fairies) and the various water-horses (shape-shifting water creatures) concerned beings thought to endanger people. In this we may be seeing the process by which pagan beliefs were downgraded to folklore, as the original beliefs were condemned as part of the conversion to Christianity and the adoption of a new spiritual outlook. The attributes once associated with pagan deities then became the characteristics of malevolent spirits, supernatural and threatening creatures and those humans who practised the forbidden arts of magic.

The shape-shifting of the Morrígan

Belief in the Morrígan's ability to shape-shift was dramatically demonstrated in the account of her meeting with Cú Chulainn in the *Cattle Raid of Cooley* (*Táin Bó Cúailnge*). In this account the following conversation revealed her ability to both change form and threaten. When her advances were rejected she replied: 'I'll get under your feet in the ford in the shape of an eel and make sure you fall.' Cú Chulainn answered: 'I'll get you between my toes and I'll break your ribs . . .' To this the Morrígan replied: 'I'll come as a grey she-wolf, and stampede cattle into the ford against you.' Cú Chulainn was undeterred, saying: 'I'll put your eye out with a stone from my sling . . .' Finally the Morrígan revealed her last threat: 'I'll come as a hornless red heifer, and lead the cattle to surge against you in the waters, whether ford or pool, and you'll not know me.' To which Cú Chulainn responded: 'I'll fire a stone at you . . . and break the leg from under you . . .'[2] All of these things eventually happened as Cú Chulainn battled opponents at the ford of Áth Traiged. The Morrígan too was injured in this battle but was healed through another shape-shifting, when she appeared as an old woman milking a cow and the exhausted Cú Chulainn was tricked into blessing her in return for three sips of milk.

Oengus Óg and the shape-shifting swan princess

Oengus Óg, the Irish god of love, was also involved in shape-shifting in order to succeed in his courtship of a girl of divine descent named Cáer. Cáer, who lived in Connacht (Connaught), could take on the form of a swan. Here it should be stressed that, unlike the experience of Aife (Aoífe), who was transformed into a crane (see below), this was a voluntary transformation, rather than the result of a curse. Furthermore, in Irish mythology swans were presented in a positive light, whereas cranes were birds of ill omen and often associated with *geasa* (taboos) against eating them. This positive role of swans was further emphasized by the tradition that four swans circled over Oengus's head while he was travelling.[3]

Having seen Cáer in a dream, Oengus searched for her for a year without success. Eventually it was revealed to him by Bodb Derg, the god of poetry and wisdom, that she was a princess of Connacht. Her divine nature was implied in her full name of Cáer *Ibormeith* ('yew-berry'), the evergreen yew tree being symbolic of immortality. It is a survival of this view of the tree in a Christianized form that explains the presence of yew trees in many ancient Christian cemeteries.

When Oengus had found Cáer, Ethal Anbúail, the girl's father, explained that she spent every other year in her swan form. The condition laid down regarding the marriage was that Oengus would be able to recognize Cáer within a flock of 151 swans. This he was able to do immediately. The recognition took place at the feast of Samhain, festival of the dead, which was also a harvest festival and a festival marking the end of the light half of the year (31 October–1 November). It was on this day that Cáer's shape-shifting occurred, along with that of the other women in her company. This association of the date with the changing of form is clearly significant within the tradition, since it was considered a time of year when the veil between this world and the spirit world was thin and communication and movement between the two might occur. In one version of the legend Oengus was able to recognize Cáer because the chain around her neck was of gold, whereas that around the other swans' necks was of silver. Cáer agreed to accept Oengus's courtship if he would allow her transformations to continue. This he agreed to, but the next year when they met he changed himself into a swan. Rising together, they circled the lake three times and sang a song that sent listeners into a sleep that lasted three days and three nights. Oengus took Cáer to his home at *Bru na Bóinne* (Palace of the Boyne) on the bend of the river Boyne, where they lived happily together. This area contains the Neolithic passage graves of Newgrange, Knowth and Dowth, and attracted a number of mythological connections.

The butterfly transformation of Étaín

Not all shape-shifting in the Irish mythological tradition was voluntary. In *The Wooing of Étaín* (*Tochmarc Étaíne*) – a story partially preserved in the *Book of the Dun Cow* (*Lebor na hUidre*) of *c*.1100, and completely preserved in another manuscript, the *Yellow Book of Lecan* ((*Leabhar Buidhe Leacáin*) of *c*.1400 – Étaín was a goddess who was transformed into a mortal, via shape-shifting, by a magical spell. The magic was cast on her by a jealous rival, Fúamnach, the wife of the god Midir. This was because Midir had returned home with the beautiful Étaín, despite already being married to Fúamnach. Fúamnach's spell first changed her into the form of a fly[4] or a purple butterfly,[5] and from this state Étaín was eventually transformed into a mortal when she was accidentally swallowed by the wife of a warrior of Ulster named Etar. This woman later gave birth to Étaín as a mortal girl. The story involved more than one set of shape-shifting since, in turn, Fúamnach had turned her into a pool of water, a maggot and, eventually, a butterfly. Even in the butterfly form there was a further episode of shape-shifting when, buffeted by the wind, Étaín landed on the cloak of Oengus Óg. Recognizing her – for he had assisted Midir in her wooing – his magic was sufficient to change her back to a woman, but only at night. Thus, partially restored, Étaín became the lover of Oengus but only for seven years, until a strong wind once more blew her away, and to the home of the warrior Etar.[6] However, one thousand years passed between her leaving the house of Oengus and finally entering the house of Etar and then falling into his wife's goblet of wine.[7]

The swan-children of Lír

A similar case of involuntary shape-shifting occurred in the famous myth of the children of Lír. The god Lír may have been the same deity as the Welsh Llŷr. However, the Irish tradition concerning the swan-children of Lír was not reflected in any similar Welsh tradition. It is possible that the suggested connection between the two is based on either a coincidence of name[8] or on common origins in an original mythology that later diverged in Ireland and Wales.

According to a late fifteenth-century account, Lír was displeased at not being chosen as king of the *Tuatha Dé Danann* and retired to live in isolation under a hill in what is now County Armagh.[9] Bodb Derg, who had been chosen king, attempted to make peace with Lír by offering him one of his daughters in marriage. Lír selected one named Aoibh (or Eve) and with her had four children. These children were a daughter, Fionnuala, and three sons, Aodh and the twins Fiachra and Conn.

When Aoibh died, Lír married her sister, Aoífe (or Eva). However, Aoífe was jealous of Lír's children by Aoibh because he greatly loved them. In order to remove this competition for Lír's affections, she ordered one of her servants to kill the children. When the servant refused, Aoífe used magic to turn the children into swans. In this state they lived for nine hundred years. This period of time was divided into three hundred years on Lough Derravaragh (County Westmeath), three hundred years in the Sea of Moyle (the narrowest stretch of sea, in the North Channel, between Ireland and the Mull of Kintyre, in Scotland) and three hundred years in the tidal estuary waters of Irrus Domnann (Sruwaddacon Bay, County Mayo). Different traditions claimed to record how the spell was finally broken and what all have in common is the strong influence of the Irish monastic writers who recorded the tradition and a connection to a Christian monk living on the coastal Inishglora Island (originally known in Irish as Inis Gluaire), near the place of the swans' final three-hundred-year sojourn. In one version the King of Leinster attacked the island sanctuary in order to secure the swans for his wife; the silver chain linking the swans was broken and the swans were consequently transformed into withered old people and died. In a second, and similar, tradition, the church bell rang as the king was removing the swans from their sanctuary; they were transformed back into humans and were baptized before they died. In the third tradition, the swan-children came to the Christian sanctuary on hearing its bell ringing; they were released from the spell by a priest, baptized and then died.

The story places this tale in the context of the events recorded in the twelfth-century *Book of Invasions of Ireland* (*Lebor Gabála Érenn*). However, the actual manuscript that records the story of the swan-children of Lír dates from much later than the composition of the *Book of Invasions of Ireland* and is either a later tradition or at least a later recording of what may have been a much older tradition. The manuscript evidence suggests that *The Tragic Story of the Children of Lír* (*Oidheadh Chlainne Lír*) was composed – in the form that now survives – in about 1500.[10] The story is now one of the most famous from Irish mythology and features in the remarkable sculpture seen today in Dublin's Garden of Remembrance, in Parnell Square. Sculpted by Oisin Kelly and inaugurated in 1966, it is dedicated to all those who died in pursuit of Irish national freedom. As four swans rise heavenward, the children of Lír fall to the ground. It is an intriguing mixture of a Christian reworking of the earlier tradition and Irish nationalism. Behind the sculpture flies the tricolour flag of the Republic of Ireland and the work itself both reminds us of the continuing influence of ancient mythology, and refers to modern political and cultural themes.

Manannán and Aife, the crane-wife

The use of magic to shape-shift (and remove) a rival was found in a number of Irish myths. A curse, similar to that which affected the children of Lír, was also used against Aife, who was sometimes regarded as a wife of Manannán, who himself was also identified as a son of Lír. According to tradition, Manannán was the originator of a spell known as the *fith-fiada*, which gave a sorcerer the power to transform another person into a different shape, particularly that of an animal. The association of this characteristic with a sea god might have been prompted by the visibly changing nature of the sea itself.[11] Manannán was also thought to own a cloak that confirmed invisibility on him. Later Manx tradition claimed he had three legs; hence the three-legged symbol on the coat of arms of the Isle of Man.[12] The connection of Manannán with shape-shifting was seen in the tradition that he slept with a queen of Ulster by disguising himself as her husband. This was a motif similar to that in Arthurian mythology of Uther Pendragon taking on the form of Gorlois, Duke of Cornwall, in order to sleep with his wife, Igraine; from which union Arthur was conceived. In the case of the shape-shifting Manannán, the child born was named Mongan and he too was believed to have had the ability to change his appearance.[13]

In the Irish mythological tradition, Manannán was linked to Aife, who was transformed into a crane. Aife's relationship with Manannán varied in different tellings of the tale. In one version, the spell was cast on her by a rival, Iuchra, who was jealous of her love for Ilbrec, who was the son of Manannán. Luring Aife into the water, Iuchra turned her into a water bird and drove her away. In this state she wandered for two hundred years until she died. In some accounts, though, she was represented as the second wife of Manannán, before being turned into a crane by his jealous first wife.[14] And in this version she lived, as a crane, in his household.[15] However, given that Manannán was considered to be a sea god, his 'house' or 'household' may simply have been a poetic device used to describe exile on the sea. On Aife's death, her skin was used by Manannán to create a magic treasure bag.[16] This crane-bag (the *corr-bolg*) included the letters of the alphabet.[17] Other treasures in the bag were reputed to be Manannán's knife and magic shirt; an anvil and leather apron that were once owned by Goibhniu, the god of smithing and the making of weapons; the shears of the King of Scotland; the horned helmet of the King of Norway; and a whaleskin belt. The magical nature of the bag was revealed in that at high tide the treasures could be seen, whereas at low tide it appeared to be empty.[18] In the twelfth-century Fenian Cycle of tales this bag came to belong to the warrior Finn (or Fionn) mac Cumhaill. While the myth does not involve Manannán in the process by which Aife was turned into a crane, it was clearly significant that her shape-shifting was connected with a god who was reputed to be a shape-shifter himself and that one version of the myth made her his crane-wife.

Sadhbh the deer-wife

A goddess and daughter of Bodb Derg, Sadhbh was changed into a deer by a wizard rival of her father named Fer Doirche ('the dark druid'). In this form she was discovered by Finn (or Fionn) mac Cumhaill, the warrior hero of the *fianna* (the bodyguard of the High King of Ireland) and a central character in the twelfth-century tales of the Fenian Cycle (the *Fianaíocht*), also known as the Ossianic Cycle. The discovery broke the spell and Sadhbh became Finn's wife. This lasted until the wizard discovered her while Finn was away and changed her back into a deer. Searching Ireland for his lost wife, Finn was unable to locate her but eventually came upon a child in the woods. Recognizing the child as his son by Sadhbh, he named him Oisín (or Ossian), meaning 'little deer'.[19] In some retellings of the story the child was being nursed by a deer.[20]

Shape-shifting appeared more than twice in this story for, at Sadhbh's original discovery by Finn, she was not harmed by his dogs, Bran and Sceolan, because they too had once been human (see below). And her final and irrevocable return to deer form occurred when she was tricked into greeting her returning husband only to discover that it was the wicked Fer Doirche, who had taken on her husband's form.

Cian and the ability to change into a pig

Cian appeared as the father of Lugh Lámhfada (Lugh of the Long Arm or, literally, the Long Hand), the sun god, in the cycle of Irish mythological tales. Since being transformed into a pig as a child by a druid he had the ability to do this whenever he was in danger. However, this shape-shifting was unable to save him when he was attacked and killed by the sons of Tuireann (see Chapter 6). They caught him and stoned him to death when he changed back into human form. Despite his importance as the father of a major Irish god, the death of Cian was only briefly described in the twelfth-century *Book of Invasions of Ireland* (*Lebor Gabála Érenn*). More details appeared in the expansion of the tradition, found in the later manuscript the *Death of the Children of Tuireann* (*Oidheadh Chlainne Tuireann*), the earliest version of which survives from the sixteenth century, with some seventeenth-century additions.

The many animal forms of Tuan mac Cairill

The tradition of shape-shifting affected not only those regarded as gods and goddesses. Heroic characters, not clearly identified as deities, could also experience it. The phenomenon occurs in the *Book of Invasions of Ireland*. In this account, Tuan was the only survivor of Partholon's settlement of Ireland (see Chapter 5). In hiding from the Nemedian invaders of Ireland he was disguised in the form of a stag, a wild boar, an eagle and finally a salmon. The salmon was eventually caught and eaten by a woman and (as in *The Wooing of Étaín*) this caused Tuan to be reborn as a human (the son of a man named Cairill).

The transformation of Líban into a salmon

In a story comparable to that of Tuan mac Cairill, a woman named Líban became a salmon and her handmaid an otter.[21] Some accounts tell of her transformation into a salmon or mermaid and her dog into the otter. In an aquatic form she survived not an invasion but the inundation of a flood that formed Lough Neagh. The account found in the *Death of Eochaidh Son of Mairid* (*Aided Echdach maic Maíred*), from the twelfth-century *Book of the Dun Cow*, then described her eventual re-emergence in the time of St Comgall, who baptized her and gave her the name *Muirghein* ('sea birth') or *Muirgheilt* ('sea prodigy').[22] Líban's name may have derived from the Irish for 'woman of water'.

Another Líban appeared in the context of myths concerning Cú Chulainn. In *The Wasting Sickness of Cú Chulainn* (*Serglige Con Culainn*) – also found in the *Book of the Dun Cow* – she was described as a seabird and then as a vengeful goddess.

The transformation of Bran and Sceolan into dogs

Bran and Sceolan, the nephews of Finn (or Fionn) mac Cumhaill, would have been human but for the fact that their mother, Uirne, had been transformed into a dog. Although she returned to human form, her two pups could not do so. Consequently, their uncle took them into his warband, the *fianna*, where they served as guards and hunting dogs. They also fought in battle. It was because of their human ancestry that they were able to recognize the real nature of Sadhbh when they came across her as a deer.

Shape-shifting in later folklore

The idea of shape-shifting spirits was later to influence aspects of Irish folklore. The *fir dhearga* ('men in red') were figures in this folklore, considered descendants of the Fomorians who had become part of the fairy world (a realm otherwise associated with the *Tuatha Dé Danann*). In some traditions they were thought to have wandered into the fairy world and become lost. A characteristic of the *fir dhearga* was shape-shifting. In this case they appeared as old men in a red coat, with long hair and a rat's tail. This latter feature suggests a human–animal overlap. Living in bogs, they were associated with the wild and dangerous. Each carried a blackthorn stick and they were believed to knock on doors at night and ask for food; it being unlucky to refuse them. The tradition claimed that, if they offered a wish in return for the meal, it was best simply to reply: '*Ná déan fochmoid fainn*' ('Do not mock us').[23]

Shape-shifting appeared in other folklore too. The *aughisky* was considered to inhabit the sea and sea loughs and to have been able to shape-shift into a horse to fatally attract a rider; other accounts considered it capable of appearing in the form of a man. A similar creature appeared in the folklore of the Isle of Man, Orkney, Shetland and Wales. As with the belief in the *fir dhearga*, these ideas may have been remnants of much earlier shape-shifting beliefs or, instead, may represent a quite different strand of more modern superstitions.

10

CÚ CHULAINN, THE HOUND OF ULSTER AND THE ULSTER CYCLE

One of the four great collections of Irish mythology is known as the Ulster Cycle (the *Ruraíocht*).[1] An alternative name, now less often used, is the Red Branch Cycle. The latter name derived from that of one of the homes of Conchobar, one of the cycle's heroic characters. This home was *Cráebruad* ('red roof-beam' or 'red branch'). The Ulster Cycle contains stories relating to the heroes of the Ulaid in what is now eastern Ulster and northern Leinster. It is from the name of this prehistoric people that the modern Irish province of Ulster takes its name. In total, the Ulster Cycle contains about eighty stories, many of them inter-related, and is an important component of the mythological traditions of Ireland. While the stories contain a large number of characters, they have a general unity of structure in purporting to have occurred in the reign of King Conchobar mac Nessa, or in a period of time close to his mythological reign. In the stories, Conchobar ruled the peoples of the Ulaid from his fortress of Emain Macha (Navan Fort, close to Armagh). Within the cycle the most prominent warrior was the king's nephew, Cú Chulainn. More of him later. The warriors most celebrated after the heroic Cú Chulainn were Conall Cernach and Ferghus mac Róich, who, though not in the same league as Cú Chulainn, were still presented as dramatic and larger-than-life personalities. Ferghus mac Róich, for example, had a first name meaning something like 'manly energy', while 'mac Róich' meant 'son of super-horse', which suggests divine origins. Ferghus appears in a number of stories, including the famous epic the *Cattle Raid of Cooley* (*Táin Bó Cúailnge*); other stories add details such as his enormous genitals and how it took seven women to satisfy him. Other leading characters in the cycle were the druid Cathbadh; the peace-making King Sencha mac Ailella; and the trouble-making Bricriu Nemhthenga ('poison tongue' or 'bitter tongue').

In the stories, the Ulster warriors were often portrayed at war with their rivals from the kingdom of Connacht, led by their queen, Medb, and her husband Ailill. Alongside these two was their ally – an Ulster warrior in exile – Ferghus mac Róich. In some accounts he was also listed as one of those who found the infant hero Cú Chulainn and later trained him as a warrior. While these are presented as historical figures there are aspects of their names and characters, as we have seen, that suggest that they began as gods or goddesses and were later written about as humans.

The nature of the stories in the Ulster Cycle

The stories within the Ulster Cycle were written in Old and Middle Irish and can be found in manuscripts dating from the twelfth to the fifteenth century. The three manuscripts that between them contain most of the stories are the *Book of the Dun Cow* (*Lebor na hUidre*), of c.1100;

the *Book of Leinster* (*Lebor Laignech*), once known as the *Lebor na Nuachongbála*, or *Book of Nuachongbáil*, compiled *c*.1160; and the *Book of Fermoy*, dating mainly from the fifteenth and sixteenth centuries but with some parts probably written as early as the fourteenth century. Some of the language in a number of the stories suggests that the tales, in some form, originated perhaps as early as the eighth century. There is evidence to indicate that the myths of the Ulster Cycle were particularly popular among the Irish elites, since they focused on the character of heroic society. This seems to have continued until the twelfth century, when the stories faced increased competition from the Fenian Cycle (the *Fianaíocht*), which seems to have had a following among less prestigious listeners.[2]

The stories themselves are dramatic, fast-paced and violent. They weave together storylines that, at times, are realistic and at others highly mythological. Supernatural heroes such as Cú Chulainn mix with gods and goddesses who otherwise appear in stories of the *Tuatha Dé Danann*. The impression of Ireland given by the Ulster Cycle is one in which a number of provincial kingdoms raided and warred with each other. A society of pagan cattle herders was dominated by a warrior aristocracy that feasted, boasted and fought. We see cattle raids, one-on-one contests between heroic champions fought on the fords of rivers, enemies disembowelled and severed heads used as trophies, great battles and symbolic conflicts. In a number of the stories protagonists' actions were restricted by certain *geasa*, or taboos. The breaking of one of these taboos could lead to the downfall of a leading figure and, in a number of cases, this was presented as a fate that the person concerned could not escape. Later Christian writers suggested that the events described in the Ulster Cycle took place around the start of the first century and were contemporary with the birth of Christ. Conchobar was alleged to have been born and died on the same days as Jesus Christ. This created a sense of

an Irish Heroic Age.[3] There is, though, nothing historical
about the events so described and even the chariots that so
often figure in the stories appear not to have had significant usage in the real Ireland of prehistory. However, some
aspects of the stories may reflect the politics and warfare
of a real society. The use of heads as trophies, the granting
to favoured warriors of the best cuts of meat (the *curadmír*, or 'champion's portion'), the influence of druids and
the way in which reputations were celebrated or threatened
by the activities of poets also sound reminiscent of Late
Iron Age society. These features also suggest the society
of early medieval Ireland and so, even if the stories reflect
some aspects of historical reality, it is difficult to pin down
exactly when that reality occurred.

The huge number of stories in the Ulster Cycle makes it
impossible to tell them all here, but some flavour of their
content can be gained from an examination of a handful
of the collection's most dramatic and revealing tales and
characters.

Cattle Raid of Cooley (*Táin Bó Cúailnge*)

The central hero in the Ulster Cycle is the warrior Cú
Chulainn. He was made the major character in perhaps the
most famous and important tale: the epic *Cattle Raid of
Cooley* (*Táin Bó Cúailnge*, often simply *The Táin*). It is certainly the longest story and has been described as Ireland's
answer to the Greek *Iliad*. According to *The Táin*, at the
age of seventeen Cú Chulainn single-handedly defended
Ulster against the armies of Queen Medb of Connacht. Cú
Chulainn appeared in a number of stories apart from *The
Táin*. Presented as the son of the god Lugh, this heroic warrior battled the surviving Fomorians, took part in many
adventures, accidentally killed his own son and eventually died in battle after being tricked into eating dog meat
(a taboo). The Ulster Cycle also saw the first appearance
of stories of the Morrígan – goddess of battle, strife and

fertility – who played an important role in the narrative of *The Táin*.

The story contained in *The Táin* is broadly as follows. Queen Medb and her husband Ailill compared their respective wealth to find that the only thing that differentiated them was Ailill's ownership of Finnbennach, the White-horned Bull. This great bull had been born into Medb's herd but had transferred its allegiance to Ailill because it had not wished to be owned by a woman. Medb, envious of this advantage enjoyed by her husband, determined to gain access to a rival beast: the great Brown Bull of Cooley (the *Donn Cúailnge*), which lived in Ulster. This bull's strength and energy was renowned and Medb desired to rent it for a year. This she succeeded in doing, but, because they had been drinking, her emissaries overplayed their hand and let it slip that, had the negotiations failed, they would have forced the Ulster men to allow the bull to be brought back into Connacht as their prize. As a consequence, the arrangement broke down and Medb raised a huge army and invaded Ulster in order to gain ownership of the great Brown Bull.

This object of the cattle raid by the army of Connacht was a bull whose prowess was graphically described in *The Táin*: 'He could bull fifty heifers every day. They'd calve at the same hour the next day, and those that didn't would burst, overwhelmed as they were by the offspring of the Brown Bull.'[4] Furthermore, the word used to describe its colour in Irish – *donn* (brown) – may have been a play on words that echoed the name of Donn, the god of the world of the dead. Such was the beast that Queen Medb desired to bring back in triumph to Connacht. The mythical nature of the protagonists is increased when we consider that 'Medb' meant 'intoxicator' and was cognate with the Old English word for 'mead'. Her character may have started as a sovereignty deity of Connacht. Similarly, her husband's name, Ailill, meant 'brilliant' or 'phantom' and suggests an original deity that had become human in later traditions.

Even larger-than-life than the Brown Bull of Cúailnge was Cú Chulainn himself. In battle his prowess was unbeatable, and 'For each of the three nights they [Medb's army] were encamped there [Druim Féine, in Conaille] he killed a hundred men, picking them off with his sling from the nearby heights of Ochaíne.'[5] This is but one of many such incidents recounted in *The Táin* as the army of Connacht came up against Cú Chulainn.

In *The Táin* the single-handed defence of Ulster by Cú Chulainn was necessary because the other men of Ulster were laid low by a curse. The cause of this disability was explained in another story, *The Nine Days' Pangs (or Debility) of the Ulstermen (Ces Noínden Ulad)*. According to the story, Macha, the wife of Crunniuc (or Crunnchu) mac Agnomain, was so prodigiously swift a runner that she was forced by her husband's boasting to race the king's chariot, even though heavily pregnant. Giving birth at the end of the race, she cried out that all who heard her scream would be cursed with the same pain that she had experienced for five days and four nights when they faced great challenges and danger. This curse then lay on the men of Ulster for nine generations. This was why they could not rally to face the army of Queen Medb.[6] In *The Táin* this disability appeared to have lasted from autumn until the end of spring and some students of Irish mythology have therefore suggested that it was originally a myth connected with winter death and spring rebirth.[7] Macha may originally have been considered a fertility and war goddess (see Chapter 6).

The Táin is graphic in its description of the violence of battle. In one incident Cú Chulainn defeated a warrior named Láríne: 'He grabbed him and shook him and squeezed him till the shit ran out of him, polluting the ford and stinking up the air all around.' Láríne was one of the few warriors who survived combat with Cú Chulainn, but only because Cú Chulainn chose not to kill him. And for Láríne the encounter was devastating: 'For the rest of his days his bowels didn't work right. He was never without chest trouble, and eating was a constant pain. Yet his is the only man who met Cú Chulainn on the Táin Bó Cúailnge and escaped with his life – not that it was much of a life.'[8]

In battle Cú Chulainn was described as having a body terribly twisted and contorted. The word in Irish that described this – *riastradh* – has been translated as 'warp-spasm'[9] and 'the Torque'.[10] 'The first Torque seized Cú Chulainn and turned him into a contorted thing, unrecognizably horrible and grotesque. Every slab and every sinew of him, joint and muscle, shuddered from head to foot like a tree in the storm or a reed in the stream. His body revolved furiously inside his skin.' This appalling transformation went on and on. Cú Chulainn's feet and knees reversed themselves, one eye was sucked in while the other hung on his cheek, his cheek peeled back to reveal his lungs and liver in his throat, a 'hero's light' shone from his forehead and a spout of dark blood rose from the front of his skull and formed a cloud of mist above him.[11] In this state of contorted rage he slaughtered his enemies in the army of Queen Medb of Connacht, on the plain of Muirthemne.

At the climax of the war, the two great bulls – the Brown Bull of Cúailnge and Finnbennach, the White-horned Bull – finally confronted each other on the Plain of Aí, in Connacht. The Brown Bull, having been brought there by the men of Connacht, let out three great bellows that provoked the native bull to mortal combat. After a ferocious battle the Brown Bull killed Finnbennach. Heading home to Ulster, the Brown Bull paused at various places – giving rise to later place names, in a way characteristic of Irish mythology – until it finally collapsed and died. After this, Ailill and Medb made a peace with the Ulster men and Cú Chulainn that lasted seven years.

The birth and upbringing of Cú Chulainn

The birth of Cú Chulainn is known from a story called *The Conception of Cú Chulainn (Compert Con Culainn)*. In the later, and better-known, version of this story, King Conchobar mac Nessa of Ulster had a sister named Deichtine. This royal princess disappeared from the Ulster court but then appeared later in the story, when the Ulstermen went hunting a flock of magical birds. On this quest they were threatened by a snowstorm and sought shelter. Their host turned out to be the god Lugh (a member of the *Tuatha Dé Danann*). That night his wife – who turned out to be Deichtine – gave birth to a son, Sétanta.

The members of the Ulster elite could not agree which of them should be Sétanta's foster father, but in an eventual compromise they all played a part. Conchobar himself acted in this capacity, while Sencha mac Ailella taught the boy judgement and flowing speech; Ferghus mac Róich taught him to protect the weak; the poet Amergin educated him and his wife, Findchóem, nursed him. In time the boy became known by a different name after he killed the fierce guard dog of Culann. When he offered to take the place of the dog he became known as 'Cú Chulainn' – 'Hound of Culann'; as a consequence he is often now known as the 'Hound of Ulster' and in stories he played a key role in defending his homeland. This is Cú Chulainn's central role in *The Táin*.

The death of Cú Chulainn's son

Although a great warrior, Cú Chulainn was hemmed in by complex taboos that stood in stark contrast to his seemingly unchallengeable strength. These are particularly pronounced in stories telling of the death of his son and his own downfall. The first taboo is related in *The Death of Aoífe's Only Son (Aided Óenfir Aoífe)*, which tells of how Cú Chulainn killed his own child. In this story, Cú Chulainn went to Scotland to be taught the skills of warfare by Scáthach, the daughter of Ardgeimm. This also features in detail in another story, *The Wooing of Emer* (*Tochmarc Emire*). While Cú Chulainn was there he met a princess named Aoífe and she became pregnant with his child. On leaving Scotland, Cú Chulainn said that when the boy, named Connla, was old enough he should come and seek his father in Ireland. Then Cú Chulainn laid down a *geis* (taboo) that was to prove the undoing of his son. According to this, Connla should not reveal his name to any man, nor refuse combat to any man. Eventually, at the age of seven, the boy went to Ireland to find his father. His warrior skills made him seem a threat to Cú Chulainn, who did not know his real identity. When the two finally met, the *geis* placed on Connla by Cú Chulainn ensured that he refused to identify himself. Without realizing who the boy was, Cú Chulainn fought and killed him. In this single combat the weapon that finally killed Connla was known as the *Gae Bulg*. This weapon also featured in *The Táin*, where it was described as opening up into thirty barbs once it had entered a man's body. It had been given to Cú Chulainn by Scáthach in Scotland. In this way the story had a grim circularity that linked the conception of Connla with his death at the hands of his own father. Other versions of the story survive in the so-called *History of Places* (the *Dindshenchas*). These survive in recensions that are found in a number of manuscripts, ranging from the twelfth-century *Book of Leinster* to a group of manuscripts dating from the fourteenth and fifteenth centuries. It is from this later material that additional information can be identified. In this later tradition, Aoífe was criticized for sending the boy to Cú Chulainn, despite being instructed so to do. This negative tone probably reflects the influence of clerical revisers and editors of the earlier tales.[12]

The death of Cú Chulainn
In *The Táin*, the story of Cú Chulainn ended with his victory. But Cathbadh the druid had predicted that Cú

Chulainn's life would be cut short. In the story *The Great Slaughter on the Plain of Muirthemne* (*Brislech Màr Maige Muirthemne*), Queen Medb – who featured so conspicuously in *The Táin* – conspired with the sons of men that Cú Chulainn had killed. These sons, bent on revenge, included Lugaid son of Cú Roí, and Erc son of Cairbre Nia Fer. Despite his great strength, Cú Chulainn was doomed by his breaking of the *geasa* that applied to him, which included a taboo against eating a dog as meat. The breaking of this taboo was forced on Cú Chulainn by another powerful taboo that dictated that he should not refuse hospitality. When an old woman offered him dog meat as a meal, he was forced to break his taboo regarding this food, and consequently he was doomed as he went into battle. This sense of a fated death is similar to that of Connla in *The Death of Aoífe's Only Son*.

Lugaid – one of those plotting the death of Cú Chulainn – had three magical spears made. It was foretold that each of these would kill a 'king'. The story was then contrived to show how this came to pass. The first of these spears killed Cú Chulainn's charioteer, who was the 'king' of chariot drivers. The second spear killed Cú Chulainn's horse, which was the 'king' of horses. The third spear mortally wounded Cú Chulainn himself, a 'king' among warriors. Facing death, Cú Chulainn tied himself to a stone so that he would face death standing up. Despite his terrible wound, his enemies were fearful of approaching him. It was only when a raven landed on his shoulder that they realized that he was dead. This was clearly a reference to the Morrígan, the goddess of battle and of death. Eventually convinced that it was safe to approach the dead hero, Lugaid went forward to cut off Cú Chulainn's head. Suddenly a supernatural light shone around Cú Chulainn; his sword fell from his dead hand and sliced off Lugaid's hand; the light finally vanished when Cú Chulainn's right hand (his sword hand) was cut off. So died Cú Chulainn, the Hound of Ulster.

In later Christian tradition, the Middle Irish story *The Phantom Chariot of Cú Chulainn* (*Siaburcharpat Con Culaind*) recounted the tradition that, when St Patrick was preaching to the still-pagan King Lóegaire, in order that the king would convert to Christianity the ghost of Cú Chulainn appeared to him. Standing in his chariot, in an image taken from the pagan mythological accounts, Cú Chulainn warned Lóegaire of the torments of hell. In this way the famous hero of an older Ireland was deployed by later Christian monastic writers to encourage conversion to the Christian faith. This account is found in the twelfth-century manuscript the *Book of the Dun Cow*.

Other characters found in the Ulster Cycle

Other stories recount the activities of more heroes of Ulster in their battles and conflicts, and these tales vary from the bloody and realistic to the highly mythical. One of these famous men was Cathbadh, the chief druid of Conchobar mac Nessa of Ulster. He appeared in a number of stories associated with foretelling the future. He predicted the death of Deirdre, a princess of Ulster who ran away from court with her lover, Naoise, in order to avoid marrying Conchobar. This Naoise had fulfilled Deirdre's desire to find a man with hair the colour of a raven, skin as white as snow and lips as red as blood. Deirdre fled to Scotland with Naoise but was tracked down. Naoise was killed and after this Deirdre was forced to marry Conchobar. Angered by her coldness towards him, Conchobar said he would punish her by giving her to the man who had killed Naoise. Taking her to him, he taunted her that she was like a ewe trapped between two rams. At this, Deirdre threw herself from his chariot, smashed her head against a rock and died. In this story Conchobar was clearly presented as the villain but in most other stories in the Ulster Cycle – such as in *The Táin* – he was portrayed favourably. The story of Deirdre was told in *The Sorrow of Deirdru/Deirdre*, also known as *The Exile of the Sons of Uisnech* (*Longas mac nUislenn*), which is found in the twelfth-century *Book of Leinster* but may originally have dated from the eighth or ninth century.[13] In *The Táin* Conchobar predicted that a youth who took up arms on a particular day would be a great warrior but die young. Overhearing him, Cú Chulainn immediately rushed to the king to ask for weapons, for he considered great fame better than long life.

Another well-known figure in the Ulster Cycle was Sencha mac Ailella, who was compelled to give just judgements or break a taboo. When he was giving a judgement based on misogyny his face broke out in a rash and remained this way until the goddess Brigid (Brigit) persuaded him to reconsider his judgement. He offered to foster the young Cú Chulainn but instead taught the young man eloquence and judgement.

More negatively portrayed was Bricriu Nemhthenga, who featured in a number of stories and each one of his appearances caused discord and conflict. In *Bricriu's Feast* (*Fled Bricrenn*), he incited the three greatest warriors of Ulster – Cú Chulainn, Conall Cernach and Lóegaire Búadach – to quarrel over the prize cut of meat at a feast, known as the *curadmír*, or 'champion's portion'. The theme of culinary competition was also taken up in *The Tale of Mac Da Thó's Pig* (*Scéla Mucce meic Da Thó*). In this story, the champions of Ulster were incited to quarrel over the carving of Mac Da Thó's pig. The conflict was the cause of much bloodshed. The story tells of how Mac Da Thó owned a fabulous dog and a fabulous pig. Facing competing bids for his fierce dog from both Medb and Ailill of Connacht and Conchobar mac Nessa of Ulster, he declared that whoever came for the dog could purchase it from him. In the meantime he slaughtered his great pig. The rest of the story was dominated by a dispute over who had the right to carve the roast animal. Bricriu stirred up bitter rivalry and disputes over who had done the greatest deeds in battle, which caused the feast to descend into bloodshed. One of the most dramatic moments in this process was when Cet mac Mágach of Connacht was about to carve the pig. At that point he was interrupted by the arrival of an even greater warrior, Conall Cernach of Ulster. Boasting that he had never spent a single day without killing a man from Connacht, had never spent a single night without plundering the wealth of Connacht, and never slept without having a Connachtman's head beneath his knee, he took Cet mac Mágach's place by the roast pig. In retaliation, Cet mac Mágach replied that his brother, Anluan, would be a greater warrior yet, if only he was there. At this, Conall Cernach declared that Anluan was indeed present and threw his severed head onto the floor – and then proceeded to carve the pig for the Ulster men. Then open warfare broke out between the men of Connacht and those from Ulster. When the survivors from Connacht eventually left they took the dog – over the ownership of which the conflict had begun and which now had appeared to prefer the Ulster men – cut off its head and stuck it on a yew tree. However, Bricriu was not always presented as so lethal and destructive. In *The Cattle Raid of Flidais* (*Táin Bó Flidais*) he was a poetic satirist, but his biting words were not as terrible in their destructive effect as they were presented in *Bricriu's Feast* and *The Tale of Mac Da Thó's Pig*.

II

FINN MAC CUMHAILL AND THE WARRIORS OF THE *FIANNA*

The tales preserved in the collection known as the Fenian Cycle (the *Fianaíocht*) – or Ossianic Cycle, after its legendary narrator, Oisín (or Ossian) – centre on the exploits of the mythical hero Finn (or Fionn) mac Cumhaill[1] and his band of warriors, the *fianna*. This term was used to describe any group of young warriors but has become particularly associated with the warband of Finn.[2] These stories tell of tests accomplished by Finn and the *fianna*, while warriors and gods and goddesses mingled in these adventures. The long-established Fenian lore attained greatest popularity around 1200, when the Fenian Cycle's outstanding story, *The Interrogation of the Old Men* (*Agallamh Na Seanórach*), also called *The Dialogue of the Ancients*, was written down. This survives in two fifteenth-century manuscripts and in one manuscript of the seventeenth century.

The 'old men' of the title were the famous Fenian poet-warriors Oisín and Caílte. These two survived the defeat and deaths of their fellow warriors of the *fianna* at the Battle of Gabhra. They eventually returned to Ireland from exile in *Tír na nÓg* (the Land of the Forever Young) to discover they had been away for three hundred years. In Ireland they met St Patrick, who questioned them about the deeds of Finn mac Cumhaill and the warrior heroes of the *fianna*. It was in their answers to these questions that the monastic writers both recorded the ancient tales from the Irish past and integrated them into the Christian culture of medieval Ireland.

The Fenian Cycle of tales is one of the four great collections of related stories that make up the bulk of the Irish mythological, legendary and semi-legendary traditions. The other three collections are the Mythological Cycle, the Ulster Cycle and the Historical Cycle, or the Cycles of the Kings. It should, though, be remembered that the names given to these collections are the inventions of much later scholars and the tales themselves are a complex mixture of ancient traditions, biblical influences and aspects of Classical stories brought into the tales by medieval Irish monastic compilers who recorded, edited, censored and reworked the accounts in order to produce the documents that survive. They certainly do not constitute the original and timeless myths of Ireland.

The focus of the stories of the Fenian Cycle

Taken at face value the stories of the Fenian Cycle[3] appear to be set in around the third century AD. In reality, they take their material from a range of sources and times; and the connection with Scotland in a number of stories reveals that they were influenced by the post-Roman settlement of Irish communities in south-west Scotland to form the kingdom of Dál Riata with its component parts on either side of the North Channel, which separates

Ireland from Scotland. Most stories, though, were set in the context of Leinster and Munster. Unlike the Ulster Cycle, much of the Fenian Cycle was written in verse and shows signs of being influenced by the Romance literature becoming popular in the twelfth century. In the stories the warriors feasted, hunted and were expected to have skills in poetry as well as in warfare. They were initiated into the warband through a series of initiation tests. While the stories contain aspects of magic and the appearance of deities recognizable from other strands in Irish mythology, there are no obvious religious teachings to be found within the tales other than an emphasis on heroic manhood and courage in battle. The stories are many and complex and just a few are outlined here to give an impression of their character.

The Cause of the Battle of Cnucha (Fotha Catha Chnucha)

The details of this battle are found in the *Book of the Dun Cow* (*Lebor na hUidre*), where the story centres on the death of Cumhaill, the father of the heroic Finn mac Cumhaill. The account explains the reason for the ancient hatred between the rivals the Clan Baíscne (first led by Cumhaill and later by Finn) and the Clan Morna (led by Goll mac Morna).[4] Goll's name (the 'one-eyed') linked him with Balor of the One Eye or Balor of the Evil Eye, of the Fomorians. This name emphasized his dangerous nature and savage origins (see Chapter 5), in contrast to Finn. At times the central figure of Goll mac Morna was replaced by another warrior, Conn Cétchathach ('Conn of the hundred battles'). The name of the battle of Cnucha later gave rise to the place name Castle Knock or Castleknock. Today it is located at Castleknock College, near Phoenix Park in Dublin, Ireland.

The Boyhood Deeds of Finn (*Macgnímartha Finn*)

This account may date from as early as the twelfth century and is reminiscent of stories connected with the boyhood of Cú Chulainn. The story starts with the death in battle of Finn's father Cumhaill, the warrior leader of the *fianna*. He was killed by Goll mac Morna. Cumhaill's pregnant wife, Muirne, called their son Demne (though he would later be known as Finn). Fearing for the boy's life, she decided to send him to safety with Cumhaill's sister, the druidess Bodhmall and her companion, Liath Luachra. These two warrior women raised him and accompanied him on a number of his early adventures.

In this stage of his life Demne went through a number of adventures that tested his ability to lead the *fianna*. These included his capturing the Salmon of Wisdom; taking part in an athletic contest in which he gained the name Finn ('the fair-haired one'); and the getting of his sword and his banner. At this time he also gained ownership of the crane-bag (*corrbolg*), which had been formed from the skin of Aife (Aoífe) by the sea god Manannán (see Chapter 9). Since the crane-bag contained the letters of the alphabet, this associates the beginning of Irish writing and poetry with Finn. In addition, he defeated Goll mac Morna, the enemy of Finn's clan in *The Cause of the Battle of Cnucha*. As a result, Finn became the unchallenged leader of the warband of the *fianna*.

Finn's successes caused his fame to spread far and wide and his guardians feared that soon Goll would learn about them and threaten him. To avoid this they sent him away. He entered service to the King of Bantry and went on to regain the lost treasure of Cumhaill, his father. It was after this that he met up with the old warriors of the *fianna* who had been defeated along with his father.

It was during these formative years that Finn inadvertently ate a morsel of the Salmon of Wisdom. It was reputed that whoever ate it would gain universal knowledge. This fortuitous event occurred while Finn was under the tute-lage of the poet Finn Eces, who for seven years had been hunting the famous salmon. When he finally caught the fish he set Finn the task of cooking it. While so doing, Finn burned his thumb on the cooking fish; and suck-ing it he suddenly gained the wisdom of the salmon. The Celtic association of the salmon with wisdom may have been prompted by the ability of the fish to return to its birthplace.[5]

Finn then travelled to the royal centre at Tara to slay Aillén 'the burner'. Aillén had gained his name from attacking Tara every Samhain (31 October) and setting it afire. In this, the story of Finn became entwined with other strands of Irish mythology since Aillén was named as a member of the *Tuatha Dé Danann*, the family of Irish gods and goddesses. Before the arrival of Finn, the *fianna* had been unable to prevent this annual destruction because Aillén put them to sleep by playing magical music. To pre-vent himself from falling under this spell, Finn breathed in poison from his own spear and so avoided falling sleep. Consequently, he was awake when the attack occurred and he killed Aillén. After this victory, Finn revealed his true identity to the court and, in return, he was given his right-ful position as leader of the *fianna*, in place of his dead father.[6]

The Pursuit of Diarmuid and Gráinne (*Tóraigheacht Dhiarmada agus Ghráinne*)

This tale concerns a love tangle involving Finn, the beautiful princess Gráinne and her lover Diarmuid Ua Duibhne. It is similar to the semi-Arthurian story of Tristan and Isolde (or Iseult). Although there are clues in the story suggesting that parts may date from the tenth century, the surviving manuscripts were all written in Modern Irish and date from no earlier than the sixteenth century. There were a number of supernatural aspects to the story: Gráinne appeared superhuman though not divine; the deity Oengus Óg was believed to have intervened; and a tree's fruit was claimed to impart immortality.[7]

At the start of the story the elderly Finn was grieving over the death of his wife Maigneis. But he sought a new wife and his choice fell on Gráinne, the daughter of High King Cormac mac Airt. She had the reputation of being the most beautiful woman in Ireland. When Finn and Gráinne first met, she was shocked to discover that Finn was older than her father. In this state of disappointment she became attracted to Diarmuid, one of Finn's young warriors in the *fianna*. In order to escape from Finn, Gráinne slipped a sleeping potion in the drink of the assembled guests and asked Diarmuid to run away with her. He at first refused, since he had promised loyalty to Finn. However, he gave in when threatened with a *geis* (taboo) that he could not break. This demonstrated Gráinne's power over him.

On the run, the two lovers hid in a forest beyond the river Shannon while Finn searched for them. They escaped capture on a number of occasions through the assistance of other members of the *fianna* and of Oengus Óg, who, as well as being god of love, was also Diarmuid's foster father. Oengus hid Gráinne in his cloak of invisibility and Diarmuid escaped by leaping over those hunting for them.

Although they had escaped from Finn, Diarmuid refused at first to sleep with Gráinne because of his loyalty to Finn. But this did not last and soon she was pregnant with the child of Diarmuid. It was then that she desired a meal of the rowan berries that were guarded by a one-eyed giant named Searbhán. Diarmuid was forced to fight Searbhán for the berries and only succeeded when he was able to use the giant's club against him. The berries of the rowan tree, it was claimed, imparted immortality. Eventually, the foster father of Diarmuid arranged a peace settlement with Finn, and Gráinne and Diarmuid lived together and raised five children.

This might have been the happy end to this tangled love story but Finn bore a deep grudge. On a boar hunt, Diarmuid was mortally wounded by the beast's tusks but could have still been saved if Finn had only given him a drink of water from his cupped hands. But twice Finn let the precious liquid slip between his fingers. A third time Finn went to the well, but on his return he found Diarmuid had died. And what became of Gráinne? Different traditions give diverging accounts of her fate after the death of Diarmuid. In one she caused her children to swear vengeance on Finn for the needless death of their father; in another she died from grief; in yet another she was reconciled with Finn.

The Battle of Ventry (Cath Finntrágha)

In its current form, the manuscript evidence for this story dates from the fifteenth century but it shows signs of using earlier material. Its central theme is how Finn and the *fianna* defended Ireland against invasion by Dáire Donn – sometimes described as 'King of the World' or 'King of Rome' – who was reputed to be the most powerful ruler in the whole of Europe. The reasons for this invasion were a mixture of the territorial ambitions of Dáire Donn, resentment regarding the heroic reputation of Finn and a desire to punish Finn for a misdeed in eloping with the King of France's wife. Clearly, Finn's marital escapades and crises had influenced more than one medieval Irish author.

According to the story, Dáire Donn landed his invasion force at Finntraighe (Ventry Bay, on the Dingle Peninsula, County Kerry), having been guided there by a disaffected member of the *fianna*. Finn summoned the warriors of all Ireland to the great battle. This included members of the *Tuatha Dé Danann* who were living in Conal Gavra (County Limerick). For a year and a day the battle raged. Finn's son Oisín faced the King of France in single combat;

the son of the King of Ulster arrived to support Finn and his *fianna* but went mad because of the frenzy of the conflict; it was only the arrival of the warriors of the *Tuatha Dé Danann* that turned the battle in Finn's favour. Finally, Finn killed Dáire Donn, along with a Greek woman-warrior, the amazon Ógarmach. It was only then that the resolve of the invaders was broken and they were routed.

The Death of Finn (*Aided Finn*)

The earliest account of Finn's death relates that he was killed in battle against the Lúagni Temrach at Áth Brea on the river Boyne. His killer was Aiclech mac Dubdrenn, who cut off his head. This account can be found in the poem *Heroes Who Were in Emain* (*Fianna bátar i nEmain*); also known as *The Deaths of Some of the Nobles of Ireland* (*Aidedha forni do huaislib Érenn*) and traditionally ascribed to the tenth-century poet Cináed húa hArtacáin. An incomplete version of this account survives in the *Book of Leinster* and in two other manuscripts. A more detailed version is found in *The Death of Finn* (*Aided Finn*). There were clearly competing versions of Finn's demise, for this work emphatically states: '*is í sin iarum Aided Finn iar fírinne in senchasa amail adfiadat na heólaig*' ('that then is the Death of Finn according to the truth of history, as the learned relate').[8]

One of these competing stories was composed in Middle Irish and dates probably from the twelfth century. It survives in two fragments,[9] which appear to represent the beginning and end of a story telling of the death of Finn. When combined, these fragments reveal how Finn died from breaking one of the *geasa* (taboos) so prominent in a number of Irish myths. The cause of Finn's death was a desire to leap the river Boyne as a demonstration of his great strength. On his way to the river he met a woman at Mullaghmast (County Kildare). Here the first fragment ends but, from what is found in the second fragment, it is clear that Finn asked her for a drink.[10] Information in *The Death of Finn* (*Aided Finn*) indicates that there was a *geis* (taboo) on Finn according to which he would swiftly die if he took a sip from a drinking horn. This taboo had been pronounced on him by his wife, Smirgat. From the second fragment, the story progressed to show how Finn drank from a spring in County Offaly. This proved his undoing since the spring was called *Adarca Iuchba* ('the Horns of Iuchba'). In this way the *geis* was broken and Finn undone, for as he leapt the Boyne he fell, struck his head on rocks and died. The location of this fatal event was later remembered as *Léim Finn* (Finn's Leap).

Other, later accounts envisaged Finn asleep in a hidden cave, from which he would emerge to save Ireland from danger. This tradition had similarities to claims regarding Arthur[11] and is a motif found connected to many famous folk heroes.

Oisín in Tír na nÓg (Oisín i Tír na nÓg)

The most famous *echtra* (adventure tale) associated with Oisín, son of Finn mac Cumhaill, involved him travelling to *Tír na nÓg*, the fabled land of youth. According to the account, one morning when the *fianna* were out hunting they encountered a beautiful girl riding a fine horse. It transpired that she was Níamh Chinn Óir (Niamh of the Golden Hair), one of the daughters of Manannán, the god of the sea. She declared her love for Oisín and together they returned to her home of *Tír na nÓg*. Oisín promised his father and the *fianna* that he would soon return to Ireland.

Living happily in *Tír na nÓg*, Niamh gave birth to Oisín's son, Oscar, and a daughter, *Plor na mBan* ('flower of women'). After what seemed to him to be no more than three years in this idyllic life, Oisín decided to return to Ireland. However, in the space of these three years, three hundred years had passed in the mortal world. Niamh loaned Oisín her white horse, Embarr, for the journey home. She gave him a solemn warning not to dismount from the horse, for, if his feet touched the ground, he would immediately become three hundred years old.

Back in Ireland, Oisín found that Finn's home, on the hill of Almu, was abandoned and in ruins; time had taken its toll. To his disgust he found his homeland was inhabited by a race of insignificant people, who bore little resemblance to the great warriors of the *fianna*. To these people the stories of Finn and the *fianna* were no more than half-remembered tales from the distant past.

While Oisín was searching for the *fianna*, he rode through Gleann na Smól (Howth, near modern Dublin) and chanced on men toiling on the hill of Tallaght, building a road. He stopped to assist them in moving a stone onto a wagon. Some accounts stated there were three hundred men and that Oisín, while on horseback, lifted the stone with one hand. However, Embarr's girth broke and Oisín fell to the ground. In an instant the three centuries caught up with him and he became ancient and withered. Niamh's horse returned alone to *Tír na nÓg*. In a scene reminiscent of the suddenly aged swan-children of Lír (see Chapter 9) some versions of the tale explain that, before Oisín died, he was visited by a Christian priest. In this case it was St Patrick himself to whom Oisín related the stories of his life before he died. As with the swan-children of Lír, this gave him the opportunity for Christian salvation and revealed the influence of the medieval Irish monastic recorders of the tradition.

The Interrogation of the Old Men (Agallamh Na Seanórach)

This great résumé of the activities of the *fianna* was supposedly set several hundred years after the death of Finn mac Cumhaill. In it the two aged heroes of the *fianna*, Finn's nephew, Caílte mac Rónáin, and Finn's son, Oisín, travelled Ireland in the company of St Patrick. During most

of the story it was Caílte who primarily informed Patrick
about the deeds of Finn and the warriors of his warband.
The account also included information designed to explain
the meanings of Irish place names.

Many of the stories explored the rivalry between Finn's
family and that of his enemy Goll mac Morna. Other stories recalled the relationship between Finn and the *fianna*
with the Otherworld and their relationship with the *Tuatha
Dé Danann*. Lastly, the account told stories connected to
St Patrick and these were often concerned with integrating
the culture of pre-Christian Ireland with the new Christian faith. There is some evidence that the author(s) adapted
pre-existing tales to suit the narrative purpose of the work.

The Fenian Brotherhood of the nineteenth century

Why did the Irish and Irish-American nineteenth-century
nationalist resistance movement take its name – the Fenian
Brotherhood – from this strand of Irish mythology as it
sought independence from British rule? In 1858 the Fenian
Brotherhood and the Irish Republican Brotherhood (IRB)
were established. Inspired by an earlier Irish nationalist
group, Young Ireland, and reacting to the horrors of the
Irish Potato Famine, they were less interested in solving
the Irish land question than in creating an Irish nationalism that would attract all groups (not just Catholics). Most
of their support came from the lower middle class in Ireland. American Fenians raided British-ruled Canada in
1866, 1870 and 1871 from bases in the USA. Many of these
Fenians had gained experience in handling weapons and in
military discipline in the American Civil War (1861–5). In
1867 there were Fenian uprisings in Chester (England) and
also in County Kerry and across Ireland. Those executed
in England for killing a prison guard while attempting to
free Fenian prisoners became known by Irish Nationalists as the 'Manchester Martyrs'. Other Fenians set off a
bomb at Clerkenwell Prison in London, killing a number

of passers-by, in another unsuccessful attempt to free jailed colleagues.

Although the Fenians failed to end British rule in nineteenth-century Ireland, they formed one of the streams flowing into the Irish nationalist and republican movement that, in the twentieth century, eventually succeeded in setting up the Republic of Ireland. Today the term 'Fenian' is still sometimes used to describe Irish nationalists, although it is more commonly used now by Unionist opponents of nationalism and as a demeaning nickname for Irish Catholics. Nevertheless, while the word is now less frequently used by Irish nationalists and republicans, in these communities it still evokes memories of the heroic resistance of the past, even if it has been superseded by other political terms.

It was John O'Mahony (a Gaelic scholar and the founding member of the Fenian Brotherhood in the USA) who coined the term 'Fenian' to describe the organization. In so doing he was influenced by the traditional Irish tales of the bands of young warriors who lived apart from the rest of Irish society and fought for the honour and protection of Ireland. Here is ample proof of the continuing fame and influence of Finn mac Cumhaill and the warriors of the *fianna*.[12]

The folklore 'afterlife' of Finn mac Cumhaill

One of the reasons why John O'Mahony gave a new lease of life to the name 'Fenian' was that the myths of Finn and the *fianna* appear to have continued to be popularly recited into the eighteenth and nineteenth centuries, well after the influence of the other mythological tales had declined and before they were 'rediscovered' by later nineteenth-century folklorists. As a result, stories of Finn continued to be invented and developed long after the medieval period. In the earlier, medieval stories, Finn was presented as superhuman or semi-divine: he reversed the transformation of his wife to a deer (see Chapter 9); he encountered the Mor-rígan in the form of three old hags; he had second sight and supernatural fighting skills; he successfully challenged Nuada of the *Tuatha Dé Danann* for the lordship of the *sídhe* of Almu.[13] This was in contrast to how his character developed in post-medieval folklore.

In these later – oral folklore – stories, Finn was often something of a figure of fun and much cruder than the character found in the medieval manuscripts. In *The Legend of Knockmany* we meet Finn – named 'Fin M'Coul' – as a giant, constructing the Giant's Causeway (County Antrim). In this form he came into conflict with another giant, Cucullin. This was clearly meant to be Cú Chulainn, although the two never met in the original medieval sto-ries. Finn went home in terror of Cucullin and only sur-vived because his wife, Oonagh, disguised him as a baby. By baking granite into her bread Oonagh tricked Cucul-lin into breaking his teeth on a loaf, only for the giant to be amazed that the 'baby' ate a loaf (which contained no granite) with ease. Testing the teeth of this amazing 'baby', Cucullin had the middle finger of his right hand bitten off, and so lost his power. Suddenly weakened, he was felled by Fin M'Coul. Other stories described Fin M'Coul as the builder of the Giant's Causeway; or the slayer of the giant who did build it.[14] In another story, he faced the humili-ating challenge of having to whistle with a mouth full of oatmeal. In these, almost slapstick, oral accounts – pop-ular among the Irish peasant communities – the stories had come a long way from the heroic medieval tales of the *fianna*.[15] In some of the oral tales there was a discernible undercurrent of anti-clericalism and Oisín's praise of Finn seemed almost a challenge to St Patrick's list of truly vir-tuous souls.[16] Clearly, within the later folklore tradition, Finn had a number of roles to play.

12

THE CYCLES OF THE KINGS: TALES OF THE TRADITIONAL KINGS OF IRELAND

This collection of tales, recorded in Old and Middle Irish, contains famous stories of the legendary kings of Ireland. These kings include such famous names as Cormac mac Airt, Niall of the Nine Hostages, Éogan Mór, Conall Corc, Guaire Aidne mac Colmáin, Diarmait mac Cerbaill, Lugaid mac Con, Conn of the Hundred Battles, Lóegaire mac Néill, Crimthann mac Fidaig and Brian Bóruma. Within these stories, a particularly notable group centre on Cormac mac Airt and his ancestors. No fewer than ten of the twenty-four stories in the Cycles of the Kings are found in this sub-group, sometimes referred to as the Cormac Cycle.[1] This Cormac was the ruler who employed Finn (or Fionn) mac Cumhaill and the warriors of the *fianna* (see Chapter 11).

The stories that centre on the kings listed above, and on

their associates, form what are often termed the Cycles of
the Kings, which are also known as the Historical Cycle.
Like the names attached to the other three 'cycles' (Mythological, Ulster, Fenian), this is a relatively modern invention
by scholars seeking to identify related groups of stories. In
the case of the Cycles of the Kings, the name was coined by
Myles Dillon in 1946.[2] The plural – Cycles – reflected the
fact that there were a number of discrete groups of related
stories that might be presented under this umbrella term.
In fact, some are so distinct that they might be regarded as
quite separate and stand-alone and it was this that prompted Alan Bruford, in 1969, to coin the term the 'Dalcassian
Cycle'[3] to describe the stories relating to the tenth-century
Brian Bóruma (often anglicized as Boru) and his family
and to differentiate them from the other tales.[4] One of the
alternative names for the overall collection of stories – the
Historical Cycle – reminds us that *some* of the kings that
featured in these tales were historical rulers, and for this
reason there was an attempt, in the 1930s, to introduce the
descriptive title 'Tales of the Traditional Kings'.[5] However,
this suggestion, although an appealing idea, never took
root. But it appears as the sub-title of this chapter because
it fairly accurately sums up the character of this large collection of stories, with its mixture of mythical, legendary,
historical and semi-historical characters.

A bridge between myth and legend

The stories found in these cycles form a bridge between
myth and legend, if by *myth* we mean stories, usually
religious, that explain origins, why things are as they are;
while *legends* attempt to explain historical events and may
involve historical characters but are told in a non-historical
way, although in some cases they also tell of mythological
characters (see Chapter 1). It is noticeable how little part
the old Irish pagan gods played in these stories. The king
who was represented as having had the closest association

with the deities of the *Tuatha Dé Danann* was Cormac mac Airt. However, while there are supernatural elements in a number of the stories, the majority focus more on the battles fought by a warrior society; and on treachery, murder and revenge. And these battles and conflicts are more reminiscent of real warfare, with nothing to compare to the kind of supernatural dramas associated with Cú Chulainn in the *Cattle Raid of Cooley* (*Táin Bó Cúailnge*). As well as containing far fewer characters drawn from the pre-Christian past, these stories also show more borrowing from other traditional folklores, from both Britain and the Classical world.

The kings that are included range from the almost entirely non-historical and mythological Labraid Loingsech, who supposedly became the High King of all of Ireland in about 431 BC, to the entirely historical Brian Bóruma (*c.*940–1014), who, unlike Labraid Loingsech, really was *Ard Rí na hÉireann* (High King of Ireland) and was also conqueror of the Vikings at the great battle of Clontarf, fought on Good Friday, 1014. Other stories stand in stark contrast to the historicity of Brian Bóruma. One of these – and perhaps the most famous tale in the Cycles of the Kings – is *The Frenzy of Sweeney* (*Buile Suibne*). This is a twelfth-century tale that was recounted in both verse and in prose. It told the story of Suibne, King of Dál nAraidi, who was cursed by St Rónán and, as a result, became half-man, half-bird. In this form he was condemned to live out his life in the woods, cut off from human companionship. The story has been translated by Trevor Joyce[6] and by Seamus Heaney,[7] and also features in the work of a number of other modern Irish poets.

The stories of the Cycles of the Kings form less of a coherent block than those found in the more mythological collections. It has memorably been said that its stories are 'less magical than in the Mythological, less heroic than in the Ulster, and less romantic than in the Fenian [Cycles]'.[8]

Nevertheless, they still contribute to the wide-ranging nature of Irish mythological and semi-mythological traditions from the early medieval period. It is noteworthy that one of the earliest appearances in literature of the Irish *leprechaun* ('tiny body')[9] can be found in stories in the Cycles of the Kings. In order to give a flavour of the kinds of stories found in these collections some contrasting ones are examined here.

The Adventures of Connla (*Echtra Connla*)

One of the stories from the collection of tales associated with Cormac mac Airt, and forming part of the Cormac Cycle sub-group within the Cycles of the Kings, is this one that shows how some of the stories in these collections had a mythological character comparable to that of many of the stories and traditions in the other cycles of tales. This tale concerns a man named Connla 'the red', or 'the fair', the son of Conn Cétchathach ('Conn of the hundred battles').

Conn Cétchathach was supposedly a High King of Ireland, and the ancestor of the *Connachta* (a group of noble families ruling Connacht – a kingdom often anglicized as Connaught – parts of Ulster and northern Leinster), and, through his descendant Niall Noígíallach ('Niall of the Nine Hostages'), the Uí Néill dynasty, which eventually conquered Ulster and Leinster (see below). Conn Cétchathach himself was associated with mythological happenings in other stories. In the late tradition found in the seventeenth-century *Annals of the Kingdom of Ireland* (*Annála Ríoghachta Éireann*) it was claimed that five roads leading to Tara (the sacred site of kingship rituals), which had never before been seen, were mysteriously discovered on the night that Conn was born. This myth indicated the future royal power of Conn and his descendants.

To return to the story of Connla: while walking with his father he met a richly dressed woman. Both Connla and Conn could hear the woman's voice but only Connla could see her. She described a magical land called *Tír na mBeó* ('Land of the Living') or *Tír na mban* ('Land of Women'), where no one grew old. This sounds very similar to *Tír na nÓg*, the Land of the Forever Young, entered via the *sídhe*, the fairy mounds in which lived the *Tuatha Dé Danann*. She invited Connla to join her there but Conn ordered his druids to prevent his son hearing her voice. The woman left but gave Connla a magic apple before she departed. For a month he ate no other food but the apple never reduced in size in all that time. After a month the woman returned and once again spoke of the strange land populated with women. Eventually Connla left with her, in a coracle made from glass. This suggests Otherworldly origins,[10] in the same way that, in Arthurian mythology, Glastonbury was described as the island of glass and a gateway to the fairy Otherworld. Connla never returned. From that day onward, Conn Cétchathach's sole remaining son became known as Art Oenfer ('Art the lone one').

This story is found in two sources: the *Book of the Dun Cow* (*Lebor na hUidre*) of c.1100 and the *Yellow Book of Lecan* (*Leabhar Buidhe Leacáin*) of c.1400. It appears to be very old and may have originated in the eighth century.

The Frenzy of Sweeney (Buile Suibne)

This dramatic story, as it currently survives, dates from the twelfth century, as do a large number of Irish mythological and legendary written sources. As well as 'The Frenzy of Sweeney', the title can also be translated as 'The Madness of Sweeney'. This story is the third and certainly the most famous of a trilogy of stories purporting to be about a seventh-century king of Ulster known as Suibne Geilt, which translates as 'mad Suibne' (or 'mad Sweeney' in its anglicized form). According to the accounts, he had lost his reason at the Battle of Mag Rath (or Moira) in 637. The preceding stories in this trilogy explained the events leading to the madness. The first story is *The Feast of Dún na nGéd* (*Fled Dúin na nGéd*), which recounted the events leading up to the battle. The second story is *The Battle of Mag Rath* (*Cath Maige Rátha*), in which were described the events of the battle itself.

In *The Frenzy of Sweeney* is the account of the persecution of the newly established Christian Church by Suibne (Sweeney), son of Colmán and King of Dál nAraide, a kingdom in eastern Ulster. A particular focus for the antagonism of Suibne was St Rónán. Furious at the sound of St Rónán's bell, he ran from his palace to attack the saint. Suibne's wife, Eórann, attempted to stop him by grabbing hold of his cloak. However, the cloak fell away from the king and, naked, he continued his assault on the saint. He threw the saint's psalter into a lake and would have attacked the saint himself had news not suddenly arrived compelling him to lead his army to the battle of Mag Rath. As Suibne left, St Rónán cursed him that he should go naked, just as he had attacked the saint. During the battle St Rónán attempted to mediate between the contending armies, in order to bring peace. Enraged, Suibne hurled two spears at the saint. Neither hit him but the second struck the saint's bell and shattered. As the broken spear shaft flew through the air, St Rónán pronounced a second curse on the king. This time it was that he would be forced to fly through the air and would eventually be killed with a spear. Attempting to return to the battle, Suibne was seized by an uncontrollable frenzy that forced him to flee from the fighting so fast that he left the ground and eventually landed in a yew tree. In this bird-like form he was gripped by madness and flew across the treetops of Ireland. His only home became a valley famous for its mad inhabitants, Glen Bolcáin (sometimes identified as Glenbuck, County Antrim).

Three times Suibne was rescued by his brother, Loingsechán, but each time his madness forced him back into the wild. One of his attempts to return to his kingdom was thwarted by St Rónán, who prayed that God would not allow Suibne to return to persecute the Church.

At long last, Suibne's wanderings brought him to the monastery of St Moling (County Carlow). It was here that he was killed by a jealous rival who transfixed him with a spear. But before he died, Suibne repented of his persecution of the Church and accepted the Christian faith. This is a feature of a number of stories that attempted to reconcile aspects of the pre-Christian past with the new Christian faith in Ireland.

It is possible that *The Frenzy of Sweeney* represented a peculiarly Irish version of a folklore motif that is found in a number of cultures, namely that of the wildman in the woods. In Welsh (and later Lowland Scottish) tradition the character of Lailoken/Myrddin occupied a similar place (see Chapter 13). It seems to have been this frenzied wildman of the northern British woods – who had second sight and had been driven mad by guilt for deaths in battle – who was reinvented as Merlin by Geoffrey of Monmouth in the *Life of Merlin* (*Vita Merlini*) of *c*.1150.

Adventures of Fergus Son of Léite (Echtra Fergusa maic Léiti)

This tale concerns how the King of Ulaid (Ulster) fell asleep on the seashore. While he lay there he was kidnapped by three leprechauns (originally *luchorpáin*) who attempted to carry him off to their home below the surface of the sea.

These diminutive beings were also referred to in the twelfth-century *Book of Invasions of Ireland* (*Lebor Gabála Érenn*), where they were called the *luchrupáin* (clearly a variant of *luchorpáin*). Here they were identified as the descendants of Noah's son Ham, as the result of the curse laid on him by his father. In Genesis, Ham was cursed because he saw his father naked and told his two brothers about it: 'Cursed be Canaan! The lowest of slaves will he be to his brothers.'[11] The reference to 'lowest of slaves' may have given rise to the Irish medieval tradition of explaining the diminutive nature of the leprechauns by reference to the descendants of Ham. Surprisingly, the Fomorian giants were also described in this same source as descendants of the same cursed son of Noah.

In the *Adventures of Fergus Son of Léite*, Fergus was saved because he woke when his feet touched the water. In addition, he managed to capture three of his would-be captors. Seeking to escape, they offered him *anmain i nanmain*, or 'a life for a life'. Fergus demanded three wishes. One of these was the ability to survive underwater, clearly one of the characteristics of his leprechaun kidnappers. However, though this wish was granted, one stretch of water, Loch Rudraige (County Down), was excluded. The implication was clear: Fergus should not venture there. This sounds reminiscent of the *geasa* (taboos) found in a number of Irish mythological tales. Predictably, Fergus could not keep away from Loch Rudraige and there he came face to face with a terrible water monster, the *muirdris*. As a consequence, his face became permanently disfigured and, because of this, he was barred from being king. This disqualification due to disability is found in a number of Irish myths and may well have reflected real ritual taboos placed on prehistoric and early medieval rulers. Fergus finally killed the monster, but died in the attempt.

In this tale the underwater home of the leprechauns revealed belief in their supernatural origins, since the underwater world appeared as one of the Otherworlds in Irish mythology. Further evidence for this interpretation can be found in the Irish word *abacc*, also used to describe the leprechauns. This may have derived from *ab*, the Irish word for river.[12] It is also possible that the name leprechaun came from the name of Lugh Lámhfada (Lugh of the Long Arm, or, literally, the Long Hand), the chief deity of the *Tuatha Dé Danann*, rather than from a hypothetical early Celtic word, *lagu* ('small').[13]

In later Irish and Scottish folklore there appeared the same theme of possible benefits gained from the capture of a leprechaun (Scottish-Gaelic *luspardan*). In some of these later traditions, the association with water continued, and with wearing red and green, colours associated with the fairy world in Irish folklore. In more modern traditions, the leprechauns were presented as shoemakers who owned a magic purse or a crock of gold; along with a continuation of the older tradition of various advantages that could be accrued from catching a leprechaun.

How King Rónán Killed his Son (*Fingal Rónáin*)

Also known as *The Death of Máel Fhothartaig Son of Rónán* (*Aided Maíl Fhothartaig Maic Rónáin*), this is an example of the many stories in the Cycles of the Kings that contain no supernatural aspects whatsoever. As such, they are clearly legendary rather than mythological. Nevertheless, aspects of this story clearly reveal folkloric features that mean it is not an historic account. In this case it is not the wildman of the woods but a terrible love triangle between a father, a son and a young stepmother. When King Rónán of Leinster remarried, his new and much younger wife was attracted to her stepson, Máel Fhothartaig. She sent her servant to inform the handsome young man, who was horrified at the suggestion. To escape the situation he left the court and travelled with fifty followers to Scotland, where he soon became famous as both a warrior and a hunter. There his two hunting dogs – Doilín and Daithlenn – gained great renown as they were even more proficient in the hunt than the dogs of the King of Scots himself.

Eventually returning to Leinster, Máel once more found himself to be the object of the young queen's unsolicited attentions. He turned for help to his foster brother, Congal. Congal advised him to go out herding cattle and informed the queen that she could meet Máel by a spot marked with white stones. When she attempted the journey, she was three times met by Congal, who abused her for her immorality. Finally, she gave up the effort and returned to court, vowing revenge. Just how this was supposed to put an end to the problem for Máel is not clear in the story. It may have been that the condemnation by Congal was hoped to have been enough to shame her into abandoning her designs on her stepson.

The plan ended in tragedy. That night the queen succeeded in making the king think that it was his son who had been pursuing her. In anger, Rónán hurled three spears, killing Máel, Congal and the court jester. Before he died Máel succeeded in persuading his father of his innocence. The story took an even bloodier turn when Congal's brother slaughtered the queen's father, mother and brother, brought their severed heads back to Leinster and threw them to her. In response, the queen committed suicide. So, with this gory finale, ends a terrible story of betrayal, jealousy and revenge. There are strong similarities between this story and the fifth-century BC Greek tragedy of Hippolytus. It is possible that both derived from a common store of folklore motifs. Alternatively, the story of Rónán and his son may have been an early medieval reworking of this established Classical story.

The Adventure of the Sons of Eochaid Mugmedón (Echtra mac nEchach Muimedóin): tales of Niall of the Nine Hostages

One of the great heroes of legendary Ireland was Niall Noígíallach ('Niall of the Nine Hostages'), son of Eochaid Mugmedón and founder of the Uí Néill dynasty, which conquered Ulster and Leinster and dominated Ireland from the sixth to the tenth century. In later years these kings looked back to the warrior Niall as the one from whom their line of kings had come. Indeed, their dynastic name meant 'descendants of Niall'. Niall himself was almost certainly a real person who lived in the late-fourth and fifth century. He appeared in the genealogies of later medieval Irish kings as their founding ancestor and was listed in the twelfth-century *Book of Invasions of Ireland* in a section that referred to historic personages, as opposed to its accounts of the mythical founders of Ireland: the Cesair, Partholonians, Fomorians, Nemedians, *Tuatha Dé Danann* and the Milesians. Niall also appears in much later Irish annals that may themselves have incorporated earlier medieval material (although nothing contemporary with his life), such as the *Annals of the Kingdom of Ireland* (*Annála Ríoghachta Éireann*) compiled, in its present form, in the 1630s in the Franciscan friary in Donegal Town.

None of these records are remotely contemporary with the activities of a real Niall but, taken together, they probably reflect something of the realities of fifth-century raiding and warfare, even if these were seen through the lens of a later society. They reveal a warrior community that raided sub-Roman Britain in a way that is amply reflected in authentic, though sparse, contemporary accounts. Later Irish medieval writers – in exaggerated accounts reminiscent of similarly inflated claims for King Arthur – even asserted that Niall campaigned against Rome itself, before turning back at the Alps. These highly legendary aspects may well have arisen from confusing attacks on Romanized Britain with attacks on Rome itself.[14] Traditional Irish accounts state that Niall died in 405, while some modern historians suggest he flourished a generation later and probably died *c.*450. The matter is difficult to categorically resolve. Until the time of Elizabeth I, in the latter half of the sixteenth century, the O'Neill earls of Ulster still claimed descent from the famous Niall of the Nine Hostages, who had lived more than a thousand years earlier.

The accounts vary as to why Niall gained his famous title of *Noígíallach* ('of the Nine Hostages'). The one called *The Death of Niall of the Nine Hostages* (*Aided Néill*

Noígíallach) claimed that the nine hostages consisted of five from the Irish provinces (Ulster, Connacht, Leinster, Munster, Meath) and four from abroad: one each from the Saxons, the Britons, the Scots and the Franks. Other accounts – such as in the tradition recorded by the seventeenth-century Irish priest and historian Seathrún Céitinn (anglicized as Geoffrey Keating) – suggested that the four foreign hostages were all Scots. Some modern historians have suggested that all four were Irish and extracted from one of the tributary communities overawed by the military might of the Uí Néill. Whatever the truth, the heroic and grandiose nature of the title was probably a result of the realpolitik of fifth-century Ireland and Britain. However, there are also mythical strands woven into the traditions of Niall and these illustrate the way in which the tales in the Cycles of the Kings act as a bridge between history, legend and mythology. In the eleventh-century account found in *The Adventure of the Sons of Eochaid Mugmedón* (*Echtra mac nEchach Muimedóin*) we are told that Niall was the son of Eochaid Mugmedón (anachronistically titled 'High King of Ireland') by a foreign woman. This woman was named as Cairenn, a princess captured during one of Eochaid Mugmedón's raids across the Irish Sea. The story describes her as a daughter of a Saxon king but her name suggests that she was Romano-British, and this was the tradition known to Seathrún Céitinn in the seventeenth century. Given the well-attested Irish raids on western Britain in the Late Roman and sub-Roman periods, it is highly plausible that an Irish chieftain or king might have a British wife who was taken on a raid. The legendary/mythical aspect, though, arose out of the conflict between Eochaid Mugmedón's existing wife and the newcomer. The former was named Mongfhionn and she persecuted the rival and the son (Niall) born to her. This was until a bard, named Torna, foresaw the future of the boy – in an example of the second sight that featured in a number of Irish legends and myths – and rescued the persecuted woman and her son.[15] The mythological and supernatural aspect was emphasized by the name of the persecutor. Another source, *The Death of Crimthann Son of Fidach* (*Aided Chrimthainn meic Fhidaig*) – found in *The Yellow Book of Lecan* (*Leabhar Buidhe Leacáin*) of *c*.1400 – claimed that the Feast of Samhain (the festival of the dead on 31 October) was alternatively called 'the Festival of Mongfhionn'.[16] This suggests that Mongfhionn may once have been regarded as a deity or a supernatural being, who was later incorporated into the tradition relating to Niall and his mother. In a similar way, *The Adventure of the Sons of Eochaid Mugmedón* recounted how a contest was later held between all of Eochaid Mugmedón's sons to decide who would succeed him. During this they came upon an ugly old hag guarding a well. The woman demanded a kiss in return for a drink. Only Niall kissed her properly; the other young men were repelled by her ugliness, although one gave her a reluctant kiss. Only then was she revealed as a beautiful woman, with the name of *Flaith* ('sovereignty'). She then bestowed on Niall the title of High King of Ireland (again, an historical anachronism). The boy who had given a reluctant kiss was granted a minor royal title. This folkloric motif of the 'loathly lady' is found in many cultures and appears in other Irish stories (for example, in the tale of Lugaid Loígde), in Arthurian accounts (the Welsh Romance tale *Peredur*, the French Chrétien de Troyes's *Perceval*, the German Wolfram von Eschenbach's *Parzival*) and in the fifteenth-century English story known as *The Wedding of Sir Gawain and Dame Ragnelle*.

A similar mixture of garbled history and strands of mythology can be discerned in *The Death of Niall of the Nine Hostages*. Like *The Death of Crimthann Son of Fidach*, this manuscript is also found in *The Yellow Book of Lecan* (*Leabhar Buidhe Leacáin*) of *c*.1400. In this account Niall was killed by Eochaid of Leinster. The root of this rivalry lay in a refusal by Niall's poet, Laidcenn mac Bairchid, to give hospitality to Eochaid. This led to Eochaid killing Laidcenn's son. In retaliation, Laidcenn recited such a powerful mocking of Leinster that nothing grew there for a year. This has a clearly mythological character. As punishment, Niall had Eochaid chained to a standing stone and sent nine warriors to kill him, but Eochaid broke free and killed them all. There is something almost Cú Chulainn-esque about this achievement. In the end, Niall himself was killed by an arrow, fired from a great distance, by Eochaid. Less mythological is the account found in the *Book of Invasions of Ireland* that told that Eochaid killed Niall during a battle fought in the English Channel. In support of this tradition is the claim in the twelfth-century *Book of Leinster* (*Lebor Laignech*), which contains a poem by Cináed Ua Hartacáin that stated that Niall raided Britain seven times and was killed by Eochaid on the last of these raids.

It is therefore with a probably historical character, but one whose achievements were celebrated in legendary terms, that we end this examination of aspects of the Cycles of the Kings.

13

MYTH, LEGEND AND HISTORY IN THE POST-ROMAN TWILIGHT: ARTHUR, KING OF BRITAIN

In the late 1960s and 1970s a burst of studies pursued the quest for the 'historical' or 'real' Arthur. Excavations at 'Arthurian sites', notably South Cadbury Castle (Somerset), accompanied a detailed scrutiny of the medieval Arthurian sources. These influenced both academic works and the writings of a huge number of Arthurian enthusiasts. Well-written books such as Leslie Alcock's *Arthur's Britain*,[1] Geoffrey Ashe's *The Quest for Arthur's Britain*[2] and John Morris's *The Age of Arthur*[3] (to name but three) took the quest in a great many directions and stimulated much debate. The last named appeared to provide such a definitive synthesis of the sources that it seemed appropriate that this once shadowy personage might actually have become such a solid figure of study that a period of sub- and post-Roman history might even be named after

him: the 'Age of Arthur'. It even seemed possible to bring
the continental exploits of Arthur mentioned in English
sources (combined with Breton texts concerning activities
abroad) into a believable construct that pointed towards a
real Arthur character who stood behind a little known, but
better evidenced, late fifth-century figure named Riotha-
mus.[4] While it was always recognized that in Welsh medieval sources Arthur *became* a mythological figure and that
medieval English works recast him as a knight, to add to
the fictional Romance tradition of a thirteenth-century
strand of French writings, it seemed possible that the historical character might finally be discerned through the
intervening mist of mythology, romance and fiction.

Since these heady days of the quest for the 'historical
Arthur' a severe reaction has set in. Even before this new
scepticism became the current academic norm, historians
such as Richard Barber, in *The Figure of Arthur*,[5] had pointed out that – counter-intuitively – the evidence for Arthur
did not suggest a historical figure who *graduated into* myth
and legend as his fame grew. In fact, the reality was the
uncomfortable truth that Arthur was a Welsh myth *before*
he became an Anglo-Norman 'semi-historical figure' in
Geoffrey of Monmouth's *History of the Kings of Britain*
(*Historia Regum Britanniae*), of *c.*1136. And then Arthur's
fame exploded through the thirteenth-century Romance
genre being formed in France, with both traditions influ-
encing later medieval Welsh reworking of the tales, before
going into sharp decline from the sixteenth century, when a
growing scepticism undermined belief in his historicity. In
short, it seems that Arthur was a myth long before he was a
man. Any attempts to mine ninth- and tenth-century Welsh
sources for historical material relating to the fifth and sixth
centuries were demolished by the detailed studies of David
Dumville,[6] Patrick Sims-Williams[7] and Barbara Yorke.[8]
Between them these insightful and critical studies demonstrated that the ninth- and tenth-century sources were

simply inadmissible as evidence for any historical study of
sub- and post-Roman Britain. At the heart of the search for
the 'real Arthur' was a literary vacuum and any attempts
to fill this void by reading *back* from sources – such as
the Welsh *History of the Britons* (*Historia Brittonum*) of
*c.*830 – were academically indefensible. These later works,
far from being straightforward collections of earlier material, were actually carefully crafted in order to meet clear
contemporary agendas. And these aims did not include the
reliable retelling of earlier historical accounts concerning
Arthur. Instead, Arthur was a potent figure in a propaganda battle set in the context of the continuing resistance of
the Welsh against the Anglo-Saxon kingdoms to their east.
This is now the received orthodoxy and the one that will
influence the role that Arthur plays in this present study of
Celtic mythology. Indeed, so strong is the new orthodoxy
that, when the highly respected early medieval historian
Nicholas Higham wrote *King Arthur: Myth-Making and
History*, he felt compelled to explain that academic historians had become 'unwilling to acknowledge or engage with
the large and enthusiastic "real Arthur" literature'.[9]

Ironically, it now seems that the 'Age of Arthur' was
actually in the 1970s. Today the search for the 'real Arthur'
has become the preserve of non-academic historians. And
while the concept of Arthur as a 'political myth' might
have been added to the idea of him as a 'cultural myth' that
had been promulgated since the late nineteenth century,
the operative word is 'myth'.

As we shall see, long before the twelfth-century explo-
sion of Arthurian literature, the legendary and even mythological king appeared in Welsh sources. And he continued
to influence Welsh storytelling throughout the Middle
Ages (see Chapter 15). But the 'Arthur of the Welsh' is a
very different king from the later medieval image familiar
to many. In these early Welsh accounts he led attacks on
mysterious Otherworld islands, hunted a mythical wild

boar and captured a magic cauldron that was a prototype of the more famous (and much later) Holy Grail. Like a magnet, Arthur gathered to himself a disparate collection of characters from Celtic myth, folklore and history. It is to this figure of myth and legend that we now turn.

Out of the ashes of defeat – a mythic warrior to promote hope in a battle for hearts and minds

By the eighth century, with Anglo-Saxon conquest dominating what we now call England and with northern Celtic Britain isolated from Celtic Wales and the Celtic south-west by this Germanic conquest, Welsh literature underwent a significant development. It changed 'from praise poetry about real men to invented stories about shadowy figures'.[10] Then, in the ninth century, the resurgence of the kingdom of Gwynedd in north-west Wales was accompanied by a reinvestigation of the past in order to meet the propaganda needs of the Welsh. By the time of the compilation of the earliest triads (see Chapter 17), in the late twelfth century, Arthur had attracted disparate tales of heroes, whose lives were then artificially connected by their presence at the Arthurian court.

The Arthur who emerged was a mysterious figure, even when writers attempted to give him a historical context. Perhaps the most striking example of this is found in *The History of the Britons* (*Historia Brittonum*). Recent academic research has concluded that this famous Latin manuscript was written *c.*830, early in the reign of King Merfyn of Gwynedd. This was a particularly critical time since the context of the early years of Merfyn's reign combined a number of key features. First, he was 'an external candidate for the kingship of Gwynedd, whose legitimacy was less than secure'; secondly, the overlordship of the Anglo-Saxon Egbert of Wessex was less threatening than the previous overlordship of the Mercians had been; thirdly, and despite this, the threat of further English aggression remained high.[11] This combination of a desire for legitimacy and a sense of threat from England coincided with a breathing space in which the propagandists of Gwynedd could construct a new take on the past. This was *The History of the Britons*, which is often attributed to a monk named Nennius, since a number of surviving manuscripts carry his name in the preface.[12] However, it now seems clear that we do not know the name of the author. And, far from being the artless 'heap of all that I could find', as its unknown author apologetically put it, the book was really a carefully constructed bid for Welsh hearts and minds. Its aim was to counter the negative view of the Welsh as being under the judgement of God that had been put forward by the sixth-century British writer Gildas and enthusiastically advanced by the eighth-century Anglo-Saxon writer Bede. In its place a heroic figure – Arthur – was historicized with a series of twelve battles as a type of Joshua, the warrior leader of Israel in the Old Testament. In this role 'Arthur-Joshua' represented an ideal Christian hero who led God's people (the Welsh) in their successful reaction to pagan Anglo-Saxon attacks. The author carefully differentiated Arthur from other Welsh rulers by describing him as '*dux bellorum*' ('leader in battles') who led the other kings against the Anglo-Saxons. This image of the invincible Arthur clearly inspired a reference to him in the Welsh poem *Y Gododdin* (*The Gododdin*). The date of the original composition of this poem is unknown but in its surviving form it dates from probably no earlier than the tenth century. Claiming to be an eyewitness of a battle fought *c.*600, its author memorably described one warrior, Gwawrddur, as '*gochore brein du ar uur caer, ceni bei ef Arthur*' ('providing food for ravens on the wall of a fortress, though he was not Arthur').[13] Clearly, by this date – and possibly independently of *The History of the Britons* – Arthur had become a byword for military strength.

The number of Arthur's battles recorded in *The History*

of the Britons (with its repetition of conflicts at certain points in order to reach the number twelve) was probably intended to represent the first twelve chapters of the Book of Joshua in the Old Testament.[14] In the same way, St Patrick was presented as a type of Moses.[15] A recent study has similarly concluded that the battle-list was not lifted from an earlier poem. Instead, it was studiously compiled by the writer of *The History of the Britons*, who contrived twelve battles from a list of nine, and Arthur's non-royal status would have lent support to Merfyn of Gwynedd's own position, since his claim to the throne was dubious.[16] The handling of Vortigern (the legendary British ruler blamed for inviting Anglo-Saxon settlement) was similarly manipulated so as to 'associate Gwynedd with the magical Emrys, who reveals himself as the virtuous Ambrosius [a British leader against the Anglo-Saxons] of Gidas's account' and to promote Snowdonia as resistant to Vortigern's wickedness, since the prophecy of eventual British triumph was revealed within Gwynedd and so lent legitimacy to this kingdom and its rulers.[17] This reminds us that there was more to mythology than a simple retelling of pre-Christian beliefs in revised forms. The Arthur of *The History of the Britons* was a myth but one created to specifically fit a Christian context. Over time, though, his myth would attract to it figures from the pagan past to form a hybrid warband and then a royal court.

That Arthur was already a figure of mythology is clear in *The History of the Britons* itself. This was partly revealed in the description of Arthur's battles. At the battle of Badon, the manuscript asserts, 'nine hundred and sixty men fell in one day from one charge by Arthur, and no-one overthrew them except himself alone'.[18] Less obviously mythical, but certainly enigmatic, is the claim that 'Arthur carried the image of St Mary, ever virgin on his shoulders'.[19] It may have been said in order to equal Bede's assertion that the heroic Anglo-Saxon king Oswald had carried a cross into battle against the Welsh. That this is a distinct possibility is shown in that, by the time the tradition was being reworked in the later (probably tenth-century) *Welsh Annals* (*Annales Cambriae*), the image of St Mary had changed to the carrying of the cross of our Lord Jesus Christ 'for three days and three nights'.[20] Furthermore, this suggests that the references to Arthur in the *Welsh Annals* were not independent of *The History of the Britons* and, far from offering corroborative evidence of an historical Arthur, were almost certainly dependent on the ninth-century account that had 'historicized' the warrior-leader in the first place. Attempts to demythologize this account have focused on the argument that the text confused the Welsh *yscuid* ('shoulders') with *yscuit* ('shield'). While this is possible, there is no rescuing the other reference to Arthur in *The History of the Britons* from the realm of myth. This 'wonder' ('*mirabile*') is found in chapter 73 and referred to a cairn in the region of Builth, in the upper Wye valley (Wales), which allegedly bore the footprint of a hunting dog belonging to Arthur. The dog was clearly huge, since its name – Cafall – meant 'horse' in Welsh. The implication was that Arthur himself was a giant. If this was not enough, the account stated that the hunt that gave rise to the paw print was in pursuit of the 'boar Troynt'. The mythological nature of this is clear since a major part of the later (possibly originally eleventh-century) story of *Culhwch and Olwen* (*Culhwch ac Olwen*) centred on the hunting of the monstrous boar Twrch Trwyth, a beast that also appeared in Irish mythology (under the name Torc Triath) and belonged to Brigid. In another Irish parallel, the Irish hero Finn (or Fionn) mac Cumhaill was also closely associated with hunting and particularly with boar hunting. This suggests that the connection between Arthur and the boar Twrch Trwyth drew on a deeper Celtic tradition of mythical heroes hunting these animals.

The account in *Culhwch and Olwen* also named both

Arthur's dog and another character's horse as Cafall (not surprising given the meaning of *cafall* in Welsh). This gigantism had clearly similarly influenced the earlier account. As if this was not enough to confirm the cairn story's mythological credentials, the writer of *The History of the Britons* also added that, if the stone was carried away for a day and a night, the next day it would be found returned to the top of the pile. It is almost certain that it was just such pre-existing myths of a great hunter and warrior that lay behind the choice of this figure to head Welsh resistance in the rewriting of history that was *The History of the Britons*. That the mythological hunt of the boar Twrch Trwyth was well known is revealed in an aside in another Welsh poem that has no Arthurian connection. In the (possibly tenth-century) *Long Song of Cynfelyn* (*Gorchan Cynfelyn*) a warrior was described as '*torch trychdrwyt*'. The meaning is obscure but it probably implied a comparison of this warrior's fighting prowess with that of the mythical boar. Arthur's reputation was similarly enhanced by his connection with the imaginary animal.

That Arthur the fabulous huntsman was also associated with equally fabulous but tragic tales is revealed in a miracle (*miraculum*) found in the same chapter of *The History of the Britons* and said to have occurred in the vicinity of Ergyng, in south-west Herefordshire, in the Welsh–English border country. This involved the grave of Arthur's son. He was allegedly both killed and buried there by Arthur himself. Although once measured, the grave, it was claimed, was never the same length when next measured. This same association of Arthur with landscape features was found in Cornwall a generation before Geoffrey of Monmouth wrote his famous account. In 1113, churchmen from Laon (France) travelling in this region found Cornishmen who insisted that Arthur's chair and oven could still be seen in the landscape and that he was not dead. Clearly, a fabulous being who left his mark across the landscape of Wales and the south-west was well established before later medieval Anglo-Norman and French writers took up the tale. Indeed, Arthur was clearly already famous when the ninth-century writer of *The History of the Britons* attempted to describe his victories as if he had once been a real person. It seems that whoever Arthur originally was (assuming that there ever was such a person) he is now irrecoverable; for at his very first recording he was already a wonder-working giant, a mythical hunter and a great warrior. In the written accounts – and these, after all, are all we have with which to trace his origins – he was a myth before he was ever a man. He may even have contained elements of Celtic myth stretching back to a pre-Christian bear god.[21] For his name may have been related to the Old Welsh word for 'bear' (*arto*; Modern Welsh *arth*). It is significant that in *The Dialogue of Arthur and the Eagle* (*Ymddiddan Arthur a'r Eryr*), Arthur was described as '*arth llu*' ('bear of the host'). This particular story will be returned to later. Suffice it to say that this bear connection may explain the association of Arthur with high and wild places.

What is clear is that, once Arthur was established as a maker of landscape features, as a supernatural hunter of supernatural beasts and *then* as a great warrior, his myth would run and run. And as it did so, it would attract names and themes from the far distant Celtic mythological past.

A warrior whose grave was 'the wonder of the world'

Scraps of poetic evidence dating from the tenth and eleventh centuries mention Arthur's name in passing but four later poems focus more closely on his exploits. Three of these are found in the *Black Book of Carmarthen* (*Llyfr Du Caerfyrddin*), also known as *Peniarth Ms 1*. This book is named after the colour of its binding and its connection with the Priory of St John the Evangelist and St Teulyddog, in Carmarthen (Wales). It is now considered to be the work of a single scribe who wrote it at different times in his life,

*c.*1250. As such, it is one of the earliest surviving manuscripts written solely in Welsh.[22] Within this collection
survives an earlier poem describing Arthur as an emperor,
after whom a troop of warriors at the battle of Llongborth
(location unknown) were named. The poem is also found
in *The Red Book of Hergest* (*Llyfr Coch Hergest*), compiled
*c.*1382–1410, and as a fragment in *The White Book of Rhydderch* (*Llyfr Gwyn Rhydderch*), compiled *c.*1350. This
poem, known as the *Elegy for Geraint Son of Erbin* (*Mar-
wnad Geraint ab Erbin*), seems to pre-date the writing of
Geoffrey of Monmouth (*c.*1136); although its description of
Arthur as emperor (Welsh '*amherwdyr*') may suggest the
influence of Geoffrey's exaggerated account of Arthur and
indicate a later date for its composition.

Also in the *Black Book of Carmarthen* are the *Stanzas
of the Graves* (*Englynion y Beddau*), which list the burial
places of Welsh heroes. This is an example of so-called
englyn poetry. This poetry, of three-line stanza construction, was an early form of Welsh poetry and the *englyn*
form dates from the ninth to the twelfth century. In this
particular poem, Arthur's grave was described as '*anoeth
bit bet y arthur*', which roughly translates as 'the wonder
of the world' or 'the most difficult thing in the world to
find'.[23] The word '*anoeth*' (translated here as 'wonder of
the world') was rarely used; for example, in Welsh prose it
occurred only in *Culhwch and Olwen*. There it was used
to describe the impossible tasks undertaken by Arthur's
warriors. This may suggest some connection between the
Stanzas of the Graves and *Culhwch and Olwen*. It is possible that the composer of the former was deliberately allud-
ing to the Arthurian tales in the latter.[24]

Another poem – also found in the *Black Book of
Carmarthen* – features a conversation between Arthur and
a gatekeeper named Glewlwyd Gavaelvawr. The contrived
conversation in this dialogue, known as *What Man is the
Porter?* (*Pa ŵr yw'r Porthor?*), was a vehicle for the writer

(via Arthur) to recount a long list of exploits, many of which drew in other mythological figures. These included 'Manawyddan son of Llŷr, profound was his counsel'.[25] While the poem says little more about this figure, his name is familiar from Irish mythology, where he was known as Manannán, the son of Lír and god of the sea. He was married to Aife (Aoífe), who was transformed into a crane. In this form she was killed and her skin was used to create a magic treasure bag. In the twelfth-century Fenian Cycle of tales this crane-bag came to belong to the warrior Finn. None of this appears in the Welsh account but it is clear that Arthur was in the company of figures from a very much older tradition. In other Welsh accounts Manawyddan was described as the brother of the god Brân. The writer of the poem in the *Black Book of Carmarthen* described battles against a hag, beings enigmatically named 'Dog-heads', nine witches and lions (which appeared to have included a monstrous animal known as 'Palug's cat').

As mythological in scope is the poem *The Spoils of Annwfn* (*Preiddeu Annwfn*). The name *Annwfn* derived from the Welsh for 'inside-world'. In this poem Arthur led an expedition into the fairy realm of the Faery Fortress (*Kaer Siddi*). The exploit demonstrated Arthur's '*gwrhyt*' ('manly courage'). This adventure clearly drew on traditions found in more than just Welsh mythology. In a similar Irish expedition, Cú Chulainn accompanied a warrior named Cú Roí on a raid on a mysterious place called Fir Fhálgae (possibly the Isle of Man) to seize a woman and a magic cauldron. This story was certainly known in Wales, since it appeared in the *Elegy on Cú Roí mac Dáiri* (*Marwnat Corröi mab Dayry*). A further Irish connection can be seen in the name of the fairy fortress, since *Siddi* (a name for the Otherworld of *Annwfn*) came from *sídhe*, the Irish word for the fairy mounds believed to be the Underworld homes of the deities of the *Tuatha Dé Danann*.

In *The Spoils of Annwfn* there are other references to this fairy fortress as the Four-cornered Fortress (*Kaer Pedry-van*), the Fort of Carousal (*Kaer Veddwit*) and the Fortress of Glass (*Kaer Wydyr*). The object of this expedition was to obtain a magic cauldron. The realm described was clearly the Otherworld, since the poem contains a specific reference to Pwyll and Pryderi, who were described as father and son in the later account in the *Mabinogi* or *Mabinogion*, in the story known as *Pwyll, Prince of Dyfed* (*Pwyll Pendevic Dyfed*), where Pwyll was described as ruler of the Otherworld. This tradition of an Arthurian raid on the Otherworld in search of a magic cauldron was also included in *Culhwch and Olwen*. A similar story of an attack on a glass tower in the middle of the sea – but launched by a party of Spanish warriors and their women – was also incorporated into *The History of the Britons*. In this version the Spanish were part of a group whose survivors went on to populate Ireland. This connection of Spain and Ireland was a feature of an Irish origin myth (see Chapter 8). It is possible that the storytellers had in mind the island of Lundy, in the Bristol Channel, when they envisaged the Fortress of Glass (*Kaer Wydyr*), since Lundy was known as *Ynys Wair* and was difficult to approach owing to its sheer-sided cliffs. Along with the islands of Bardsey and Grassholm, it was considered an entry point to the Otherworld.

What seems clear from these poems is that the earliest written Welsh records relating to Arthur saw him as a strangely detached figure who gathered names to himself: Cai and Bedwyr were semi-mythical warriors with extraordinary exploits; Gwenhwyfar was his wife, whose character and significance would be expanded on in later traditions; Medrawd (or Melvas/Melwas) was apparently Arthur's enemy; others, such as Manawyddan son of Llŷr and Pwyll and Pryderi, were drawn from pre-Christian mythology. Arthur was the connecting hero whose exploits joined these otherwise disparate figures. What is abundantly clear is that he was not an historical character. This is almost certainly why he is absent from every surviving early Welsh royal genealogy. It is as if Arthur was always something of an outsider, despite his fame. This status continued until the twelfth-century imaginary ancestry that Geoffrey of Monmouth created for him. Before this, despite occasional references to his sons, Arthur was essentially rootless. He and his warriors were rather like the mythical Irish hero Finn mac Cumhaill and his band of warriors, the *fianna*. Incidentally, Geoffrey of Monmouth's claim that Arthur's father was called Uther Pendragon is usually taken as a literary conceit playing on the idea of ancient British kingship through the name or title Pendragon, meaning 'head-dragon' or 'ruler'. However, the Welsh word *uthr* ('awesome'/'terrifying') does appear associated with Arthur in a poem called *The Conversation of Gwyddnau Garanhir and Gwyn ap Nudd* (*Ymddiddan Gwyddnau Garanhir a Gwyn ap Nudd*) and found in the mid thirteenth-century *Black Book of Carmarthen*. A line in this poem ran, when describing a warrior named Llachau, 'son of Arthur, awesome in songs' ('*uthir ig kertev*').[26] This may have been influenced by Geoffrey of Monmouth, who wrote over a century earlier, or it may have been that Geoffrey drew on an older common source and made the description '*uthr*' into a personal name.

The once and future king

Once established, this dramatic figure appeared in a number of later written accounts, which will be explored separately in due course owing to their importance as sources of varied myths (Arthur appears alongside other mythological heroes in the discussion of the *Mabinogi* in Chapter 14, with legendary but historical figures in the *Mabinogi* in Chapter 15, has walk-on parts in the Welsh Romance tales explored in Chapter 16, and finally appears among the heroes of the Welsh triads in Chapter 17). He did, though, appear in other genres apart from these. In a number of saints' lives dating from the late eleventh and early twelfth centuries we again meet the king. In the *Life of St Cadoc* (*c*.1050) he was portrayed in a negative tone as a warrior who threatened a girl on the run until dissuaded by his more honourable companions. That he was playing dice on top of a hill may have been a survival of the Arthur-of-the-high-places theme referred to earlier. In another part of this *Life*, St Cadoc arbitrated between Arthur and a warlord who had killed three of his men. Arthur demanded that the cattle granted in compensation should be of a magical colour: red and white. However, they turned to bracken as soon as Arthur took them. At the point when a now penitent Arthur submitted to the saint the *Life* described him by the Latin title '*rex*' ('king'), which reinforced the significance of the grant of privileges to St Cadoc's monastery and also probably constitutes the earliest recorded use of this title for Arthur.[27] In the *Life of St Carannog* (early twelfth century) Arthur was portrayed as a dragon slayer. In the *Life of St Padarn* (twelfth century), where he was simply referred to as 'a certain tyrant', the earth swallowed him up to his chin. Other *Lives*, however – of St Cadoc, St Efflam and St Gildas – envisaged him as ruler of the whole of Great Britain, although he was portrayed as a rather do-nothing king in the *Life of St Illtud*.[28] This last work may reflect how the figure of Arthur became a gathering place for stories in which he played little or no part.

Themes that feature large in other sources were sometimes referred to with little detail in these accounts, such as the violation and abduction of Gwenhwyfar by Melvas/Melwas (Medrawd) in the *Life of St Gildas* (*c*.1130). That Melvas was king of the 'summer country' may be nothing more than a reference to Somerset, given a Glastonbury connection in this account. But it may have been an echo of older myths concerning the abduction of a royal woman by an Otherworld ruler. This is given added emphasis by the fact that this *Life* was the first manuscript to connect

Arthur with Glastonbury and the first to contain a description of Glastonbury as having a 'mystical, supernatural nature'. With echoes of the island mentioned in *The Spoils of Annwfn*, Arthur rescued Gwenhwyfar from a castle on the 'Island of Glass'.[29] Arthur, in this *Life*, was described by the Latin title '*tyrannus*', which may have had a pejorative meaning (linked to 'tyrant'), alongside the alternative sense of 'lesser king'. The abduction of Gwenhwyfar was also the subject of another story that may date from the twelfth century but survives in only two manuscripts, from the sixteenth and seventeenth centuries. This is *The Dialogue of Melwas and Gwenhwyfar* (*Ymddiddan rhwng Melwas a Gwenhwyfar*). In it Gwenhwyfar scorned the courage of Melwas. As in the *Life of St Gildas*, Melvas/ Melwas was described as being from *Ynys Wydrin* ('Isle of Glass'). These allusions certainly suggest Otherworld connections and later fourteenth- and fifteenth-century Welsh poets seem to have believed this was the case when they described his use of magic and how he went to '*i eithá byd*' ('the end of the world').[30] This Otherworld connection was strengthened by the fact that Gwenhwyfar's name meant something like 'White-phantom' and also suggested an Otherworld being. Other accounts described her as the daughter of a giant; this is a characteristic she shared with Olwen, the heroine in *Culhwch and Olwen*.

The characterization of Arthur as being subject to the saints' authority in these *Lives* was picked up in *The Dialogue of Arthur and the Eagle* (*Ymddiddan Arthur a'r Eryr*). This may date from as early as the twelfth century but survives only in a manuscript of the fourteenth century. In it Arthur received basic Christian instruction from an eagle that was actually Arthur's deceased nephew. The presentation of Arthur as one needing Christian instruction is reminiscent of the Irish tradition that envisaged Oisín (or Ossian) in dialogue with St Patrick in *The Interrogation of the Old Men* (*Agallamh Na Seanórach*). It may suggest

that, in this strand of Welsh storytelling, Arthur's credentials as a Christian figure were open to question. This may
have been due to a realization of his questionable (mythical) origins or may, more prosaically, have been due to clerical distrust of the secular aristocracy. What is clear is that
the Arthur of *The Dialogue of Arthur and the Eagle* was a
long way from the Arthur presented in *The History of the
Britons* and in the *Welsh Annals* as a victorious Christian
conqueror.

It was on this foundation of a famous but troubled king
that Geoffrey of Monmouth built his edifice – made up of
Welsh traditions, Anglo-Norman knightly preoccupations,
Classical themes and imagination – which would carry the
Arthurian legend forward for the next eight hundred years.
He also put together one of the most enduring pairings
in literature: Arthur and Merlin – who was described as
a prophet and a magician. Merlin first appeared in Geoffrey's *Prophecies of Merlin* (*Prophetiae Merlini*) and then in
his *History of the Kings of Britain*; the former was written
in the 1130s while Geoffrey was still working on the latter,
and it was later incorporated into this larger work. Finally,
around 1150, he wrote the *Life of Merlin*. However, before
Geoffrey there was no relationship between these two
characters. Merlin had an identity quite separate from that
of Arthur. It is clear that Geoffrey's Merlin represented
a name that was, in Welsh, originally spelled Myrddin.
Geoffrey largely created the character of Merlin but he
almost certainly based him on an earlier figure. While no
Welsh text referring to Merlin pre-dates Geoffrey, aspects
of these suggest that they represent – at least in part – the
survival of an earlier folklore character: the Wildman in
the Woods. The *Black Book of Carmarthen* contains a text,
The Apple-trees (*Yr Afallennau*), which depicted Myrddin
living wild in the Caledonian Forest of Scotland in misery
and madness after the battle of Arfderydd.[31] A similar,
Scottish tradition existed concerning a Wild Man named

Lailoken, who was mentioned in the *Life of St Kentigern* (*c*.1185). It is possible that this character lay behind Geoffrey's Merlin. It is also highly likely that the original was a figure of folklore and not a real person. Once associated with Arthur, the myth of Merlin gained great momentum and the two remain linked in the popular imagination. It is appropriate that this all too brief examination of the character of Arthur ends with myth and folklore.

14

WELSH MYTHOLOGICAL HEROES OF THE *MABINOGI*

The term '*Mabinogi*', or '*Mabinogion*', was first coined in the nineteenth century.[1] It was and is often used to describe eleven anonymous medieval Welsh tales that are found in the *White Book of Rhydderch* (*Llyfr Gwyn Rhydderch*), of *c.*1350, and in the *Red Book of Hergest* (*Llyfr Coch Hergest*), of *c.*1382–1410. The overall collection consists of the core stories that are the so-called four tales of the 'Four Branches of the Mabinogi'; there are also four associated stories; in addition, the modern collection contains another three stories that today are often included as part of the eleven tales of the *Mabinogi*, although these three were, in fact, Welsh versions of Arthurian tales that also appeared in the work of the medieval French writer Chrétien de Troyes.

The Four Branches of the Mabinogi are a collection of four interconnected prose stories from medieval Wales.

The collective name *Mabinogi* derives from the Welsh word *mab* ('boy', 'youth'). In time this conveyed the meaning 'tale of a hero's boyhood', and it eventually came to mean simply 'a tale'.[2] A form of the name that is often used – *Mabinogion* – was coined by the nineteenth-century editor and translator of these tales, Lady Charlotte Guest. In error she thought it was the plural of the word *mabinogi*, which appears at the end of each of the four core tales. The form *Mabinogion* does, though, appear once in the manuscripts that Lady Charlotte Guest translated (at the end of the first story, *Pwyll, Prince of Dyfed*), although this is now considered to be a scribal error in this particular manuscript. All four stories vary in their date of composition, author, content and styles. Consequently, 'the term *Mabinogion* is no more than a label, and a modern-day one at that'.[3]

In these four core tales forming the four 'branches' of the *Mabinogi* proper we find characters drawn from pre-Christian Celtic mythology, Welsh versions of common folk tales and accounts of early medieval heroes. Overall, though, it is mythology that dominates these four stories. However, they are more than simply records of older traditions. It is clear that the compiler used these earlier stories as a way of drawing out moral principles that he felt relevant to his own society. These principles were not explicitly stated in the stories: rather they are implied. The stories are *Pwyll, Prince of Dyfed* (*Pwyll Pendevic Dyfed*), who was forced by circumstances to be temporary ruler of the Otherworld; *Branwen Daughter of Llŷr* (*Branwen ferch Llŷr*) and her marriage to the King of Ireland; *Manawyddan Son of Llŷr* (*Manawyddan fab Llŷr*), who found his kingdom placed under a spell; and *Math Son of Mathonwy* (*Math fab Mathonwy*), who needed to rest his feet in the lap of a virgin, unless he was at war, or he would die. Each of these stories ends with a colophon (a brief description) stating: 'so ends this branch of the mabinogi'. Another linking feature is that a character named Pryderi appears in all four stories.

This Pryderi was considered to be the son of Pwyll, Prince of Dyfed, and Rhiannon, the daughter of Hyfaidd Hen. Consequently, Pryderi had Otherworld connections, since Pwyll was at one time ruler of the Otherworld. The super-human growth to adulthood exhibited by Pryderi demon-strated his distinctive nature and was probably intended to indicate supernatural origins. Pryderi was born, fostered, inherited a kingdom and got married in the first story, or 'branch'; he was hardly mentioned in the second branch; in the third branch he was imprisoned by magic and then freed; in the fourth and final branch his death in battle was described. These four stories will be explored in this chapter.

The four additional stories, which we might call 'asso-ciated tales', were drawn from separate traditions and include *The Dream of Macsen Wledig* (*Breuddwyd Macsen Wledig*); *Lludd and Llefelys* (*Lludd a Llefelys*); *Culhwch and Olwen* (*Culhwch ac Olwen*), also known as *How Cul-hwch won Olwen* (*Mal y kauas Culhwch Olwen*); and *The Dream of Rhonabwy* (*Breuddwyd Rhonabwy*). Of these, *Culhwch and Olwen* and *The Dream of Rhonabwy* con-tain early Welsh traditions about King Arthur. These four stories tend to either be loosely linked to semi-historical characters or to include characters who might have some connection with history, or they attempt to reconstruct a legendary past. And, most significantly, they do not appear to have drawn on such an old source of mythology as the stories that constitute the 'Four Branches'. We might say that they represent the area where myth meets history and so are *legendary* Welsh stories, although they do not constitute a clearly delineated group. However, at the very least, they are sufficiently different from the 'Four Branch-es' and the three 'Welsh Romances' to justify separating them, at least for convenience. These 'associated tales' will be explored in Chapter 15.

Finally, we come to the last group, the Welsh Romances.

These are the tales of *Peredur Son of Efrawg* (*Peredur fab Efrawg*); *Geraint and Enid* (*Geraint ac Enid*); and *Owain, or the Lady of the Fountain* (*Owain, neu Iarlles y Ffynnon*). Critics have debated whether these are simply based on the late twelfth-century French writer Chrétien de Troyes's Romances – *Perceval*, *Erec et Enide* and *Yvain* – or if they derive from a shared original.[4] However, the Welsh stories are not direct translations and also include material not found in Chrétien's work. Therefore, they form a distinct group of Welsh stories, but ones written in the popular medieval Romance genre. Into them their author wove strands of an older Welsh mythology. As such, they are decidedly different from the other groups of stories found in the *Mabinogi* collection. These three Welsh Romances will be explored in Chapter 16.

Pwyll, Prince of Dyfed (*Pwyll Pendevic Dyfed*)

In this story, Pwyll was out hunting when a stag he was pursuing was brought down by another pack of hunting dogs. These were strikingly different from his own dogs in that 'they were a gleaming shining white, and their ears were red'.[5] Welsh traditions named such animals *cwn annwfn*[6] ('hounds of Annwfn'). Comparison with other stories reveals that these colours were regarded as particularly indicative of Otherworld origins. It is significant that in the *Life of St Cadoc*, of c.1050, Arthur demanded that cattle granted in compensation should be of the same colours: red and white. However, they turned to bracken as soon as he took ownership of them. Similarly, in *The History of the Britons* (*Historia Brittonum*) the two fighting dragons (see Chapter 15 and the tale of *Lludd and Llefelys*) that represented the Welsh and the Anglo-Saxons were described as being red (Wales) and white (Anglo-Saxons). Clearly, red and white were highly significant colours.

Having let his own dogs feast on the stag brought down by the other pack, Pwyll was then challenged by the owner of the other dogs. It turned out that he was Arawn, King of Annwfn. Arawn and Pwyll made an arrangement to make up for Pwyll's unintentional discourtesy over the stag. By this arrangement, the two would take on each other's form and change places, and, as Arawn, Pwyll would rid him of his long-standing enemy – Hafgan.[7]

This exchange then took place and it lasted for a year. Pwyll honourably slept with the wife of Arawn but did not have sexual relations with her, even though she was the most beautiful woman he had ever seen. Exactly one year after the meeting by the body of the stag, Pwyll, in the form of Arawn, met Hafgan in the middle of a ford. Clearly, this was considered a liminal place at the boundary of their jurisdictions. It is interesting to note that in Irish tradition the Badbh was believed to show herself as the 'Washer at the Ford' (see Chapter 7) and so made this place a boundary between this world and the Otherworld. Similarly, one of the Morrígan's attempts to defeat Cú Chulainn in the *Cattle Raid of Cooley* (*Táin Bó Cúailnge*) occurred at the ford of Áth Traiged (see Chapter 9). The same sense of a significant place clearly underlay this location in *Pwyll, Prince of Dyfed*. Guided by advice given a year before by Arawn, Pwyll dispatched Hafgan with one blow and declined the invitation to deliver a second blow as a coup de grâce. On several occasions previously, Arawn had given Hafgan more than one blow and this had led to his magically surviving. As a result of this victory, Pwyll became the sole ruler of Annwfn, which became a united kingdom under Arawn when the character swap had ended.

Once they were back in their correct places, Arawn discovered that Pwyll had not slept with his wife; while Pwyll discovered that in his absence Dyfed had been ruled justly, kindly and generously. Each was therefore grateful to the other. Arawn needed the courage of Pwyll and Pwyll needed the wisdom of Arawn.[8] As a result, they became firm friends and, since Pwyll had united Annwfn, 'the name Pwyll, prince of Dyfed, fell into disuse, and he was called Pwyll Pen Annwfn from then on'.[9]

This Otherworld connection was then reinforced by the next part of the story. Pwyll was told that anyone visiting the mound of Gorsedd Arberth,[10] which may have been in the Prescelly Mountains (Pembrokeshire),[11] would either be injured or see something wonderful. This is very reminiscent of the Irish traditions concerning fairy realms under the *sídhe*, the fairy mounds that were considered to be the Underworld homes of the *Tuatha Dé Danann*. From the mound Pwyll saw a woman on a pale-white horse. After sending a servant on foot to enquire who she was, he discovered that she could not be caught even though her horse appeared to be merely ambling. The same thing occurred when another servant tried to catch her on horseback; a similar attempt to catch up with her on horseback failed the next day too. The close connection between this rider and the (possibly fairy) mound and with horses has caused some to suggest that she was a Welsh version of the goddess Epona, whose cult has left evidence from the Roman period in Britain and on the continent. This link is possible but cannot be proved.

Finally, Pwyll himself pursued the woman, and he was able to meet with her because he asked her to stop for the sake of the man she loved most. This turned out to be Pwyll and so she stopped. When questioned, she revealed that she was Rhiannon, the daughter of Hyfaidd Hen, and was to be given in marriage to another man but loved only Pwyll. Her name may have originally derived from that of a Celtic goddess, Rigantona (the Brittonic name combines the words 'great' and 'queen'). Since the attraction was mutual, Pwyll agreed to meet her again to try to prevent the marriage. However, he was tricked into making a promise to a stranger and this was none other than Gwawl son of Clud,[12] the man to whom Rhiannon was promised in marriage. The trick delivered Rhiannon to Gwawl.

Rhiannon, not surprisingly, was annoyed and commented that no man had ever been as stupid as Pwyll.

Not to be outwitted, Pwyll later tricked Gwawl into getting into a bag, where he became trapped and was beaten by members of Pwyll's retinue. This was apparently the first time that the game 'Badger in the Bag' was played. Sadly, it is likely that this game was known to the first hearers of this story and involved the baiting (and killing) of a real badger.

Eventually, with the rival defeated, Pwyll married Rhiannon and she bore him a son. But on the night the boy was born he vanished while his mother and her six attendants slept. In order to protect themselves from blame, the attendants set up Rhiannon so it would appear that she had killed and eaten the baby. Unable to prove her innocence against the united testimony of her attendants, Rhiannon accepted a punishment that for seven years she would sit by a mounting block and carry all those who wished it to the royal court and tell them of her guilt.

In the next stage of the story a mystery affecting the mare of Teyrnon Twrf Liant, the lord of Gwent Is Coed, was solved. This character's name, Teyrnon, derived from that of a Celtic god, Tigernonos (containing the Brittonic words 'great' and 'lord'). His epithet, Twrf Liant, may have meant something like 'roaring flood tide'. Given the proximity of Gwent Is Coed to the river Severn, it is possible that Teyrnon was originally a deity associated with this river and its dramatic tidal movements. If so, he was only a name by the time this story was written, since no supernatural attributes were accorded him, although the matter of the clawed beast at May Eve (see below) may suggest that at one time he was associated with a longer myth.

Every May Eve Teyrnon's magnificent mare gave birth but her foal vanished. From other events that were said to occur at this time of year (the screaming dragon in the story of *Lludd and Llefelys* and the battle between Gwyn

ap Nudd and Gwythyr fab Greidyawl for the hand of
Creiddylad, the daughter of Lludd Silver-hand in *Culhwch and Olwen*, both discussed in Chapter 15) it is clear
that May Eve and May Day were considered a time when
the veil between this world and the Otherworld was thin.
One night Teyrnon thwarted a great clawed beast that was
stealing the foal but, on returning home after chasing it, he
found a boy in swaddling clothes by his door. Strangely,
the storyteller made no attempt to explain the connection
between the clawed beast and the child left at the door. Perhaps the implication was that the beast had earlier taken
the child, but this was not made clear.

Teyrnon and his wife named the boy Gwri Wallt Euryn
('Gwri of Golden Hair') and raised him as their own.
Eventually, however, the boy's supernatural growth and
likeness to Pwyll caused Teyrnon to take the boy to court,
where he was reunited with his parents. Rhiannon's innocence was proved, the boy was renamed Pryderi and the
story ended happily. Teyrnon was offered rich rewards
but declined them all. Pryderi went on to become ruler of
Dyfed on the death of Pwyll.

The compiler of this story wove together a number of
mythological themes – the temporary rule of the Otherworld, the lady on the horse that could not be caught, the
May Eve conflict and the mysterious boy with supernatural growth – to produce a memorable story but one that
was also heavily dependent on an underlying stratum of
Welsh mythology. And this stratum was recognizably part
of a wider body of Celtic myth.

Branwen Daughter of Llŷr (*Branwen ferch Llŷr*)
This story begins with an insight into the medieval Welsh
perspective on the past. It occurred, so the tale goes, when
'Bendigeidfran son of Llŷr was crowned king over this
island and invested with the crown of London'.[13] This land
was called 'The Island of the Mighty'. Medieval realities

then dictated that, despite this apparent domination of what had actually later become England, he was residing at Harlech (Wales) with his entourage. Bendigeidfran's name derived from 'blessed' and 'Brân', a deity.[14] An Irish Bran travelled to the Otherworld and Bendigeidfran's gigantic size, ownership of a magic cauldron and talking severed head suggest he was originally part of an independent myth.

Also interesting is that the compiler of the story noted that he was there in the company of his brother, Manawyddan son of Llŷr. This character was the Welsh form of the Irish Manannán the son of Lír, who was also god of the sea and married to Aife (Aoífe), who was transformed into a crane. In this form she was killed and her skin was used to create a magic treasure bag. None of this mythological information was woven into the simple statement that forms part of the opening of this story and this is characteristic of the way that the Welsh storytellers often drew on characters from a mythical past without necessarily commenting on their significance. The absence of any comment about such a character's mythological origins may have been either because the sense of magical being was enough – without further elaboration – or because the writer was unaware of the myth behind the name. Furthermore, there was no connection between this character and the sea in Welsh traditions.[15]

While Bendigeidfran was at Harlech, a fleet appeared from Ireland. Travelling in this was Matholwch, King of Ireland, with a proposal to unite Britain and Ireland by marrying Branwen daughter of Llŷr. This was agreed and the marriage duly took place. Incidentally, Bendigeidfran's gigantic size was indicated in an aside that explained that the event occurred in tents because he was too big to fit into a house. The success of this union, however, was almost immediately marred by a vicious maiming of Matholwch's horses by Efnysien (one of Bendigeidfran's two half-brothers on his mother's side). The act was solely motivated by malice and the writer had earlier indicated that this brother was a man who created discord and enmity (in true folk-tale contrast with his brother Nysien, who brought harmony and reconciliation). Their mother was the daughter of Beli son of Mynogan (the former's name may have derived from the name of a Gaulish god, Belinus).

Not surprisingly, Matholwch was both confused (because the family had just let him marry the most beautiful girl) and angry. He made to leave for Ireland. However, Bendigeidfran offered generous compensation for the horse maiming and made it clear that he had nothing to do with it. In addition – since Matholwch still seemed sad – Bendigeidfran offered him a magical cauldron. The properties of this cauldron were that it would revive the dead, although they would not regain the power of speech. This was clearly a survival of a very well-established Celtic belief in magical cauldrons. Archaeology supports this statement as the silver Gundestrup Cauldron – found in Denmark in 1891 – is a remarkable example of both workmanship and visual mythology. The cauldron is 69 cm in diameter and 42 cm in height; it weighs almost 9 kg. Probably made *c*.130–1 BC, it represents Celtic art of the La Tène Culture. It is decorated with mythical scenes that include a cross-legged antlered figure holding a snake, bull hunting, male and female figures with wheels, and warriors being dipped headfirst into a cauldron.[16] With over a millennium separating the cauldron in Denmark and the literary reference in Wales, this is a remarkable illustration of the continuity of Celtic mythology and the once-widespread nature of these beliefs. Other magical cauldrons included the cauldron of the Irishman Diwrnach Wyddel in *Culhwch and Olwen* and that sought by Arthur in *The Spoils of Annwfn* (*Preiddeu Annwfn*).

The storyteller interwove an Irish connection, since Bendigeidfran explained that the cauldron had been brought to Britain by an Irishman named Llasar Llaes Gyfnewid. To this, Matholwch added the information that he knew this man and his wife and a cauldron he carried. He had given the couple hospitality but they had caused such discord that they had been driven from Ireland through being placed in an iron house that was heated to white heat until they broke out and fled to Wales. The Otherworld origin of the cauldron was underscored by the explanation that Matholwch had seen the man, his wife and the cauldron emerge from a lake. The couple were both huge and their son was born as a fully armed warrior.

After this, Matholwch returned to Ireland, and Branwen with him. But soon the Irish grew incensed at the original insult done to Matholwch and punished Branwen by putting her to work in the kitchen, where each day she was struck on the head. As well as the offence given to her, this was additionally shocking because to strike a queen, or even to knock anything from her hand, was a high crime in medieval Welsh law.[17] This crime of striking a queen appears also in *Peredur Son of Efrawg*, where Arthur's queen was struck (see Chapter 16).

In time, Branwen taught a starling to speak and the bird took news of her plight to her brother, Bendigeidfran. In response, he mounted an invasion of Ireland. So huge was he that he waded across the sea from Wales, although the story notes that the sea between the two countries was not then so wide. This curiously telescopes traditions of a time when all of Britain was Celtic (the early fifth century) and a time before the Irish Sea was fully formed (millennia earlier in prehistory, after the last Ice Age). That the two ideas existed as ancient traditions seems clear, but their telescoping illustrates the flexibility of such folk tales and their manipulation of imprecise memories of ancient events.

On Branwen's advice, Matholwch offered peace to Bendigeidfran. This involved giving Ireland to his son by Branwen, building a house big enough for Bendigeidfran (along with his army and the retinue of Matholwch too). However, Matholwch hoped to trick Bendigeidfran by hiding two hundred armed Irish warriors in the house. These, though, were discovered and killed by Efnysien – who had caused all the trouble in the first place – by squeezing the hide bag containing each warrior until his fingers sank into the brain through the skull. The ambush thwarted, peace was then made. But the malicious Efnysien contrived to destroy this fragile peace. When the new king of Ireland – Gwern, the son of Branwen and Matholwch – came to speak with him at the feast, the vicious Efnysien threw the boy into the fire. The malevolent and divisive nature of Efnysien was a personification of the cause of strife, and a similar device is found in a number of folk tales and mythologies. A character reminiscent of his destructive influence is the Norse figure of Loki.

In the ensuing battle, the Irish made use of the magic cauldron to revive their dead until a repentant Efnysien (realizing that he had caused the defeat of the British, although he seemed to feel no remorse for the burning of Gwern) tricked the Irish into throwing him into the cauldron. Inside, he stretched out and shattered the cauldron into four pieces and his own heart was shattered too.

In this way, a victory of sorts went to Bendigeidfran but only seven of his men survived, while he himself was wounded in the foot by a poisoned spear. He then ordered that his own head be cut off and taken to London. There it was to be buried, facing France and protecting Britain from invasion. This would be done, he said, over a long period of time, during which the head should reside for seven years at Harlech, with the birds of Rhiannon singing (a point undeveloped in the story) and then for eighty years in Gwales in Penfro. This latter place was also known as Ynys Gwales and was the island today called Grassholm, which lies eight miles off the south-west coast of Pembrokeshire (Wales). The birds of Rhiannon were also mentioned in *Culhwch and Olwen*, where they were said to be able to wake the dead and send the living to sleep.

When Bendigeidfran's head was brought back to Wales, Branwen died of a broken heart as she reflected on the destruction she had witnessed. The men carrying the head also discovered that in their absence Britain had been conquered by Caswallon son of Beli. He had defeated those left behind by Bendigeidfran through the use of a cloak of invisibility.

Having taken the head to Gwales in Penfro, the men resided there for eighty years and during that time they did not feel their sorrows, and with the head with them it was as if Bendigeidfran had not died. At last, though, they broke a taboo that had been laid on them by Bendigeidfran and opened a door facing Cornwall. At this, their sorrows returned and they hurried to London in order to bury the head. Its burial became known as one of the 'Three Fortunate Concealments' and its later uncovering as one of the 'Three Unfortunate Disclosures'. The fatal blow to Branwen of seeing Bendigeidfran's head brought back to Wales became known as one of the 'Three Harmful Blows' (see Chapter 17).

Back in Ireland, the island was eventually repopulated by the offspring of five women who survived the slaughter and from these derived the five provinces of Ireland.

Manawyddan Son of Llŷr (*Manawyddan fab Llŷr*)

After the head of Bendigeidfran had been buried, his brother Manawyddan son of Llŷr was saddened and did not know where to live, since he did not want to claim help from his cousin, Caswallon, who had replaced Bendigeidfran as ruler of the Island of the Mighty (Britain), as mentioned in the last story. At this point, Pryderi (son of Pwyll, Prince of Dyfed and Rhiannon) offered Manawyddan marriage to his widowed mother and the rule of Dyfed. This, Manawyddan accepted.

All seemed well. Pryderi made homage to Caswallon at Oxford (continuing to recall the time when British rulers dominated England) and Manawyddan planned to do so, too. This was until one evening when they went up to the mound of Gorsedd Arberth. It was from this mound that Pwyll had first seen Rhiannon in the tale *Pwyll, Prince of Dyfed*. Once again, an Otherworld event occurred. This time a mist fell and when it rose they discovered that everyone in Dyfed had vanished.

Deserted in their own realm, they finally resolved to travel to England and live as craftworkers. Following this decision, they worked as pommel-makers in Hereford, shield-makers in another, unnamed, city and shoemakers in another town. In each place they were forced to leave due to the enmity of other craftspeople caused by the excellence of the workmanship of the newcomers.

At last they returned to Dyfed. Here Pryderi and Manawyddan hunted a gleaming white boar that led them towards a mysterious tower. While the nature of this boar was not explored in this story, it was clearly linked to tales of magical boars found in a number of Welsh traditions, such as *Culhwch and Olwen* with the hunting of the boar called Twrch Trwyth and a similar Arthurian tradition found in *The History of the Britons*. The dogs pursued the boar into the tower and, against Manawyddan's advice, Pryderi went inside in order to rescue his dogs. There, he took hold of a golden bowl by a well, only to find his hands stuck to the bowl, his feet stuck to the floor and his power of speech gone.

Returning to Rhiannon, Manawyddan recounted the events and she went out to look for Pryderi, only to find herself in the same predicament. At this point, with a loud noise and in a great mist, the tower vanished, taking Pryderi and Rhiannon with it. This left only Manawyddan and Cigfa, the daughter of the wife of Pryderi. Once again the two travelled to England only to find the same negative response to their craft skills. Finally, they returned once more to Dyfed and farming. However, they were still dogged with misfortune as their wheat was stolen by an army of mice. Through lying in wait to discover the nature of the thieves, Manawyddan succeeded in catching one fat mouse. He was resolved to hang the mouse-thief (despite being advised that it was better to let it go by Cigfa). After constructing a tiny gallows on Gorsedd Arberth, Manawyddan prepared to hang the mouse. A passing, threadbare cleric tried to dissuade him but to no avail; he was similarly followed by a priest and eventually a bishop. The bishop offered a high price for the life of the mouse, but Manawyddan demanded more. His 'price' was the restoration of Pryderi and Rhiannon, along with the removal of the enchantment from Dyfed. Just why Manawyddan thought that the passing bishop would be able to deliver this is not made clear in the story. However, it soon transpired that the 'bishop' was really Llwyd son of Cil Coed and that he had enchanted Dyfed as revenge for the 'Badger in the bag' trick played on Gwawl son of Clud, by Pwyll, as recounted in the story of *Pwyll, Prince of Dyfed*. Llwyd and Gwawl were friends. And the fat mouse was the pregnant wife of Llwyd. After finally securing from Llwyd the promise that no retribution would fall on Dyfed, Pryderi and Rhiannon or Manawyddan himself, the spell was lifted, Pryderi and Rhiannon were restored to Manawyddan and the mouse was released. Due to how Pryderi and Rhiannon had been imprisoned (Pryderi had gate-hammers – possibly knockers – hung around his neck and Rhiannon had the collars of draught-animals hung around hers), the story was also known as 'the Mabinogi of the Collar and the Hammer'.[18]

Math Son of Mathonwy (*Math fab Mathonwy*)
Math son of Mathonwy was ruler of Gwynedd at the same time that Pryderi son of Pwyll ruled Dyfed. Math had a curious and debilitating affliction. To stay alive he had to

rest his feet in the lap of a virgin, unless he was at war. The virgin's name was Goewin. However, she was desired by a man named Gilfaethwy son of Dôn; and his brother, Gwydion, resolved to assist him to achieve his goal. The female name Dôn derived from the name of a Celtic goddess, Dana or Danu.[19] The name of this goddess gave rise to the river names Danube (central Europe) and Don (Scotland) and the Irish race of gods and goddesses the *Tuatha Dé Danann*. These men were the nephews of Math and the later magical skills of Gwydion suggest there was once a body of mythological literature centred on this 'divine family' that has been largely lost.

Gwydion's plan involved causing a war between Gwynedd and Dyfed that would take Math away from his kingdom. The war was provoked through Gwydion telling Math that Pryderi had gained a new kind of fine-tasting animal – the pig. It is interesting, given the mythical nature of a number of pigs in Welsh stories that Gwydion reported that Pryderi had gained these animals from Annwfn (the Otherworld). In negotiations with Pryderi for some pigs, Gwydion offered fine stallions and hounds. The deal was accepted but the stallions and hounds were conjured by magic and vanished once the exchange had taken place. This caused Pryderi to raise an army and war broke out with Gwynedd. While Math was away, Gilfaethwy took Goewin against her will, in Math's own bed. At the culmination of the war it was decided that Gwydion should face Pryderi in single combat. This took place but Gwydion killed Pryderi through the use of magic combined with his warrior skills.

When Math returned home from battle he discovered the outrage perpetrated against Goewin by his own nephews and he was furious. In order to make amends, he married Goewin and punished his nephews. Using magic (this was the first mention in the story of Math having this ability) he turned Gilfaethwy into a hind and Gwydion into a stag.

There are echoes of the shape-shifting so prominent in Irish mythology in this (see Chapter 9). After a year, they returned having mated and produced a fawn. Math then turned them into a boar and sow but in reverse order of the gender of the previous enchantment. Again, a year passed and then they returned with their offspring. Then Math turned them into wolves with the same result. Having been so humiliated, they were finally returned to human form.

In the next phase of the story, it was then necessary to choose a new virgin for Math to rest his feet on. The choice fell on his niece, Aranrhod daughter of Dôn. However, she failed a virginity test as, when she stepped over Math's magic wand, she dropped a child and another small thing that Gwydion seized, wrapped in silk and put in a chest. The child that was dropped was named Dylan Eil Ton, who took on the nature of the sea and swam like a fish. Later (not in this story), he was killed by his uncle Gofannon, whose name may have been connected to that of the Irish god of smithing, Goibhniu. The 'thing' that had been wrapped in silk turned into a boy who was raised by Gwydion. As with Pryderi in *Pwyll, Prince of Dyfed*, he grew at a supernatural speed but Aranrhod, his mother, would not name him or raise him. Furthermore, she said that he would have no name until she provided it and clearly she had no intention of so doing.

Gwydion took the boy away on a magically created ship and disguised their appearance, and they became shoemakers. In this form Aranrhod unknowingly approached them. The boy threw a sharp object at a wren landing on the deck and Aranrhod unknowingly named him as Lleu Llaw Gyffes ('the fair-haired one with the skilful hand'). Angry at being tricked, she then said he would not get weapons until she provided them. Again, she was tricked into arming the boy because Gwydion made her fear that she faced an attack and again he and the boy were disguised. She then said that he would not find a wife but

Math and Gwydion conjured a woman out of flowers, who was named Blodeuedd ('flowers'). However, she betrayed Lleu and plotted his death. She tricked him into revealing he could only be killed in the unlikely setting of having one foot on the edge of a bath-tub and the other foot on the back of a billy goat. This, Blodeuedd contrived to do and her lover killed Lleu. He changed into an eagle and vanished.

Although Lleu had vanished, Gwydion resolved to find him. Following a sow, he at last came to where Lleu was, still in the form of an eagle. With magic he returned him to human form and Blodeuedd was punished by being turned into an owl named Blodeuwedd ('flower face'). Her lover was forced to stand where he had killed Lleu and have a spear thrown at him. His servants refused to take the blow for him, earning notoriety as one of the 'Three Disloyal Retinues' (which seems harsh given that he had committed the earlier crime). Lleu threw the spear and it pierced a stone to kill Blodeuedd's lover. Following this, Lleu went on to rule Gwynedd.

So ended the fourth branch of the *Mabinogi*.

15

WHERE MYTH MEETS HISTORY: LEGENDARY WELSH STORIES

The first two of these four stories – *The Dream of Macsen Wledig* (*Breuddwyd Macsen Wledig*) and *Lludd and Llefelys* (*Lludd a Llefelys*) – explore traditions concerning early British history. In this there is a curious interplay between legendary history and mythology. These are, in effect, interpretations of British history that also include motifs from folklore.

The final two stories – *Culhwch and Olwen* (*Culhwch ac Olwen*), also known as *How Culhwch won Olwen* (*Mal y kauas Culhwch Olwen*), and *The Dream of Rhonabwy* (*Breuddwyd Rhonabwy*) – are Arthurian in nature. As such, both attempt to set their stories in a Dark Age past. Of the two, *Culhwch and Olwen* is the more imbued with mythology and really stands out as a distinct tale in a genre all its own. *The Dream of Rhonabwy*, though, provides something of a bridge between the worlds of myth and legend. It sets itself in the context of the politics of the rule of Madog of Powys (died 1160), looks back to the battle of Badon or Baddon (a real event) and names Arthur's rival as Owain son of Urien of Rheged, a kingdom centred on the Solway Firth but whose lands stretched over north-west England and eastwards into Yorkshire. Owain and Urien were historic rulers in the 'Old North' (northern Britain before the Anglo-Saxon conquests) in the sixth century. While Owain has been very much transmuted into a myth-ical character, he was originally a real warrior. Similarly, another enemy is Osla Gyllellfawr ('big knife'). Described as leader of the Saxon armies at Badon, he also appeared in *Culhwch and Olwen* as a member of Arthur's retinue. He may have represented a garbled version of the name of the eighth-century Mercian ruler, Offa.[1] Another possibility that has been suggested is that he represented Octha, son of the Anglo-Saxon Hengest;[2] or Octha son of Oisc, who was son of Hengest according to the eighth-century Anglo-Saxon historian Bede. As with Owain, we see an attempt to adapt history. Though very different, these two stories both attempt to reconstruct a period of history when Brit-ain was under the rule of one leader: Arthur. While this was clearly imaginary, there is something historical within this, as it reminded readers of a time when there was a common Celtic culture across what had later become 'Eng-land' and 'Wales'. As such the motivation was a reinvention of history and not simply a retelling of mythology.

The Dream of Macsen Wledig (Breuddwyd Macsen Wledig)

This legendary tale was based on a real character from Late Roman Britain. This was Magnus Maximus, who was pro-claimed emperor by the Roman troops in Britain in AD 383. Although defeated and killed when he extended his ambi-tions to the continent, he was later claimed as ancestor in a number of Welsh royal genealogies. In these he was remembered as Macsen (or Maxen) Wledig. Wledig was from the Welsh *gwledig*, or 'lord'.

In the story, the Emperor Macsen fell asleep after a day's hunting and dreamed of a journey across rivers and mountains to a great castle where a huge fleet was anchored. Reaching a wonderful land, he encountered a castle decorated with gold, silver and jewels. Two seated youths were playing *gwyddbwyll* (not unlike chess), the name formed from *gwydd* (wood) and *bwyll* (wisdom/intelligence),[3] in the company of a man on an ivory throne, carving *gwyddbwyll* pieces, and a beautiful maiden. At this point Macsen woke but could not stop thinking of the woman. So preoccupied was he that he neglected all affairs of state and all communication with the imperial household. This neglect soon sparked opposition to his rule and, at last, he shared his dream with his counsellors. They advised him to send out three messengers to seek out the beautiful woman. This was done, but to no avail.

At last the emperor returned to the place in which he had experienced the dream and his servants finally saw the land in question from the top of a high mountain. These servants then travelled there. Their quest eventually took them to Snowdonia and the Menai Straits. There they finally found the castle (at Caernarfon) that featured in the dream, complete with the two youths, the *gwyddbwyll*-piece carver and the beautiful woman. They proclaimed her Empress of Rome but she replied that if Macsen loved her, he should come and get her.

When her reply reached him, Macsen at once travelled to Britain. He defeated the British, who were led by Beli son of Manogan. The name of Beli may have been derived from the name of a Gaulish god, Belinus.[4] This character was included as an ancestor in a number of Welsh stories in the *Mabinogi*. Then Macsen travelled on to north Wales. As before, when his messengers had reached there, he found two men – Cynan and Gadeon – playing *gwyddbwyll* and their father – Eudaf son of Caradog – still carving pieces for the *gwyddbwyll*. The beautiful woman he discovered to be named Elen Luyddog. That night she became his bride. In return, Macsen made her father ruler of Britain and built for her three great castles: at Caernarfon, Caerleon and Carmarthen. The predominance of Caernarfon within the story may point to it being part of the well-evidenced campaign of the court of Gwynedd to reinvent the past in order to bolster its claims of overlordship within Wales in the medieval period.

For seven years Macsen remained in Britain. In this time he built roads and fortresses. The writer clearly made Macsen responsible for all of the Roman infrastructure, whose ruins could still be seen in the medieval landscape. Due to staying so long away from Rome, Macsen was deposed but then marched on Rome to regain his throne. Despite conquering France and Burgundy, Macsen was unable to take Rome. Only the arrival of Elen, along with her brothers, changed this. The Britons – unbeknown to Macsen – stormed Rome and in a battle that raged three days and three nights (clearly a mythological trope in this case) recaptured the city and presented it to Macsen.

In return for this, the two brothers were given leave to conquer any land they wished. They seized the Armorican region of Gaul (France), killing the men but sparing the women. In order to have their British speech 'uncorrupted' they cut out the tongues of the women that they took as wives. This, it is asserted, is the origin of Brittany and its language, so closely related to British. This story was based on a manipulation of the Welsh name for Brittany (*Llydaw*) by claiming it derived from *lled taw* (half-silent). This was inspired by a fiction that first appeared in the ninth-century *History of the Britons* (*Historia Brittonum*).

This legendary history is an intriguing interweaving of fact and fiction. Flavius Magnus Maximus Augustus was actually Spanish by birth and a Roman general who served in Britain. In 383 he rebelled against the emperor, Gratian, and seized control of Britain. This was by no means a unique event since the large concentration of Roman military forces in Britain presented opportunities for a number of ambitious generals on several occasions. Taking troops from Britain, Magnus seized control of Gaul, killed Gratian, and threatened Italy. Given local recruitment in this period of Roman rule it is likely that a significant number of the units taken to Gaul would have been British in composition.

Unable to suppress him, Emperor Theodosius (ruling the Eastern Roman Empire) negotiated and Magnus was recognized as emperor in Britain, Gaul and Spain, governing from Trier. In 387, Magnus invaded Italy, was defeated, retreated to Aquileia (in Italy, on the northern coast of the Adriatic), surrendered and was executed in 388. There is no persuasive evidence to suggest that he married a British woman.

Where the legend intersects with history is the probable movement of British troops out of the country under Magnus. It may also reflect a glimpse of reality in its, otherwise fictional, account of the settlement of Armorica by British forces and the speechless local wives. This clearly was an attempt to explain the strong connections between Britain and Brittany. The *History of the Britons* also claimed that Brittany was garrisoned by British troops under Magnus Maximus. This is a real possibility and echoes of it may faintly reverberate through the account in *The Dream of Macsen Wledig*. Similarly, the movement of troops out of Britain in 383 may have been accompanied by arrangements made between imperial authorities and the local governing councils of the British *civitates* (local government areas) for local defence. Such arrangements may lie behind the fictional claim that Magnus made Eudaf son of Caradog the ruler of Britain after him. The arrangements may also have become entangled in popular memory with the decision by the Roman Emperor Honorius, in 410, to instruct the British to organize their own defence in the absence of imperial troops, who had been moved to the continent by another British-based 'rebel-emperor', Constantine III.

What is certain is that the memory of Magnus Maximus influenced later Welsh thinking. With a little historical reconstruction, it could be claimed that it was not the Romans who had conquered Britain but the British who had captured Rome. The presence of such a successful rebel-emperor in Britain again reinforced the British connection. The invention of a British wife personified this. As a result, the later (early medieval) Welsh kingdoms of Powys and Gwent claimed Magnus as an ancestor. An inscription on the Pillar of Eliseg (Llangollen, Denbighshire, Wales), dating from the 850s, claims that the semi-legendary British ruler Vortigern was married to Sevira, 'the daughter of Maximus the king, who killed the king of the Romans'[5] and so was a founder of the kingdom of Powys. This was almost certainly propaganda in response to claims to pre-eminence by the rulers of Gwynedd (within which kingdom *The History of the Britons* was written c.830). Nevertheless, it shows the extent to which the memory of Magnus Maximus affected later Welsh rulers.

The legend of Macsen Wledig continues to exert a powerful grip on the Welsh imagination. The legend has become a myth of national survival against the odds. The patriotic Welsh folksong entitled *Yma o Hyd (Still Here)*, released by Dafydd Iwan in 1981, opens with celebrating how, despite it being 1,600 years since Magnus Maximus left Wales, the culture and language of the Welsh still survives as the chorus asserts:

We're still here today! We're still here today
Despite everything and everyone
We're still here today

Its final verse sums up the power of the myth of Macsen Wledig:

> Remember that old Prince Macsen, left our country as one
> Let's shout out to all the nations 'We'll be here until King-
>   dom come!'[6]

Lludd and Llefelys (*Lludd a Llefelys*)

This story tells the deeds of Lludd, King of Britain. Inter-estingly, it first appeared as an addition to the thirteenth-century Welsh translation of Geoffrey of Monmouth's twelfth-century *History of the Kings of Britain* (*Historia Regum Britanniae*). The story claimed that Lludd was son of Beli the Great: a mythical name that was included in *The Dream of Macsen Wledig* and other stories. The account claims that he ruled shortly before the first Roman inva-sion by Julius Caesar. Lludd was not an historical charac-ter but the story writer believed this to be the case. Lludd, in this account, overcame three plagues that threatened Britain with the assistance of his brother, Llefelys, king of France. The three plagues appear to represent invaders who threatened the independence of Britain. Coming after over a millennium of invasions (Romans, Picts, Scots, Anglo-Saxons, Vikings, Normans) this certainly resonated with Welsh historical experiences.

The first plague that threatened Britain was that of the Coraniaid. These were a race who could hear every word that was spoken and so could thwart all resistance to their oppression. In order to prevent the consultation between Lludd and Llefelys concerning resistance to the Coraniaid being overheard, the conversation was conducted through a long horn of bronze. Surprised by the hostile words each heard the other say, they discovered that there was a demon in the horn making trouble but the demon was driven out by pouring wine into the horn. The solution to the Corani-aid was found in insects provided by Llefelys, which were crushed in water and, when scattered over the Coraniaid, proved poisonous to them.

The second plague took the form of two fighting dragons whose screams on every May Eve were heard above every hearth in Britain and made women barren and drove young men and maidens mad. In addition, the whole land was rendered infertile. It turned out that one dragon represented the British people and the other one represented a foreign people (unnamed) that was trying to overcome them. This plague was defeated by digging a hole in the exact centre of Britain and placing a vat of mead, covered by silk, inside it. When the dragons had finished fighting, they sank to the earth in the form of little pigs (once again, pigs were connected with mythical events), drank the mead and fell asleep. This done, the sheet was wrapped round them and they were placed in a stone chest. This was buried at Dinas Emrys in Eryri (Snowdonia).

This tradition is particularly interesting because it is very similar to one found in the ninth-century *History of the Britons*. In that book the semi-historical character Vortigern was described as attempting to build a fortress in Snowdonia. However, the building kept collapsing and Vortigern was informed that the matter would only be solved if he scattered on the ground there the blood of a boy born without a father. Such a boy was eventually found but he revealed to Vortigern the cause of his trouble. Beneath the building site, there was a pool, along with two dragons fighting. The red dragon represented the Welsh and the white dragon the Anglo-Saxons. The Welsh, he was assured, would eventually be victorious. The boy revealed his name as Ambrosius. The site of the failed building project was remembered in the Welsh landscape as Dinas Emrys (fortress of Ambrosius). What is interesting is that the writer of *Lludd and Llefelys* referred to it by this name in his telling of the dragon-plague without any reference to the earlier story, which had apparently inspired it. One possibility is that there was a yet older tradition that was embellished differently in *The History of the Britons* and in *Lludd and Llefelys* (while in the latter still using the place name that only made sense because of the earlier tradition in *The History of the Britons*). The alternative is that the later account simply lifted and remodelled the earlier Ambrosius/dragons story in order to explain how the dragons became imprisoned at that spot but kept the place name without recognizing the inconsistency this caused, since at the 'time' of the original burial it could not have been named after the (later) Ambrosius. Also interesting is that the name of the boy represented a memory of Ambrosius Aurelius, who appeared in a sixth-century account written by the British cleric Gildas[7] and who was an historical character who led a sub-Roman resistance to the Anglo-Saxons in the fifth century. By the time of the writing of *The History of the Britons* he had become fully mythologized.

The third plague was that of a powerful magician whose magic caused all the royal court to sleep while he stole all the food and provisions. This plague was defeated by Lludd standing guard by night. To keep himself awake, while his court was being enchanted to sleep, he immersed himself in cold water again and again. At last, a giant armoured man entered the court to seize the provisions. Lludd battled him to submission and spared him on condition that the man restored all that had been taken and submitted to Lludd as a vassal. At this the story rather abruptly ends.

Culhwch and Olwen (*Culhwch ac Olwen*)

This story, also known as *How Culhwch won Olwen* (*Mal y kauas Culhwch Olwen*), opens with the strange tale of the birth of Culhwch. His mother, Goleuddydd (the queen and wife of Cilydd son of Celyddon Wledig), went mad in pregnancy and eventually gave birth in a pig-run. Although the queen's senses returned just before the birth, it was fear of the pigs that caused her to go into labour. As a consequence, the child was named Culhwch, from *cul* (narrow passage/run) and *hwch* (pig). Hence: 'pig-run'. This is significant since pigs were to have a prominent place in the story, as in a significant number of Welsh myths. Soon after this event, Goleuddydd died and Cilydd agreed to his dying wife's request that he would not remarry until a two-headed briar grew on her grave. In order to prevent such a remarriage she charged her chaplain with clearing her grave of any plants. Every morning the king sent a servant to check on the grave – but no briar was there to be seen. But after seven years the chaplain forgot and the briars grew on the grave.

Cilydd was told by his counsellors that a suitable wife was known but already married to a king named Doged. He then, shockingly, killed King Doged and took his wife, daughter and land. This woman became stepmother to Culhwch and when he was reluctant to marry her daughter, the stepmother cursed him that he would therefore not have a woman until he could gain Olwen, the daughter of Ysbaddaden, Chief Giant. Culhwch realized he would not achieve this goal of winning Olwen on his own and so set out for Arthur's court to enlist help.

In overcoming the obstacles in their way, a cast of mythical and semi-mythical beings embarked on a dramatic and fast-moving set of adventures. In this story Arthur held court at Celli Wig in Cornwall at the centre of a fabulous band of warriors. When Culhwch reached the court, the wide array of warriors there included characters from history and mythology. Alongside the historical reference to Gwilenhin, King of France (probably a reference to William the Conqueror, died 1087), and Fflergant, king of Brittany (Alan IV, Duke of Brittany, died 1119), were mentions of Irish mythological heroes. These included Welsh forms of the names of Cú Chulainn, Conchobar mac Nessa (a hero king in the Ulster Cycle) and Ferghus mac Róich, who was a warrior of the Red Branch of Ulster and was one of those who found the infant hero Cú Chulainn and later trained him as a warrior. Welsh myth was represented by Manawyddan son of Llŷr (who appeared in Irish mythology as Manannán son of Lír), along with an unlikely group drawn from giants, monsters and even saints.[8]

From this warrior-band, six were chosen to accompany Culhwch on his quest. These included Cai, Bedwyr and Gwalchmei (Arthur's nephew). Reaching a shepherd's hut, they learned that Olwen washed her hair there every Saturday. When she appeared, white flowers sprang up in her footprints, hence her name, meaning 'white track'.[9] She responded positively to the suit of Culhwch but advised him that Ysbaddaden would set him difficult tasks to overcome because he was fated to die when his daughter married.

Finally reaching the home of the giant, Culhwch was given forty tasks to accomplish. These tasks were described by the Welsh word *anoetheu*, meaning 'things hard to come by'.[10] Time and again Culhwch confidently replied to Ysbaddaden: 'It is easy for me to get that, though you may think that it's not easy'; which provoked the giant to demand yet another task be accomplished with the words: 'Though you may get that, there is something you will not get . . .'[11] The rest of the story was built around the tackling of some of these tasks, although only twenty-one were actually accomplished. This and the untidy telling of the tale raises the question of whether this was an ancient story, or whether the characters of Culhwch and Olwen were invented by the compiler of the story in order to draw together a range of pre-existing Arthurian tales.[12] The jury remains out on this question. What is clear is that one of the mythological themes running through the story certainly was very old indeed because it was first referred to, in passing, *c.*830 by the writer of *The History of the Britons*. And this was the hunting of a gigantic boar.

The most famous story within *Culhwch and Olwen* tells of the hunting of the great boar Twrch Trwyth. This hunt appeared in the tale because the boar had between his ears a razor, comb and a pair of scissors required by Ysbaddaden to prepare his hair for the wedding. Before this boar-hunt took place, though, Culhwch killed the giant Wrnach whose sword was needed to kill the boar. He tricked the giant by offering to sharpen his sword but, instead, killed the giant with it. Then the companions enlisted Arthur's help to free Mabon ap Modron from prison in Gloucester because only he could handle Drudwyn, the hunting dog needed to chase down the boar. Mabon was the Gaulish god Maponos and Modron was the Celtic mother goddess Matrona.[13] The Welsh redactions of Geoffrey of Monmouth's *History of the Kings of Britain* – the *Chronicle of the Kings* (*Brut y Brenhinedd*) – associated the goddess with *Ynys Afallach* (Island of Afallach), which was the Welsh name for Geoffrey's *Insula Avalonsis* (Isle of Avalon). Later in the story of Culhwch, a reference to Mabon son of Mellt (lightning) was also probably a reference to this deity.

Next they killed Ysgithrwyn Pen Baedd ('white tusk chief of boars'), the wildest boar in Britain, because they needed his sharp tusk with which to shave Ysbaddaden. The great boar-hunt of Twrch Trwyth then began. This turned into an exhausting cross-country hunt that went from Ireland to Wales and southwards to the river Severn, where the hunters took from Twrch Trwyth the razor and scissors that lay between his ears. Twrch Trwyth then escaped to Cornwall where the comb was finally taken from him; then the boar was driven into the sea and vanished (presumably drowned). In this hunt, land was wasted and many hunters were killed.

After this, Arthur killed the Black Witch, whose blood was needed to soften the beard of Ysbaddaden. That done,

Culhwch cut the hair of Ysbaddaden and shaved him to the bone. The giant died and Culhwch married Olwen. This hunting of Twrch Trwyth represented a mythological event that resonated with many aspects of Celtic pre-Christian beliefs: the magical boar, the impossible quest, the realms of giants and witches, and the eventual triumph of the warriors who accomplish their tasks.

A similar connection of this story with mythical beings occurred in the reference to Gwyn ap (son of) Nudd, who was unable to take part in the boar-hunt so central to the tale, but who, on every May Day until the world's end, fought with Gwythyr fab (son of) Greidyawl (or Greidol) for the hand of Creiddylad daughter of Lludd Silver-hand. This is interesting for two reasons: firstly, it reminds us of the significance of May Day within the Celtic ritual year (see Chapter 4); secondly, it links beliefs about this day with a specific mythological being – Lludd Silver-hand. As with a number of Welsh references to beings once regarded as gods, or culture-heroes, the reference was undeveloped and the significance of the 'event' described was not explored by the writer. It is likely that the writer of *Culhwch and Olwen* was no longer aware of the religious beliefs once associated with this character from the pre-Christian past. Instead, Lludd Silver-hand had simply become one of many half-remembered magical beings who were certainly not venerated as gods by the time that *Culhwch and Olwen* was written down. Indeed, it is likely that this once-divine status had been completely forgotten. But evidence from other sources reveals that Lludd Silver-hand was a Welsh form of the Irish Nuada Airgedlámh (Nuada of the Silver Hand). In Welsh the name became Nudd Llaw Ereint or Lludd Llaw Ereint (Nudd/Lludd of the Silver Hand). Were it not for the Irish evidence, the reference in this Welsh source would remain enigmatic. However, the Irish evidence (see Chapter 6) unpackaged a much more complex mythological construction within which it was envisaged that this being was the

King of Erin (Ireland) and leader of the *Tuatha Dé Danann*. Having lost his hand – and consequently his right to rule – in the first battle of Magh Tuireadh, against the *Firbolg*, he had a silver hand fashioned by Dian Cécht, and died in the second battle of Magh Tuireadh, against the Fomorians, having previously regained his throne. None of this complex set of old beliefs is apparent in the passing reference preserved in *Culhwch and Olwen* but it reminds us of a number of common threads that linked Celtic beliefs on both sides of the Irish Sea and probably further afield, although we often lack the surviving evidence to trace this wider connectivity confidently. What is particularly puzzling in the Welsh version is that Lludd Silver-hand shared the same name as the father of Gwyn ap Nudd (Lludd and Nudd being different forms of the same name and both derived from the name Nodens, a Romano-British deity venerated as a healer god, sun god and sea god). Whether this was due to a complex mythological genealogy in which Gwyn ap Nudd contested to mate with his own sister – Creiddylad daughter of Lludd Silver-hand – or simply due to a duplication or confusion in the transmission of older oral traditions into written form, is now impossible to decide.

About Creiddylad we know even less. The writer of *Culhwch and Olwen* described her as 'the magnanimous maiden' and 'the most majestic maiden there ever was in the Three Islands of Britain and her Three Adjacent Islands'.[14] Later in the account the writer provided a more detailed explanation of how she had gone off with Gwythyr but before he could sleep with her she had been seized by force by Gwyn. Gwythyr raised an army to recapture her but was defeated. Among those captured by Gwyn was Cyledyr Wyllt son of Nwython. Gwyn killed Nwython and forced Cyledyr to eat his own father's heart, which caused him to lose his sanity. Arthur then went north, released those held prisoner by Gwyn and arranged the yearly contest between Gwyn and Gwythyr, with the proviso that whichever one triumphed on Judgment Day would have Creiddylad.

All of this passes in something of an aside in *Culhwch and Olwen* and seems to have been designed simply to enhance the prestige of Arthur's highly eclectic court and, of course, the prestige of Arthur himself. However, this aside was clearly the tip of a mythological iceberg. The combination of competition for sexual relations with a being who appeared to personify Britain, the annual May Day competition, and the faint possibility that Gwyn and Creiddylad were brother and sister may suggest that this was originally a spring fertility myth in which the personification of the land was competed for by rival deities every year. This is particularly likely since Gwyn ap Nudd was considered the ruler of the Otherworld. It is a little reminiscent of the Irish tradition within which Boann (a personification of the river Boyne) was the wife of the river god Nechtan or Echmar, but also mated with the Daghda. This does not mean that the Welsh account was a version of this Irish one; rather it implies similar mythological themes apparent in both Celtic cultures. This may also have informed the tradition of the Arthur/Gwenhwyfar/Melvas triangle and abduction-theme. This is even more likely given the mythical character of all three of these three figures and the Otherworld connections of the last two. And all this from a passing reference in *Culhwch and Olwen*. It reminds us of both the large amount of mythological information 'fossilized' in these medieval accounts, but also of how much we do not know.

It is also interesting that Cornwall was envisaged as being Arthur's domain in this story. On his mother's side he was said to have been related to the 'chief elder of Cornwall'. The only time Arthur appeared distressed at the destruction caused by the boar was when it left Wales for Cornwall. The twelfth-century writer Geoffrey of Monmouth referred to Arthur with the Latin title of *'aper*

Cornubiae' (boar of Cornwall), which linked Arthur both to the famous boar-hunt and to the south-west of England.

Further enhancing the dramatic nature of Arthur's authority in the story were the names given to each of his possessions. His sword was *Caledfwlch* (hard notch), his spear was *Rhongomyniad* (spear-striker), his shield was *Wyneb Gwrthucher* (face-to-evening), his knife was *Carnwennan* (white-hilted-one) and finally – as if ironically – his wife was *Gwenhwyfar* (meaning something like 'white phantom').

The Dream of Rhonabwy (*Breuddwyd Rhonabwy*)

The style of this story, along with a hint in its colophon (the brief description of the tale), suggests that, unlike the other stories, this never had an oral history but, instead, only ever existed as a work of literature. It also rather parodies the Arthurian myths and style of storytelling.

The hero Rhonabwy sought shelter in the home of Heilyn Goch. The squalid conditions, with ankle-deep cow urine and excrement, along with flea-infested beds, seem to have been deliberately designed to satirize the knightly quest so central to the 'Three Romances' (see Chapter 16) and even the fast-paced action narrative of *Culhwch and Olwen*. It was in this filthy and insanitary situation that Rhonabwy lay down on a yellow ox-hide and dreamed his dream.

In the dream itself, Rhonabwy was guided by a character named Iddog who was responsible for causing the battle of Camlan in which Arthur was killed. However, the timescale in the story was then telescoped and the reader finds the focus has shifted to just before the battle of Badon, an earlier battle, with the location being near the river Severn. The enemy to be fought at the coming battle was named as Osla Gyllellfawr. Although no ethnic label was attached to this figure, all other British/Welsh traditions (from the sixth-century account of Gildas onwards) claimed that the battle of Badon was fought between the British and the Anglo-Saxons. The implication from this is that Osla Gyll-ellfawr was considered to be an Anglo-Saxon; hence the reason why some scholars have thought he represented the fifth-century, semi-legendary Anglo-Saxon leader, Octha (or Oisc), or the much later (eighth-century) historic Mercian king, Offa. Either way, the battle was clearly of epic proportions. Those gathered for battle were presented as much larger than the men from Rhonabwy's time. To Rhonabwy's guide, Arthur asked: 'Where did you find these little men?'[15]

Then, a great surprise. Instead of the battle, the story described a board game of *gwyddbwyll* between Arthur and one of his own supporters, Owain son of Urien. This 'battle' in the *Dream of Rhonabwy* replaced the forthcoming battle with the Anglo-Saxons. While Arthur and Owain competed on the gaming-board, Arthur's men and Owain's ravens fought and slew each other in a strange conflict that was reported to the two leaders as they played. Finally, Arthur crushed the gaming-pieces and a truce was declared. Another truce was declared with Osla Gyllellfawr. The story came to an end and Arthur set off for Cornwall.

At the end of the dream the writer made no attempt to describe the significance of what had just been recounted. Readers were left to draw their own conclusions and perhaps this was the writer's motive. Alternatively, the pointlessness of what had just been described might have simply been yet another parody of contemporary mythological and legendary stories with their high drama, violence and doing of great deeds.

16

WHERE WELSH MYTH MEETS 'ROMANCE'

All of these final three stories have as their centre King Arthur's court at Caerleon on Usk. Each story consists of a journey embarked on by a hero who faces tests and challenges. In meeting these, the hero proves himself in each story. In this they are reminiscent of the late twelfth-century French 'Romances' that came to dominate Arthurian literature in the Middle Ages and were a genre of literature written for the wealthy lay aristocracy. These Romances, which combined stories of courtly love with knightly adventures embodying a moral teaching, have been described as the 'literature of chivalry'. This form of literature was intended to teach the aristocracy how to behave correctly in order to protect and maintain the medieval social order.[1] At the same time, the Romances aimed to provide engaging entertainment and, in order to do so, drew on popular themes, but explored and combined these in new ways.

Themes were chosen from Classical history and literature and included tales of Alexander the Great and the Trojan Wars; others drew on the more recent past by focusing on the eighth-century Frankish king Charlemagne and his warriors. Perhaps the most famous of these Romances was *The Song of Roland* (*La Chanson de Roland*), the oldest manuscript of which dates from between 1140 and 1170 and was written in Anglo-Norman, although it was probably composed in the early twelfth century. This transformed a violent border skirmish into epic heroism through the introduction of legendary swords and magic horns, alongside themes of treachery and revenge.

Given the popularity of Arthurian and Celtic-originated themes in Brittany, and with Welsh themes publicized and enjoyed by a wider continental audience owing to the popularity of Geoffrey of Monmouth's *History of the Kings of Britain* (*Historia Regum Britanniae*), *c.*1136, it is not surprising that these Arthur-related stories were picked up by French Romance writers such as Chrétien de Troyes (died *c.*1190). It was Chrétien, more than any other writer, who launched the genre of 'Arthurian Romance'. In his stories Arthur was never the centre of the plot; rather the tales, while focused on the Arthurian court, were more concerned with the trials, tribulations and triumphs of other members connected to the court. It was Chrétien who brought pre-existing stories and traditions – such as the love between Tristan and Isolde (or Iseult), the relationship between Lancelot and Guinevere and the mysterious Grail – to a wider and highly appreciative audience.

The relevance to any study of Celtic mythology is that, while Geoffrey of Monmouth, Chrétien de Troyes and other twelfth- and thirteenth-century writers were highly creative in their building of plots and back-stories, they drew much of their inspiration from Celtic traditions. These had survived in Wales and Brittany and, under their influence, became medieval bestsellers. Under the layers of fiction, contrived connections and dramatic plots, hints from a Celtic mythological past can still be made out.

This brings us to the three 'Romances' in the *Mabinogi*. They apparently represent reintroductions of these Romance stories into Wales itself. This reminds us of the complex 'cross-pollination' that occurred with regard to the transmission of mythical themes in the medieval period. However, although these three stories are very different from the other tales in the *Mabinogi* and share the common features outlined above, they do not constitute a coherent whole. They were certainly not the work of one single author and are not grouped together in the surviving Welsh manuscripts.

While it is reasonable to group them as 'Romances' shot through with myth, they are very different from the French stories they appear to be based on. They are very Welsh and contain material distinct from the French tales. This has led some modern authors to challenge whether they should be described as 'Romances' at all.[2] Nevertheless, there are good reasons for examining them as a group and also for considering them as a Romance-Myth hybrid form of literature: there is a well-established tradition of grouping them and studying them together; they are significantly different from the other stories in the *Mabinogi*; they share common features with each other, even though they do not form a homogenous literary group; and they were clearly heavily influenced by French Romance literature. In short, there is enough common ground within these stories to justify focusing on them as a recognizable group. Here, we will look particularly at their mythical content within the overall storyline.

A recent analysis of the three stories has suggested that they represent a Welsh selection of acceptable themes from the French Romance genre. These included action, knightly education and the balancing of knightly duties with love. On the other hand, it seems that other themes were rejected:

courtly details, characterization that developed feelings and motives, and authorial asides. The Welsh writers selected the bits that suited their own purposes. In short, they can be said to represent 'three hybrid texts, typical of a post-colonial world'.[3]

Peredur Son of Efrawg (*Peredur fab Efrawg*)

In this thirteenth-century story, the hero – Peredur – was transformed on a journey from an unsophisticated rustic to an accomplished knight. He then won the (rather reluctant) love of a lady named Angharad, before spending fourteen years in Constantinople with an empress whose admiration he had gained. Following this, he embarked on a dangerous journey that took him to the Castle of Wonders. Here, he defeated the witches of Caerloyw (Gloucester).

Peredur was brought up by his mother in an all-female household. This was to protect him from the dangers of a knightly career since just such a career had led to the deaths of his father and his brother. However, the appearance of three knights kindled his curiosity and he travelled to Arthur's court.

There, he set out to avenge an insult earlier done to Gwenhwyfar, wife of Arthur. This had involved a knight pouring wine over her and striking her on the ear. To strike a queen was a particularly grave insult and was specifically referenced in Welsh laws. This theme of an assault on Gwenhwyfar occurred in a number of Welsh traditions. The abduction of Gwenhwyfar has already been examined in Chapter 13 and a specific reference to an enemy (Melvas/Melwas, also known as Medrawd) striking a blow on her appeared in the triad entitled the *Three Unrestrained Ravagings of the Island of Britain* (see Chapter 17). After killing the offending knight, Peredur underwent a number of adventures that trained him in chivalry.

However, the most important features of the story in terms of mythology can be observed in the training that he underwent in the courts of his two uncles. At one court, his lame uncle advised him never to question the significance of an event that he observed. This had consequences when he visited the court of the other uncle. Here, he witnessed a strange procession of a bleeding lance and a head on a platter. Minding his previous education, he asked no question concerning the significance of this event.

In later adventures he learned warfare at the court of the witches of Caerloyw and then returned to Arthur's court. A later set of adventures took him to Constantinople and the love of the empress. The training by the witches was similar to the training of the Irish hero, Cú Chulainn, in the skills of warfare by Scáthach, the daughter of Ardgeimm (see Chapter 10).

When he eventually returned to Arthur's court, he was berated by a woman for not asking about the significance of the lance and the head on a platter. Had he done so, she instructed him, he would have healed the king and restored the land to prosperity. Furthermore, he discovered that the witches of Caerloyw were responsible for beheading his own cousin and laming his uncle. It was Peredur who was fated to avenge these family hurts.

There are hints here of much older Celtic traditions. The lame first uncle suggests a motif similar to the wounding of Bendigeidfran with a poisoned spear, in *Branwen Daughter of Llŷr* (*Branwen ferch Llŷr*). And the fact that the uncle was fishing with two lads when Peredur arrived suggests he was meant to represent the Fisher-King who was central to Chrétien de Troyes's French account of the appearance of the grail (*graal*) in his version of this story. The severed head – though differently presented and interpreted – was also similar to the beheading of Bendigeidfran in this earlier story (see Chapter 14). This is not to suggest any direct connection between *Peredur Son of Efrawg* and *Branwen Daughter of Llŷr*; rather, it implies certain common motifs that were drawn on by medieval Welsh storytellers and formed part of a wider and older pool of Celtic mythological themes. The head-cult theme was also found in Irish literature such as that involving Mac Cécht, a warrior who fought at the battle celebrated in *The Destruction of Da Derga's Hostel* (*Togail Bruidne Dá Derga*). In this, he championed the doomed king, Conaire, killed the man who beheaded Conaire and then gave the king's head a last drink. The theme of avenging a wronged kinsman also found in *Peredur Son of Efrawg* was, again, a dominant one in the Welsh (and Irish) traditions.

The head on the platter was different from the grail that was described in Chrétien de Troyes's *Perceval, the Story of the Grail* (*Perceval, le Conte del Graal*). In that account, Perceval (Peredur in Welsh) saw the procession in the hall of the wounded Fisher-King. However, both accounts were quite different from what the Arthurian tradition of the Holy Grail would eventually develop into and both works described the dish as a platter, not as the cup or chalice that would eventually be envisaged. In fact, the French word *graal* meant a platter or the kind of broad dish that might support the serving of a large fish such as a pike.[4] This suggests earlier strands of mythological imagery that would eventually be Christianized by the Burgundian poet Robert de Boron in his story *Joseph of Arimathea* (*Joseph d'Arimathie*), *c.*1202. By the time of this later development of the theme, the *graal* had become a Christian chalice containing Christ's blood. It had become what in English would be written as 'the Holy Grail'. Chrétien de Troyes had already hinted at how this might develop when, in another description of the *graal*, he explained that the Fisher-King was sustained by a single Mass wafer brought to him on the *graal*. This was, though, quite absent from the description of the object in *Peredur Son of Efrawg*. In the latter, the description was more in keeping with a world of magic cauldrons and talking-heads.

Other mythological features of the story included the

hunt for a magical animal (a unicorn, in this case) and a magic *gwyddbwyll* board found in the Castle of Wonders.[5] The hunt was a common occurrence in a large number of Celtic tales. As well as reflecting an aspect of everyday experience, the fact that the animal sought was magical turned the hunt's surprises and uncertainties into a quest and a test. It could therefore become both a way that the prowess of a hero was tested and a means by which some Otherworldly object or knowledge could be gained. Other features included the claim of Peredur's male cousin that he had the ability to appear as a woman. This shape-shifting was a common feature in Celtic mythology and occurred often in the Irish literature as well as in the Welsh. Marvels in this story included lions guarding a castle, giants, dead men who could be revived in tubs of warm water (reminiscent of the cauldron of Bendigeidfran, in *Branwen Daughter of Llŷr*) and magic stones. At times, the presence of the marvellous does not seem to have had any significance attached to it, such as the episode of a half-burning tree. Overall, it can be difficult to identify a common theme in the story and at least one interpretation is that the present narrative was composed using a number of separate stories that were 'connected by the identity of the hero and little else'.[6] Furthermore, there is a fragment of a story involving the hero Gwalchmai that may only have been included because the compiler found it alongside other material of interest to him. The end section may simply have been added in an attempt to pull the story together. However, despite this failure of plot and structure, the account still succeeded as a series of exciting adventures.

Finally, the name of Peredur was probably taken from that of Peredur arfau dur (Peredur 'of steel weapons') recorded in the tenth-century poem *Y Gododdin* (*The Gododdin*), which looked back to a battle fought *c*.600. This described warriors of the Old North and was consistent with a trend noted in a number of Welsh stories whereby the name of a real hero from the past was used in the telling of a story that was far removed from reality. The intention was probably twofold. Firstly, to provide a familiar name that was already associated with heroic deeds in order to make the story more appealing to an audience and, secondly, to make the story feel more authentic as if it really had occurred in a distant – but real – Celtic past. The story of *Peredur Son of Efrawg* was also given a northern connection through the name of Peredur's father. Efrawg or Efrog derived from the Welsh form of the place name York.

Geraint and Enid (*Geraint ac Enid*)

This story – also known as *Geraint Son of Erbin* (*Geraint fab Erbin*) – united romantic themes and reminders of knightly duty. Geraint won his bride but became so preoccupied with her that he neglected his duties as a knight. He then misinterpreted her anxiety for love for another. This caused him to take her on an exhausting journey until, at last, they were finally reconciled.

Of all the three 'Welsh Romances', this one is closest to the corresponding French Romance, *Erec and Enide* (*Erec et Enide*), although the name of the hero was changed from the Breton personal name Erec to the Welsh personal name Geraint. This was probably because the thirteenth-century Welsh adapter of the story wanted to celebrate a well-known British hero: Geraint of Dumnonia (south-west Britain), who reigned in the late sixth or early seventh century.

In the story, Geraint competed in a tournament and won the hand of Enid. Recalled to rule his ancestral lands, Geraint neglected his duties because he was so enamoured with Enid. She inadvertently communicated to him his courtiers' criticisms and he, rather puzzlingly, took this as a confession of infidelity on Enid's part. Through a series of adventures she eventually persuaded him of her faithfulness. After this, Geraint defeated the 'Knight of the Hedge of Mist', an image of magical-mist reminiscent of that found in *Manawyddan Son of Llŷr* (*Manawyddan fab Llŷr*), where mist was also associated with Otherworld enchantment (see Chapter 14). Another mythological feature was the joust that led to Geraint's defeat of the 'Knight of the Sparrowhawk' (*Marchawc y Llamysten* in Welsh); this knight was revealed to be Edern son of Nudd. While nothing was made of the mythological nature of this character in this story, other evidence shows that he was originally considered to be the brother of the equally mythological Gwyn son of Nudd, who annually fought Gwythyr son of Greidyawl for the hand of Creiddylad daughter of Lludd Silver-hand (see Chapter 15). And Nudd was the Welsh equivalent of the Irish deity Nuada Airgedlámh (Nuada of the Silver Hand). In a curious inconsistency, at the end of the joust neither Geraint nor Enid claimed the prize of the sparrowhawk; the writer apparently forgot this detail.[7]

Another link to other myths was the naming of Arthur's hunting dog as Cafall in a stag hunt. The name derived from the Latin *caballus* (horse); this was Arthur's gigantic dog referred to in the ninth-century *History of the Britons* (*Historia Brittonum*) and in the later story *Culhwch and Olwen* (*Culhwch ac Olwen*).

The earlier part of the story in *Geraint and Enid* was clearly set in the geographical context of south-west Wales, although the later part of the story – when he and his wife faced their joint journey – had no clear geographical context.[8] However, it is likely that much of the story was a resetting of a Breton Celtic tale. The evidence for this is that in Chrétien de Troyes's version of the story the hero was known by the Breton personal name *Guerec* (French: Erec). Alongside this it should be noted that the female personal name Enid may have been derived from the Breton *Bro Wened*, the name for Vannes, on the Gulf of Morbihan (Brittany, France). Consequently, this might have represented a Breton version of a mythological mating of the ruler with the land, found in a number of Irish examples. In the case of Erec and Enid, it may have been envisaged as a mating of *Guerec* (representing the male ruler) with *Bro Wened* (the female land).[9] This is particularly persuasive since the Breton personal name *Guerec* would earlier have been written as *Weroc*. The area around Vannes took its name from someone who had borne this name and the area-name was *Bro Weroc* ('land of (G)weroc').[10] That two personal names derived from alternative names (*Bro Wened* and *Bro Weroc*) for the same area of Brittany is surely too significant to be considered a coincidence. The suggestion that this story originated as a myth of sovereignty is very persuasive.

A similar Irish parallel would be the mating of the Daghda with Boann, who was the wife of the river god Nechtan. Another Irish example of a character who probably originated as a being considered to be a sovereignty goddess was that of Queen Medb of Connacht;[11] similar Irish sovereignty deities were Ériu, Banbha and Fódla, the wives of the kings of the *Tuatha Dé Danann* at the time of the invasion of the Milesians.

Owain, or the Lady of the Fountain (*Owain, neu Iarlles y Ffynnon*)

This thirteenth-century tale provides something of a mirror-image to the issues explored in *Geraint and Enid*. This story tells how Owain won his bride but then neglected her since he preferred to stay at Arthur's court. However, he was eventually brought to face the error of his ways and the couple were eventually reunited. The character Owain took his name from a real historic ruler: Owain son of Urien, who ruled in north-west Britain in the sixth century in the kingdom of Rheged. By the twelfth century Owain had become fully mythologized and had been brought into the circle of warriors associated with Arthur. For example, in *The Dream of Rhonabwy* (*Breuddwyd Rhonabwy*) it was Owain's ravens who battled Arthur's men before the battle of Badon, while Arthur and Owain played a board-game (see Chapter 15). In this story, too, the warriors of Owain were described as 'the Flight of Ravens'.[12]

The story is concise and focused, and centred on three journeys to a magic well. The Welsh word used, *ffynnon*, can be translated as 'fountain' or 'well'. The magic well was a similar motif to the well found in *Manawyddan Son of Llŷr* (*Manawyddan fab Llŷr*) that led to the enchantment of Pryderi (see Chapter 14). The combination of knightly duty and romantic love was interwoven through Owain defeating the 'Knight of the Fountain' and his subsequent marriage to his widow, the 'Lady of the Fountain' of the title of the story. When he returned to Arthur's court he forgot his wife. However, when he realized this, he lost his reason. Eventually – through the assistance of a lion – Owain was restored to health, overcame obstacles and was reunited with his wife. In many ways this story was closer than the other two to the French Romance of *Yvain*, written by Chrétien de Troyes.

Welsh mythological themes surfaced in the story in a number of ways, including in the characters involved. Owain and Cai were well known companions of Arthur by the time this story was written and had long since become detached from reality. Arthur's gatekeeper, Glewlwyd Gafaelfawr ('Brave Grey Mighty Grasp'), also appeared in *Culhwch and Olwen* and in *Geraint and Enid*. The enchanted well has already been noted but Arthur and Gwalchmai's expedition to the spring, leading to a three-day battle with its defender, was clearly so numbered in order to denote mythical significance. The association between visits to the spring and storms that occurred[13] underscored this liminal place where this world and the Otherworld met. The throwing of a basinful of water onto the stone by the spring had the effect of both provoking a hailstorm and challenging the defender. The threefold occurrence of this event – firstly by Cynon, then by Owain and finally by Arthur – emphasized repeatedly the enchanted nature of this source of water. This emphasis on enchanted water was a common motif in Celtic mythology. It is surely significant that an alternative title for the whole story, found in one manuscript, gave Owain the title of: *Earl of the Basin* (*Iarll y Kawg*).[14] It suggested that the experience at the enchanted well was more significant than the love-interest encapsulated in the more common title. Overall, mythological themes permeated this story, as they did in both the other Welsh versions of the Romances.

17

HEROES AND VILLAINS OF THE WELSH TRIADS

A particular kind of Welsh medieval literature recorded traditions about events, heroes and villains from the mythological and legendary past by grouping them into related bundles of threes. This number combined the sacred number three with a mnemonic device designed to aid recall. This triad device was used in Welsh medieval legal codes as well as in poetry and proverbs.[1] These collections of poetic traditions are known as the *Triads of the Island of Britain* (*Trioedd Ynys Prydein*).[2]

The oldest manuscript containing triads is called *Peniarth 16* and dates from the fifteenth century. However, aspects of its orthography (spellings and style) point to it having been copied from an early thirteenth-century original.[3] Another small collection of triads survives in the 'Triad of Horses' in the *Black Book of Carmarthen* (*Llyfr Du Caerfyrddin*), written *c.*1250; yet others are found in the fragmentary survival of triads – from a once much fuller collection – in the *White Book of Rhydderch* (*Llyfr Gwyn Rhydderch*) compiled *c.*1350; and this fragmentary collection survives intact in the *Red Book of Hergest* (*Llyfr Coch Hergest*), compiled *c.*1382–1410.[4] This has led a number of experts to conclude that the oldest triads date from the thirteenth and fourteenth centuries,[5] or even the twelfth and thirteenth centuries,[6] but appear to have been based on a collection put together in the eleventh or twelfth century.[7] This original compiler remains unknown, but overall the triads come from a mixed source. Some may have been derived from very early oral traditions since they contain stories and themes similar to earlier works such as *Culhwch and Olwen* (*Culhwch ac Olwen*) and other stories found in the *Mabinogi*. Others, though, appear to have been influenced by the twelfth-century work of Geoffrey of Monmouth, in his *History of the Kings of Britain* (*Historia Regum Britanniae*). A number of these later additions reflect the growing popularity of Arthur in medieval Wales; in these his name appears to have replaced those of earlier heroes. This is particularly noticeable in cases in which Arthur was added as a fourth example to trump the other three in the original triad. Five of the triads refer to traditions concerning Camlan – the last and fatal battle fought by Arthur.[8] None of the triads in their current form are much older than the ninth century.

Overall, three main themes dominate and categorize the triads. These are Welsh mythology (and semi-mythology); medieval Welsh legendary perspectives (and reconstructions) of the pre-Saxon 'Roman past' and the traumas associated with the loss of much of Britain to the Anglo-Saxons; and, finally, the exploits of legendary characters from what might be termed the 'Welsh Heroic Age'. These last stories centred on events in the sixth and seventh century that occurred in Wales and in the 'Old North' (British areas of what later became northern England and southern

Scotland).[9] As such, they preserved echoes of ancient traditions both legendary and mythological and, as Rachel Bromwich memorably put it, 'are based on the debris of saga
literature'.[10] A number of the triads combined tales from
more than one of these three categories as if consciously
designed to create a sense of unified Welsh 'history'.

In this chapter a selection of the many triads are recounted in order to give an insight into the ways in which these
mythological and legendary stories drew on medieval
Welsh views of beliefs and events that were set in the distant and not so distant past.

Triad heroes and villains of the mythological past: echoes of ancient beliefs

Beli son of Mynogan, whose name appears to have been
derived from the name of a Gaulish god, Belinus, appeared
in the triad named *The Three Silver Hosts of the Island of
Britain*. In this triad the tradition claimed that Caswallawn
son of Beli, Gwennwynwyn and Gwanar sons of Lliaw son
of Nwyfre, and Arianrhod daughter of Beli led an army
out of Britain to campaign in foreign parts. There is no evidence that the writer of the triad had any idea that Beli had
once been a deity and the triad lacks detail, so it is unclear
what the significance was of this movement of armies. It
may simply have been that the names of magical characters
of indeterminate status were added to common cultural
themes in order to lend them increased grandeur or mystery. In the Welsh case the theme of armies leaving Britain may have been half-remembered echoes of real events:
the withdrawal of Roman forces leading to the collapse of
Celtic Britain in the fifth century.

Another reference to Beli occurred in the triad of the
Three Dishonoured Men who were in the Island of Britain,
which referred to Afarwy son of Lludd son of Beli. This
preserved the names of two originally pagan gods. Beli
has already been referred to and Lludd was a reference to

Lludd Llaw Ereint (Lludd of the Silver Hand), the same deity referred to in Irish mythology as Nuada Airgedlámh (Nuada of the Silver Hand). Furthermore, Rhun son of Beli was named as one of the *Three Red Ravagers of the Island of Britain* and it is clear that by the early medieval period, Beli was perceived as the ancestor of a number of Welsh 'rulers' who were also non-historical. The second of these 'Red Ravagers' was named as Lleu Llaw Gyffes ('the fair-haired one with the skilful hand'), who also appeared in the *Mabinogi* in the tale of *Math Son of Mathonwy* (*Math fab Mathonwy*). The triad appears to have been constructed so as to juxtapose magical 'ancestors' as the protagonists in dramatic conflicts of the past.

Beli's son, Caswallawn, was named as the first of the *Three Golden Shoemakers of the Island of Britain*. The magical nature of this tale was emphasized by the wording of the second example in this triad, which referred to the activities of Manawyddan son of Llŷr as occurring, '*pan uu hut ar dyuet*' ('when there was an enchantment on Dyfed').[11] The nature of this 'enchantment' was unexplained; apparently the initiated were expected to know its meaning.

The name of another deity from the pre-Christian past was preserved in the *Three Exalted Prisoners of the Island of Britain*. This was in the second example in this triad and involved Mabon son of Modron. These characters represented Mabon, the Celtic sun god Maponos, and Modron, who was the Celtic mother goddess Matrona. Mabon also appeared, as the husband of a woman named Emerchred, in the second of the *Three Faithful Women of the Island of Britain*. In the *Three Exalted Prisoners* it was concluded that a fourth and even more exalted prisoner than the three named was Arthur. In a later repetition of this triad the author named the places in which this fourth prisoner was kept: 'three nights in prison in Caer Oeth and Anoeth' and then 'three nights imprisoned by Gwen Pendragon', followed by 'three nights in an enchanted prison under the Stone of Echymeint'.[12] The mention of 'Anoeth' (the Otherworld) alongside another magical prison reveals how thoroughly the traditions concerning Arthur mixed myth with pseudo-history by the time that the triads were written down.

The triad the *Three Fortunate Concealments of the Island of Britain* contained a reference to a myth found in the *Mabinogi* in the story of *Branwen Daughter of Llŷr* (*Branwen ferch Llŷr*) and discussed in Chapters 14 and 16. This triad concerned the burial of the head of Brân the Blessed son of Llŷr in London, to ward off Saxon invasion. The name of Brân the Blessed appeared in the *Mabinogi* in the form Bendigeidfran (derived from 'blessed' and the name 'Brân'). Llŷr was a form of the name that appeared in Irish mythology as Lír, the sea god. The second concealment was of the dragons under Dinas Emrys by Lludd son of Beli, which was also mentioned in the *Mabinogi* tale *Lludd and Llefelys* (*Lludd a Llefelys*), discussed in Chapter 15. This triad connected mythological names (Lludd and Beli) with legendary events (Vortigern and the Anglo-Saxon invasions) that were themselves the subject of other accounts. In this case these other accounts described how the hidden dragons were eventually discovered in the fifth century as portents of the conflict between the Welsh and the Saxons. Llŷr was also mentioned in the triad curiously known as the *Three Prostrate Chieftains of the Island of Britain*, which referred to Manawyddan son of Llŷr. Manawyddan was a Welsh form of the name found in Irish mythology as Manannán the son of Lír and god of the sea. There was, though, no connection between Manawyddan and the sea in Welsh mythology, although he was named as the brother of a giant: the aforementioned Bendigeidfran (Brân). The strange name for this triad was prompted by a tradition that those remembered in it would not seek a dominion, which nobody could deny them, though even this explanation is puzzling.

An event mentioned in *Branwen Daughter of Llŷr* also appeared in the triad of the *Three Harmful Blows of the Island of Britain*. The first of these was the violence allowed against Branwen by her Irish husband, Matholwch. In the triad the blow was described as being delivered by Matholwch himself, rather than by those in the court-kitchen, as described in the *Mabinogi*.

Mythology and magic were entwined in the first of the *Three Great Enchantments of the Island of Britain*. This involved Math son of Mathonwy teaching the skill of enchantment to Gwydion son of Dôn. Math was referred to in the *Mabinogi* tale of *Math Son of Mathonwy* in which to stay alive he had to rest his feet in the lap of a virgin, unless he was at war. The female name Dôn derived from the name of a Celtic goddess, Dana or Danu.[13] The aim of this triad was clearly to explain how Gwydion came to possess the magical power associated with him in other stories.

Another magical tale reflected in both the *Mabinogi* and the triads informed the triad of the *Three Faithless War-Bands of the Islands of Britain*. The first part of this triad focused on a story also found in *Math Son of Mathonwy*. This involved retainers who would not stand between their lord, Goronwy the Radiant, and a spear-thrust. This man had been responsible for the murder of Lleu Llaw Gyffes ('the fair-haired one with the skilful hand') in order to gain possession of his wife, Blodeuedd, and the spear-thrust was the punishment for that earlier crime. As a result, the warband of Goronwy the Radiant were remembered with dishonour (which given his guilt for the murder of Llaw seems harsh but reveals the unquestioning loyalty theoretically expected of retainers).

Less obviously identifiable was the target of the third of the *Three Fortunate Assassinations* but he still was, nevertheless, clearly mythological in nature. This was Gwrgi Garwlwyd. The name translates as 'Man-hound

Rough-grey' and was probably originally a reference to a werewolf. That this being killed a Welsh person every day and two on Saturday (to avoid killing on Sunday) corroborates this identification since he was clearly considered monstrous, until he was killed by Diffydell son of Dysgyfdawd. So too were the objects of the first of these 'Fortunate Assassinations'; these were the Two Birds of Gwenddolau who were alleged to feast on the corpses of two Welsh people for lunch and two for supper, and who were killed by Gall son of Dysgyfdawd. Incidentally, this Dysgyfdawd also appeared as the father of the assassin of the historic Æthelfrith of Northumbria in the second of the 'Fortunate Assassinations'. Quite why he was so closely associated with assassin-children was not made clear in the triad. He was identified as being from Deira and Bernicia (Northumbria), and was also described as being a bard in the triad *Three Chieftains of Deira and Bernicia, and the Three were Sons of a Bard*. The triad, though, invented this piece of 'history', since Æthelfrith of Northumbria was actually killed by fellow Anglo-Saxons in 617.

Given the place of pigs within Welsh mythology it will come as no surprise to learn that they feature in one of the most detailed and developed of the triads. This is the *Three Powerful Swineherds of the Island of Britain*. The first of these swineherds was named as being Pryderi son of Pwyll, Lord of Annwfn, which immediately indicated the Otherworld nature of this story, since *Annwfn* derived from the Welsh for 'inside-world'. The pigs he tended were the seven animals that his father, Pwyll, had given to his foster father, Penndaran Dyfed. Pwyll's ownership of pigs from the Otherworld also featured in the *Mabinogi* tale, *Math Son of Mathonwy*.

The second 'Powerful Swineherd' was Drystan son of Tallwch, who tended the swine of March son of Meirchyawn. Even the combined force of Arthur and his warriors March, Cai and Bedwyr was unable to take as much as one piglet from Drystan, which the triad summed up in the memorable line: '*nac o dreis. nac o dwyll. nac o ledrat y gantaw*' ('not by force, nor by deception, nor by stealth').[14]

The third 'Powerful Swineherd' was Coll son of Coll-frewy, who was responsible for the swine of Dallwyr Dallben, kept at Glyn Dallwyr, in Cornwall. One of his sows – Henwen – was due to farrow but a prophecy said that Britain would suffer from what she was carrying. Consequently, Arthur gathered an army to destroy Henwen. What then followed was a pig-hunt a little reminiscent of the hunt for the magical boar, Twrch Trwyth, in *Culhwch and Olwen*. At a number of places the sow dropped items that (according to the triad) helped explain why these places were famous for these things: a grain of wheat and a bee in Gwent; a grain of barley and a grain of wheat in Pembrokeshire. In addition, she brought forth a wolf cub and a young eagle at the Hill of Cyferthwch in Arfon (Gwynedd), whose owners suffered unspecified problems owing to the presence of these animals in their households. Finally, at Llanfair in Arfon, she gave birth to a kitten under the Black Rock. Coll, the swineherd, threw it into the sea and it was found on the seashore of Môn (Anglesey) by the sons of Palug. As a result, it became known as 'Palug's Cat' and it caused great harm to them and to the island. It was remembered, in a separate triad, as one of the *Three Great Oppressions of Môn*, alongside the very historical Northumbrian ruler, Edwin, King of Lloegr (England).

This terrible cat was also remembered in the story *What Man is the Porter?* (*Pa wŷr yw'r Porthor?*), in which it was killed by the Arthurian warrior Cai, but only after it had killed many, since 'Nine score fierce [warriors] would fall as her food'.[15] The nature of this story, once shorn of its pig-related mythology, may suggest a real event that became attached to the tale of Henwen. A kitten rescued from the seashore that grew up to eat warriors suggests the animal was probably really a leopard cub or panther cub, sent as a diplomatic gift to the Welsh prince of Gwynedd and lost at sea. Some later traditions claim it was speckled,[16] so emphasizing its leopard-like appearance. Strange as all this sounds, it is not as unlikely as it may at first appear. Imported Byzantine pottery (from the Eastern Roman Empire) has been recovered in north-west Wales as well as in south-west England; and a sixth- or seventh-century Byzantine intaglio (engraved gem from a ring) has been found at Cefn Cwmwd on Anglesey. These suggest that after the fall of the Roman Empire diplomatic gifts from the surviving Eastern Roman Empire continued to reach western Britain as part of far-flung Byzantine diplomacy. So, an exotic connection between Anglesey and the Mediterranean world is, in fact, proven. A big-cat cub, sent as a diplomatic gift, is a real possibility. There is a hint of this in a line of the earliest version of the poem *What Man is the Porter?*, where a confusion in the manuscript suggests that Cai might have gone to Anglesey to fight either 'hosts' (an army) or 'lions'.[17] Apparently, one of the scribes who later copied out the poem found it rather puzzling and substituted the word 'hosts' for the earlier word 'lions'. This is understandable, as it was more likely that a warrior might fight an army on Anglesey than a giant cat. However, the hint is revealing and suggests that it was actually a big-cat that was involved and that the kitten was something altogether more deadly than the average pet. Probably lost in a shipwreck, it was later found on an Anglesey beach. Its new owners, the unsuspecting sons of Palug, had no idea just what they had rescued! And its appetite grew.

Triad heroes and villains of Roman Britain and the Saxon invasions: where history meets legend, part I

The Three Silver Hosts of the Island of Britain entwines historical events with mythical and legendary characters. Each of these 'hosts' were, it was claimed, armies that left

Britain in order to fight abroad. In this survive echoes of Roman forces withdrawn at various points towards the end of Roman rule. In one case a character named Yrp took the British host to Llychlyn (an indeterminate place, sometimes associated with Scandinavia, at other times with an Otherworld beneath the sea). Some of those who went with him settled on two islands near the 'Greek Sea'.[18] The second host was that of the famous counter-invasion that led to the legendary capture of Rome by Elen of the Hosts and Macsen Wledig, and was based on the historic bid for imperial power by Magnus Maximus in 383. This host also, according to the triad, went to Llychlyn, which is in contrast with the specific claim that Rome was the target in *The Dream of Macsen Wledig* (*Breuddwyd Macsen Wledig*), as explored in Chapter 15. The third host allegedly pursued the men of Caesar (an enigmatic claim) and was led by Caswallawn son of Beli, and Gwennwynwyn and Gwanar sons of Lliaw son of Nwyfre, and Arianrhod daughter of Beli.

Macsen Wledig also briefly appeared in the *Three Chief Officers of the Island of Britain*, which named his son as Owain. This conflated two historical characters into a fictional family relationship: the fourth-century Magnus Maximus and the sixth-century Owain of Rheged (see below).

The triad of the *Three Dishonoured Men who were in the Island of Britain* combined legendary accounts relating to both the Roman and the Anglo-Saxon invasions. The first of these 'Dishonoured Men' was Afarwy son of Lludd son of Beli, who invited Julius Caesar to Britain. The second was Gwrtheyrn the Thin, who invited the Anglo-Saxons into Britain. This was a reference to Vortigern, a British ruler of the fifth century referred to by the eighth-century Anglo-Saxon historian, Bede, and described in the British account in the ninth-century *History of the Britons* (*Historia Brittonum*). This triad clearly reflected something of the medieval popularity of Arthur since it claimed that Gwrtheyrn also exiled Uther Pendragon (father of Arthur in medieval accounts)[19] who later went on to kill Gwrtheyrn. This then led on to the third act of dishonour, which was the betrayal of Arthur by Medrawd (also known as Melvas/Melwas) and led to Arthur's death at the battle of Camlan.

Another reference to Julius Caesar can be found in the *Three Unfortunate Counsels of the Island of Britain*. Caesar featured in the first of these, which was the British decision to allow the horses of the Romans (under Caesar's command) a footing on the British seashore. The second example was the British decision to allow the Anglo-Saxons, Horsa and Hengest (and Hengest's daughter, Ronwen), into Britain. The third was Arthur's decision to divide his army at the battle of Camlan.

We have already seen a reference to the *Three Fortunate Concealments of the Island of Britain*. But the triad of the *Three Unfortunate Disclosures* set the later disastrous revealing of these secrets, that should have remain concealed, in the period of history that witnessed the Anglo-Saxon invasions in the fifth and sixth centuries. Two of these 'Unfortunate Disclosures' involved Vortigern. In the first, he disclosed the bones of Gwerthefyr the Blessed (said to protect the harbours of Britain) in order to gain the love of Ronwen (in Welsh legend the daughter of the Anglo-Saxon leader, Hengest); in the second, he disclosed the hidden dragons. The third 'Unfortunate Disclosure' was when Arthur revealed the head of Brân the Blessed because he wanted Britain defended only by his military might. In each of these three triads the writer presented a combination of hubris and lust as the reasons for the loss of much of Britain to the Anglo-Saxons.

Actions leading to the death of Arthur at the battle of Camlan featured in a number of triads. In the second of the *Three Harmful Blows of the Island of Britain* it was allegedly the blow struck by Gwenhwyfach on Arthur's queen, Gwenhwyfar, that led to the battle. In the first of the *Three Unrestrained Ravagings of the Island of Britain* the blow was struck by Medrawd (see Chapter 16). While Camlan was not specifically mentioned in this particular triad, other Welsh traditions named the conflict between Medrawd and Arthur as a major cause of Arthur's demise. As mentioned, the third of the *Three Unfortunate Counsels of the Island of Britain* described Arthur's fateful decision to divide his forces with Medrawd at Camlan. As if to emphasize the numerical significance, the compiler of this triad stated that the division was threefold.

Interestingly, the triads also insisted that Arthur had no fewer than three queens named Gwenhwyfar. These were: Gwenhwyfar daughter of Cywryd Gwent, Gwenhwyfar daughter of Gwythyr and Gwenhwyfar daughter of Gogfran the Giant. These three were named in the *Three Great Queens of Arthur*.

Triad heroes and villains of the 'Welsh Heroic Age': where history meets legend, part II

A number of historical rulers from Wales and the 'Old North' also played a part in the triads. Some had merely walk-on parts such as those in the *Three Fair Princes of the Island of Britain*. These were: Owain son of Urien, Rhun son of Maelgwn and Rhufawn the Radiant son of Dewrarth Wledig. Owain son of Urien ruled in north-west Britain in the kingdom of Rheged in the sixth century (see Chapter 16). Rhun was a mid sixth-century ruler of Gwynedd. The third 'Fair Prince', Rhufawn, was an Arthurian warrior mentioned in *Culhwch and Olwen*.

Owain and his associates featured in a number of triads. Owain's bard, Dygynnelw, appeared as the first of the *Three Red-Speared Bards of the Island of Britain*. And Owain's horse, Karnaflawc, was recalled as the first of the *Three Plundered Horses of the Island of Britain*.

Incidentally, Owain of Rheged's father, Urien, was recalled in the triad *Three Savage Men of the Island of Britain, who performed the Three Unfortunate Assassinations*, where his death was laid at the door of Llofan Llaw Ddifro. This same Urien was also remembered in the *Three Battle-Leaders of the Island of Britain* who gained revenge for the wrongs done to them from their graves. The triad-writer did not explain how. Another son of Urien – Rhiwallawn – was recalled in the second of the *Three Fettered War-Bands of the Islands of Britain*, which described him fighting the Saxons. The writer of this triad explained that its name arose from the unlikely decision of these warriors to place horses' fetters on their own feet in battle; presumably as a restraint to ensure they did not flee in the face of enemy attack. The third of these triads also involved a battle with the Saxon enemy. This time the enemy king was Edwin of Northumbria (died 633) and the Welsh warband was led by Belyn of Llyn, the battle being fought at Bryn Edwin in Rhos (northern Wales).

Edwin also featured in the *Three Defilements of the Severn*. This triad featured Cadwallawn and the armies of the Cymry (Welsh) on one side and Edwin with the armies of Lloegr (England) on the other. So great was this conflict, according to this triad, that the river Severn 'was defiled from its source to its mouth', presumably meaning that the waters were stained with blood due to battle. This triad then went on to record other 'defilements' that were anything but self-explanatory. The second was 'the gift of Golydan from Einiawn son of Bedd, king of Cornwall' (which seems to explain nothing), while the third was due in some way to 'Calam the horse of Iddon son of Ner from Maelgwn . . .'[20] Of these, only the first is readily understandable and the others seem lost in obscurity. The third, though, did involve another very famous king: Maelgwn of Gwynedd (died *c.*547 of plague).

A mixture of enigmatic and historical characters is found

in the triad the *Three Roving Fleets of the Island of Britain*. The first ('The Fleet of Llawr Son of Eiryf') appears to derive from a character whose name may be translated as 'Solitary son of Number'.[21] On the other hand, the 'Fleets of Divwg Son of Alan/Alban' and the 'Fleet of Solor/Dolor Son of Murthach/Mwrchath King of Man' seem to have referred to actual events shorn of myth and legend but we cannot tell in what period they were set.

The third of the *Three Unrestrained Ravagings of the Island of Britain* described Aeddan the Wily coming to the court of Rhydderch the Generous at Alclud and stripping it of all its resources. Aeddan the Wily (in Welsh, Aeddan Fradog) was Aedán mac Gabráin, king of the Scots-Irish kingdom of Dál Riata (in Argyll, Scotland), *c.*600.[22] The raid in question was on the stronghold of the British kingdom of Strathclyde at Dumbarton.

Another historical character to be remembered in a triad was Geraint son of Erbin, who was named as one of the *Three Seafarers of the Island of Britain* and was probably Geraint of Dumnonia (south-west Britain), who reigned in the late sixth or early seventh century. Or the ruler, who was later dimly remembered, may have been the king named Geraint, who was mentioned by the Anglo-Saxon, Aldhelm, and who was attacked by the West Saxons *c.*710.[23]

Some Welsh wishful thinking lay behind the second of the *Three Fortunate Assassinations*. This involved the killing of Edelfled, king of Lloegr (England), by Ysgafnell son of Dysgyfdawd. In fact, as we have seen, the Northumbrian king, Æthelfrith, was actually killed in battle against the East Anglian king, Rædwald in 617. What is interesting is that in another triad – *Three Chieftains of Deira and Bernicia, and the Three were Sons of a Bard* – Ysgafnell was placed in the right geographical context, since Æthelfrith was a Bernician king who annexed Deira. However, this annexation was of another Anglo-Saxon kingdom and it seems that, by the time he did it, British power had been eclipsed in the north-east of what was becoming England.

It is rather appropriate that this brief overview of the triads ends with legend presented as history; for the writers of the triads – though informed by Welsh history – viewed it through the lens of mythology and legend.

18

THE MYTHOLOGY OF THE NORTH

Echoes of earlier mythologies have survived among the Gaelic-speaking population of western Scotland; this is a region that is historically, linguistically and culturally closely linked to Ireland. During the fifth century this connection was strengthened when areas of the western coastlands were settled by a tribal group called the Scotti, whose original home was in the Irish petty-kingdom of Dál Riata in County Antrim. Increasingly influential, these Scots-Irish eventually united with the Picts (see below), in 844, to form a united kingdom under Cináed (Kenneth) mac Ailp'n.[1] The matter, though, may have been even more complex with movement occurring in *both directions* across the North Channel and a number of experts now conclude that the evidence is lacking for a single dedicated colonization of Argyll by a single Irish group.

Even more complex is the fact that the linguistic shift

in the area from British (Brittonic) speech to Gaelic is not reflected in the archaeology, which suggests continuity from the late first century AD to the seventh century. Furthermore, the possibility that Gaelic-speaking British immigrants may have been present in north-east Ireland may help explain the presence of Gaelic speakers on both sides of the North Channel by the seventh century.[2] In short, the relationship between south-west Scotland and north-east Ireland was highly complex, with reciprocal movement of linguistically related peoples affecting both areas. What is clear, though, is that Scotland was greatly influenced by Irish Gaelic culture by the seventh century and probably had been for a long time before this.

In addition, Scottish myths also survive from the time when southern Scotland was British and closely integrated into the British kingdoms of what we now call northern England. Before the Anglo-Saxon conquests, of course, there was no such thing as 'England' and before the expansion of Scots-Irish power there was no such thing as 'Scotland' either. Consequently, these northern British kingdoms (Rheged, Gododdin and Strathclyde) once dominated Cumbria, Lothian and what would later become south-west Scotland.

And some of the myths of the North may also have had their roots in that mysterious people of northern Scotland – the Picts. Part of the enigma of the Picts derives from the fact that they have left no written records. This is in contrast to the British kingdoms of southern Scotland who – despite succumbing to a combination of Anglo-Saxon and Scots-Irish assault – have left a literature that was preserved in Wales as a remnant of the 'Old North'. The Scots-Irish who migrated from northern Ireland and colonized south-west Scotland, and whose expansion of power finally eclipsed both the northern British and the even more northerly Picts (and who eventually gave their name to Scotland), have also left a range of written records preserved in both Scotland and in Ireland. So, who were the Picts? The current thinking is that the Picts, far from being a separate ethnic group, were simply the descendants of the Iron Age population of Scotland and almost certainly spoke a P-Celtic Brittonic language related to the British language that eventually developed into Welsh.[3]

This theory, though, is not accepted by all scholars. In the eighth century, the Anglo-Saxon churchman Bede recorded the opinion that there were five languages spoken in Britain: English, British, Scots (Gaelic), Pictish and Latin. In corroboration, when the Irish churchman, Columba, visited the court of Brude, the Pictish High-king, situated on the banks of the river Ness, he required a translator; this suggests that Brude spoke a language distinctly different to Columba's Gaelic. This has led some experts to question whether the Picts were actually a Celtic people at all. If not, their speech may have represented the survival of a Bronze Age language that pre-dated the arrival of the Celtic languages in the British Isles. There is also the possibility that connections with the Baltic may have meant that Pictish contained elements of a Finnic language[4] (Finno-Ugrian being the only surviving non-Indo-European language in northern Europe). Bede thought that it was possible that the Picts were descended from 'Scythians', a term that he used to describe Scandinavia.

On balance though, the most likely answer is that the Picts were, in fact, Celtic;[5] a Brittonic people who spoke a form of P-Celtic that was not always readily understood by speakers of the other Celtic languages in Britain and may have been related to Gaulish.[6] This unintelligibility may have been a matter of dialect or accent. In support of this is the evidence of the Pictish place names of north-east Scotland, which clearly derive from an Indo-European language and not from a lost 'Bronze Age language'. Another interpretation suggests that Pictish was a British language but contained elements of Scottish-Gaelic[7] owing to the proximity of Ireland and frequent trade contacts as well as settlement. Consequently, it would have had features familiar to Irish travellers like Columba without being completely intelligible. So, we will assume that the Picts were a Celtic people and that whatever mythology they contributed to the myths of the North, these form part of the Celtic heritage of the British Isles. However, since they differed little from the other Celtic peoples, it is unlikely that this contribution is now readily distinguishable.

It seems therefore that there was a triple conduit of Celtic mythology that fed into what survives in Scotland – an Irish stream, a British stream and a Pictish stream – but all are likely to have had similar characteristics. Some of these traditions survive in early sources, while many others were only recorded in the sixteenth century and later, as students of folklore collected stories and traditions recounted in rural areas. An example of this is Sir James MacGregor's collection known as *The Dean of Lismore's Book*, which was compiled in the sixteenth century. Many more stories were recorded in the nineteenth and early twentieth centuries. This, of course, poses a problem: how many represent survival of an earlier mythology and how many are much later developments without ancient roots? The same problem occurs in assessing the nature of any folklore and opinions differ widely. It can be difficult to achieve a consensus. What is probably a reasonable approach is to conclude that those that appear to echo aspects of mythology preserved elsewhere (in better attested earlier accounts) were probably survivals of beliefs of some antiquity. This is the approach followed here and, consequently, a number of parallels will be drawn between Scottish myths and Irish and Welsh mythologies.

Water-horses and other water monsters

A number of related beliefs concerned dangerous shape-shifting creatures thought to inhabit stretches of water.

The *each uisge* (Scottish-Gaelic for 'water-horse') was
a water spirit, also called the *aughisky* or *capall* (or *each*)
uisce in Ireland. Sometimes known as the *kelpie* (from the
Scottish Gaelic *cailpeach/colpach*, 'colt' or 'bullock'),[8] it
was thought that it could assume the shape of a horse and,
in that form, would graze beside water. This was thought
to happen in November more than any other month. However, if a traveller mounted the 'horse' it would dive into
the water and drown its rider, before devouring the victim.
A similar creature was known on Orkney as the *tangie*;
in the Shetlands as the *shoopiltee* or *searrach uisge*; on the
Isle of Man as the *cabyll-ushtey* or the *glashtin;* and was
called the *ceffyl dŵr* in Wales.[9] Irish tradition claimed that
the seventh-century saint, Féchine of Fore, forced an *each
uisce* to pull his chariot after his horse died. This empha-
sizes the common stratum under both Scottish and Irish
mythology.[10]

Some accounts claimed the water spirit was capable of
transforming itself into a beautiful woman in order to lure
men to their deaths; or a man; or a giant bird. In the form
of a woman it was called the *glaistig*. Other versions of the
tradition claimed it was a large, bull-like animal with a
horse's neck and head. Regarding this, it is significant that
the word *kelpie* (as noted above) could mean both 'bullock'
and 'colt'. Still other versions claimed that it had a serpen-
tine neck and head. This form sounds very much like the
beast often described as the Loch Ness Monster.

The Loch Ness Monster is perhaps the most famous
mythical water-beast in the world. Loch Ness was not the
only stretch of water renowned for its monster. In Ireland
Lough Ree and Lough Fedda were also reputed to be the
homes of water monsters. The monster in Loch Ness was
mentioned in Adomnán's *Life of Saint Columba*, which
was written in the late seventh century.[11] In this account
the Irish saint Columba (died 597) came across the burial
of a man who had been savaged in the loch. By invoking the

name of God and making the sign of the cross, Columba triumphed over the monster, which fled.[12] While this is a remarkably early record of a tradition concerning a monster in Loch Ness, there is the distinct possibility that the monster served a pragmatic role in Adomnán's narrative. It has been noted that in his account of the miracle-working acts of the Irish-born saint, all Columba's encounters with animals in the Gaelic areas of Dál Riata were friendly ones, while all his hostile encounters occurred in Pictish-ruled areas. These included triumphing over a wild boar on Skye, as well as the encounter with the murderous beast of Loch Ness. In this, Adomnán may well have been following a conscious agenda that involved portraying the Scots-Irish positively, in direct contrast to the Picts, who were presented as a hostile people (this hostility extending even to the creatures of their land).[13] In which case, the mythology of the Loch Ness Monster may have owed its earliest recording to the complicated ecclesiastical politics that involved the alliance between the Gaelic-speaking monastic community of Iona and the ruling elite of Dál Riata; it was this latter group who eventually came to dominate Pictland and led the Gaelic cultural colonization of Scotland.

The *boobrie* (also known as the *tarbh boibhre*) was another shape-shifting monster with some similarity to the water-horses discussed earlier. It was thought to be able to take on the form of a horse or a cow (a similar equine/bovine duality associated with the name of the kelpie); or even of a gigantic insect with tentacles capable of sucking the blood from a horse. It could also take on the form of a bird. The *boobrie* ate calves, lambs and otters.[14]

The *Cailleach Bheur* (Beira, the Queen of Winter) and Bride, the Queen of Summer

Sometimes also called Beira, Queen of Winter,[15] this being's Gaelic name was the *Cailleach Bheur*. The name derived from the Old Irish for 'veiled one' and has come to mean 'old woman' in Modern Irish and Scottish-Gaelic. In late winter her rule was threatened by Angus of the White Steed and his beautiful wife Bride. Raising storms in January and February to keep out these spirits of spring, the *Cailleach Bheur* also stirred the whirlpool of Corryvreckan, caused rivers to overflow and the late winter and early spring snow to fall. As winter gave way to spring, the *Cailleach Bheur* replenished her strength by drinking from the Well of Youth found on the Green Island of the West. The well was actually a spring bubbling from a crevice in the rock. This then sustained her through the summer until once more she ruled as Queen of Winter. It was essential that she drank from the well before a bird drank from it or a dog barked. If she failed to do this she would die. Having drunk, she then became youthful again, only to mature over the warm months until becoming old at the onset of winter. Non-Gaelic speakers of the north-east also spoke of a storm-causer named 'Gentle Annie' whose name may have been derived from Anu in Irish mythology and preserved in the Paps of Anu in County Kerry.[16]

In other tellings of this tale it was thought that the *Cailleach Bheur* formed many of the lochs, released rivers from the earth, created the hills and shaped the glens. Loch Awe, in Argyll, it was claimed, was formed because she forgot to replace the lid on a well at Ben Cruachan and the water poured out by night to form the loch. Consequently, she was known as *Cailleach nan Cruachan*. A similar story involved one of her maids, named Nessa. The maid was late in covering another well, which also poured out. Frightened, the girl ran away, only to be turned by the *Cailleach Bheur* into the river Nessa. This motif of a river being formed from an overflowing well also featured in the Irish myth concerning Boann and the origins of the river Boyne.

The whirlpool of the Corryvreckan was where the *Cailleach Bheur* washed her shawl. There, in the sea between the islands of Jura and Scarba, was where her 'washing pot' was located. It was also there that she drowned Breckan, the son of a king of the Scots.

The giant-sons of the *Cailleach Bheur* were known as the *Fooar* and lived in the mountains and deep caves. Some were horned like deer, while others had many heads. The gigantic size of these creatures indicated their Otherworld origins in a way found in both Welsh and Irish mythology. One encounter with a family of such gigantic beings was said to have involved a man named 'Finlay the hunter', who eventually triumphed over all the giant family, including the great hag who presided over it.

Since the *Cailleach Bheur* was considered a being of the wild places it is not surprising to learn that folklore associated her with wild animals: eagles, foxes, deer, goats, sheep and wild cattle.[17] Mountainous places associated with her included Beinn na Caillich on the Isle of Skye; and in Glen Cailleach (Perthshire) a number of strangely shaped stones at Tigh nan Cailleach were thought to represent the *Cailleach Bheur*, Bodach her husband and their children.

A similarly fearsome female creature associated with the *Cailleach Bheur* was the Thunder Hag. Wreaking havoc on Scotland, she was eventually felled by a spear thrown by a hero named Conall Curlew.

Another monstrous creature of the wild places was the West Highland *fachan*. Envisaged as having one leg, one arm and one eye, and armed with a flail, it was also known as the *athach* or the *direach*. One was said to frequent the lonely Glen Eitive.[18]

Bride, on the other hand, was remembered in Gaelic folklore as the bringer of summer growth and fertility. In some areas she was associated with snakes and a rhyme ran:

Today is the Day of Bride,
The serpent shall come from his hole,
I will not molest the serpent,
And the serpent will not molest me.[19]

On Bride's Day milk was poured on the ground, porridge was thrown into the sea. In other areas of Scotland
the sea-being (probably once considered a deity) being
honoured was called Shony.[20]

Beings of the sea: Blue Men, Finmen, mermaids and the seal-people

Between the Inner and Outer Hebrides were thought to
reside a particularly dangerous kind of aquatic being that
resembled humans. These were the Blue Men of the stretch
of water between Lewis and the Shant islands; they sank
boats but spared sailors who could complete the half-lines
of poetry they called out.[21] When on calm days the Minch
was turbulent it was thought to be because the swimming
of the Blue Men stirred up the sea.

On the Orkneys this belief in sea-beings included the
so-called Finmen. Tall and dark, they could conjure up a
fleet of phantom boats or make their own boat invisible.
Destroying the tackle of any fisherman who dared enter
their aquatic territory, they also let slip the anchor of
offending boats and allowed the tide to carry them away.
Alternatively, they would smash a boat's oars or hole the
vessel. However, marking the line-sinker and the fishing
boat with the sign of the Christian cross would keep the
Finmen away. An obsession with silver meant that a Finman
pursuing a fishing boat could be distracted by throwing a
silver coin into the sea. Finmen were also believed to sometimes kidnap human women to make them their wives.

On Orkney, mermaids were thought to be the daughters
of the Finfolk. A number of mermaid-related beliefs were
recorded by Orcadian folklorist, Walter Traill Dennison
(1826–94). The mermaids were thought to be beautiful,
with long, golden hair and white skin – but from the waist
down they were fish. Only by gaining a human husband
could a mermaid shed her fishtail and walk on dry land.
If she failed in this she was doomed to a life of increasing

ugliness. If a young man vanished in the turbulent waters around Orkney, the disappearance was often blamed on a mermaid.

On Stronsay, the rock formation in Mill Bay known as the 'Mermaid's Chair' was considered the place from which a mermaid would calm the stormy sea with her singing. This characteristic of singing was one shared with sirens from Classical mythology. This may have been because the belief in mermaids was influenced by these foreign traditions. Alternatively, the two traditions may have developed independently. As well as calming the sea, a mermaid could also charm a man with her singing. A charm to break this spell was:

> Geud tak a care o' me! Geud's neem,
> I hear de mermaid sing;
> Hid's bonnie, bonnie, bit no sae bonnie,
> As Geud's bells I heeven ring.[22]

Orcadian traditions also included beliefs in the 'selkies' or seal-people. These seal-people were, it was believed, able to transform themselves into humans. How frequently this occurred varied within different traditions. Some said it happened only on Midsummer's Eve, other accounts suggested every ninth night. Then they would dance on the beach by moonlight. In order to return to the sea the selkies had to put on their sealskin once more. If it was lost or stolen then they could no longer transform themselves back into seals. There is something in this reminiscent of the shape-shifters that are so common a feature in Irish mythology. Furthermore, it was thought that selkie-men (being highly attractive) would come ashore in the hope of seducing human women. Other accounts spoke of selkie-girls (also thought to be beautiful) captured by human men who denied them their sealskins, keeping them as captive-wives on land.[23]

By the time folklorists recorded these beliefs, the Fin-folk and the seal-people were considered distinct races of aquatic beings. The former were regarded as malevolent, with the latter being considered fairly benign. However, on Shetland the two were not so differentiated and the seal-appearance was simply one of the methods used by the shape-shifting Finfolk. Consequently, it is likely that the original myth was of a more threatening race of under-water beings reminiscent of the Irish Fomorians, living in their underwater fortress (see Chapter 5).

The idea of the 'Land under Waves' that featured in a number of traditions relating to beings living in under-water worlds may in part have been based on reflections in still waters, especially in lochs.

The fairy-folk

This term covers rather a large range of Otherworld crea-tures known from Scottish folklore and having paral-lels with Irish rural beliefs and similar beliefs found in a number of cultures.

On Orkney, as in Ireland, the fairy-folk were thought to inhabit prehistoric burial mounds. On Orkney the term *trow* was often used to describe the inhabitants of these mounds. This may represent a mixture of Celtic fairy-beliefs and a belief in trolls originating from the Vikings. The Orcadian fairies and *trows* could differ in appear-ance but both were much feared. It is difficult to unravel the original beliefs that lay behind the concept of such fairies. One possibility is that they represented defeated former inhabitants who were driven into subjugation, extinction or living on the margins by later colonists (par-ticularly the Norse in the northern and western isles). The fact that the word *pight* (Pict) became interchangeable with fairy and *trow* on Orkney may support this inter-pretation.

Generally, though, the most likely explanation is that

the Scottish fairy-folk were all that remained of beliefs in pagan gods and goddesses from before the Christian conversion. The tradition would then bear a close resemblance to the Irish medieval beliefs concerning the *Tuatha Dé Danann* after they had relinquished control of Ireland to the Milesians. In this Irish tradition, the *Tuatha Dé Danann* then became the inhabitants of the Otherworld of *Tír na nÓg*, which was often entered through prehistoric burial mounds, the fairy *sídhe* (see Chapter 8). Evidence supporting this interpretation can be found in Orcadian folklore that both fairies and selkies were descended from the Fallen Angels, and whether they fell to earth or into the sea resulted in them becoming either fairies or selkies. This was clearly influenced by medieval and later Christian beliefs that sought to bring the Celtic mythologies into line with biblical cosmology.

Scottish fairies were often associated with green, which was therefore considered an unlucky colour for a woman to wear. Hence the proverb:

A Graham in green
Should never be seen.[24]

Human interaction with fairy-folk appeared in a number of Scottish traditions (as in Ireland). One particularly notable example was the so-called 'Fairy-Flag' of the MacLeods of Dunvegan Castle. The story associated with this faded piece of cloth is that it was all that was left behind when a fairy-wife of a MacLeod chief returned to the Otherworld. This idea of a human–fairy liaison also featured in Irish traditions.

Similar to these diminutive Otherworld beings were 'bogeys' or 'bogles' of various kinds. Some, such as brownies, were considered helpful. Other bogeys were believed to be destructive; such as the 'bogart'.[25] In Highland areas the form of this name was *bodach*. A similar creature was the *boggan* or *bócan* (also referred to in Ireland), which was thought generally to be dangerous but occasionally friendly. It was thought that a *boggan* would attach itself to a particular family and one tradition named an example of this as having been an attachment to the Coluinn (or Colann) gun Cheann of the MacDonalds of Morar, in the western Highlands.

Variously described as 'brown elves' (a borrowing from Germanic mythology) or 'household goblins', brownies were generally considered to live in rural cottages and to carry out work for 'their' families while the humans slept. They were described as wearing brown clothing. Their supposed helpfulness was the reason why, in 1915, this name was chosen for what was then the youngest group in the Girl Guides Association. Earlier, in 1914, this group had been named 'Rosebuds'[26] but the name was unpopular with the young female members. They took their eventual name from a book (*The Brownies*) written in 1870 by Juliana Horatia Ewing. In this book children were encouraged to act like helpful brownies, rather than behaving like lazy bogarts. Bogarts also appeared in the mythology of Cornwall, where they were considered a form of brownie; and a similar creature was thought to exist in Wales (called a *bucca*) and on the Isle of Man (called a *fenodyree*).

The belief in brownies may have had its origins in pre-Christian beliefs in household spirits thought to represent the spiritual character and identity of a family; or even the spirit of an ancestor. This interpretation is reinforced by the Hebridean tradition of giving a milk-offering to the *gruagach*, a form of brownie.[27] It was thought that children were more likely to see them than adults and that, if offered payment or a new suit of clothes to replace their ragged ones, they would disappear.

Similarly elven, but regarded as a solitary creature of the

woods, was the *ghillie dhu* whose clothes were made from leaves. It was thought to usually live in birch woods.[28]

Water-spirits at the fords and personified rivers

A number of water spirits were thought to reside at fords threatening travellers; this was a tactic associated with the kelpie.[29] This is reminiscent of the similar connection made between female spirits and deities and fords found in Irish mythology.

Folklore also suggested the association of rivers with beings who were once probably thought of as goddesses in local pre-Christian mythology. Examples include the river Forth, which was known as the 'deaf or soundless one' and the river Clyde, which was known as 'the purifying one', probably owing to its scouring the surrounding land when in flood.[30] This personification of rivers was also a feature of Irish mythology and underlies a number of river-names that survive in what are, or were, Celtic-speaking areas.

The 'Scottish Arthur'

Scottish traditions concerning Arthur are not represented by a body of literature to match that of Wales or indeed France (with its Romance traditions). Nevertheless, there were medieval Scottish works that focused on the illegitimate birth of Arthur as a counterargument to Edward I of England's claim that his own right to lordship over Scotland was based on the rule of Arthur. These medieval works included John of Fordun's *Chronicle of the Scottish People* (*Chronica Gentis Scotorum*), written *c*.1385, and Walter Bower's mid fifteenth-century *Scotichronicon*, which emphasized the illegitimacy of Arthur's birth as a result of Merlin's 'unlawful arts'. This was expressed even more strongly in the mid fifteenth-century *Scottis Originale*, which described Arthur as a 'whore's son' contaminated by Merlin's magic.[31] Clearly, the magical nature of Arthur, as detailed by Geoffrey of Monmouth in the twelfth century, could be turned against the famous king. On the other hand, other Scottish commentators (like the Welsh and Cornish) countered English propaganda by stating that Arthur was their (i.e. British) champion and that he did not conquer them; rather they were inheritors of his kingdom.[32] Other accounts placed Scottish knights in Arthur's entourage. These included the fifteenth-century *Gologros and Gawaine*, which celebrated that Gawain was a prince of Lothian or the Orkneys.

Below this educated and political manipulation of the Arthur-myth existed a different stratum of beliefs that represented a more populist view of the mythical Arthur. In these traditions, as in the comparable Welsh sources, Arthur was the gigantic figure who left his mark on the landscape. Consequently, Arthur's Seat is still the name of the landscape feature outside Edinburgh and, as early as the 1170s, Arthur's Bower was located at Carlisle, while a number of locations in the Scottish Lowlands bear testimony to the fame of Arthur. Gaelic sources located his court at Dumbarton and at Dunbuck.[33] Much later folklore named Drumelzier, near Peebles, as the site of Merlin's grave. The Eldon Hills near Melrose were the location of an encounter between Canonbie Dick and Arthur's knights sleeping in a cave, but Dick blew a horn, rather than drawing a sword that he found there, which rendered him ineligible to wake the sleepers. Arthur's O'en near Falkirk was called *Furnus Arthuri* in 1293, although it was actually a ruined Roman building. William of Worcester, in 1478, claimed Arthur kept his Round Table at Stirling Castle and a sixteenth-century source claimed that a feature there was the *Tabyll Round*, and this is sometimes located at the centre of a formal garden constructed there in the seventeenth century. A cairn east of Laurencekirk (Aberdeenshire) is called Arthurhouse, while a land grant of 1339 named a *Fons Arthuri* (Arthur's Fountain) near

Crawford, in Strathclyde on the upper Clyde. Ben Arthur is the name of a Highland peak west of Loch Long (Argyll and Bute) and Dumbarrow Hill in Tayside is sometimes called Arthur's Seat. Also on Tayside, near Coupar Angus, was Arthur's Stone.[34] These were attempts to name landscape features according to their connection with the mythical king and to locate Arthur in an imagined local landscape of a type seen as early as the ninth century in Wales, in the geographical features mentioned in *The History of the Britons* (*Historia Brittonum*).

Later folklore traditions also revealed that a wilder and even more mythological Arthur, reminiscent of the hero of the Welsh boar-hunt, was also preserved in Scottish accounts. A sixteenth-century rhyme, the *Complaynt of Scotland*, encapsulated this wild-hunting Arthur, who was a long way from the courtly concerns of the better educated:

Arthour knycht he raid on nycht,
With gyltin spur and candil lycht.[35]

(Arthur knight he rides by night,
With gilded spur and candle light.)

Perhaps the most curious survival of this tradition of a Scottish Arthur of night, wind and storm was in Beatrix Potter's *The Tale of Squirrel Nutkin*. In it the mischievous squirrel recited a rhyme that ran:

Arthur O'Bower has broken his band,
He comes roaring up the land!
The King of Scots with all his power,
Cannot turn Arthur of the Bower![36]

After this recitation, Nutkin made a sound like the wind and so gave away the meaning of the riddling rhyme.

With this combination of medieval fame, allied with a more ancient strand of Celtic mythology, this brief exploration of Scottish mythology closes.

19

THE MYTHOLOGY OF THE 'WEST WELSH': CORNISH MYTHS AND LEGENDS

The Cornish are the descendants of the 'West Welsh', who once spoke a language related to the other P-Celtic Brittonic languages (Primitive Welsh, Cumbric, Cornish and Breton).[1] Although ostensibly conquered by the West Saxon king, Egbert, in 814, Cornwall remained peripheral to Wessex and the later emerging kingdom of England in the late-ninth and early-tenth century. In the Viking Wars, the Cornish were allied at times with the Scandinavian enemies of Wessex and remained relatively independent of direct West Saxon rule. In 927, the Anglo-Saxon king, Æthelstan, fixed the border with the 'West Welsh' (the Cornish) on the river Tamar and with the Welsh at the river Wye.[2] Before its eventual annexation by the Anglo-Saxon state of England, after resisting Anglo-Saxon military expansion for centuries, Cornwall had a distinctive Celtic identity derived from the survival of British language and culture in the south-west as part of the Celtic kingdom of Dumnonia. However, its Celtic legacy survived in a sense of separate identity, an immediately noticeable landscape of Celtic place names, traditions and stories that formed part of a culture that had once been common across Britain and a language (*Kernewek*, Cornish) that finally seems to have died out in the eighteenth century. The last fluent speaker of Cornish is popularly believed to have been Dolly Pentreath, a fish-seller in the fishing village of Mousehole who died in 1777, although this assertion remains disputed. The language has been revived in the twentieth century. What is clear is that Cornwall has a varied tradition of mythology and legend that is derived from its Celtic roots, although at a number of points this was influenced by the manipulation of those myths and legends by non-Celtic cultures.

Arthur of the 'West Welsh'

Unlike Wales, Cornwall has not preserved any of its early medieval Romance tradition regarding Arthur (assuming any existed in the first place) but a number of other traditions concerning Arthur have survived in a class of literature known as the Cornish *drolls*. In the early modern period *droll*-tellers were itinerant storytellers who travelled between villages recounting traditional stories, embellished with their own flair and imagination. As with many such oral accounts it can be difficult to differentiate the ancient material from the modern additions. Nevertheless, the nature of some of the strands within the *drolls* suggests that some at least were of considerable age.

That Arthur was a popular character within these tales is supported by a significant Arthurian component in a play, called *The Life of St Kea* (*Bewnans Ke*), from the second half of the sixteenth century. Written in Middle Cornish, it offers tantalizing evidence to suggest that there was once a substantial amount of Arthurian material in Old and

Middle Cornish that has since been lost. In *The Life of St Kea*, the saint returned from Brittany to attempt to prevent a civil war between Arthur and his nephew, Modred (a name also appearing in Welsh sources in the forms Medrawd or Melvas/Melwas). The cause of the conflict was the abduction of Guinevere by Modred. The abduction of Arthur's wife was well known in Welsh medieval sources and there is no conclusive evidence that *The Life of St Kea* preserved an independent Cornish contribution to this legend. It is, in fact, more likely that it retold, in Cornish, a tale already well known from the Welsh (and perhaps Breton) sources. Parts of it also appear derived from Geoffrey of Monmouth's twelfth-century *History of the Kings of Britain* (*Historia Regum Britanniae*).[3]

Cornwall featured in a number of medieval Arthurian stories. Geoffrey of Monmouth located both Arthur's conception and birth at Tintagel and entwined this with the magic of Merlin, which allowed Uther Pendragon to take on the form of Gorlois, Duke of Cornwall, in order to seduce his wife, Ygerna. One of the suggested locations for Arthur's court was at Kelliwic or Celliwig, in Cornwall; this is a claim found in a number of medieval sources including *What Man is the Porter?* (*Pa wr yw'r Porthor?*) and *Culhwch and Olwen* (*Culhwch ac Olwen*). St Michael's Mount featured as the location of Arthur's battle with a monstrous giant in Geoffrey of Monmouth's work and in Sir Thomas Malory's *Le Morte d'Arthur* (*The Death of Arthur*), which was printed in 1485. However, these are not Cornish medieval traditions; rather, they are Norman, Welsh and English medieval traditions *about* Cornwall. Whether the same beliefs were held in Cornwall at the time is difficult to tell, since the later Cornish evidence may have been derived from the earlier non-Cornish sources rather than offering corroboration.

Nevertheless, there clearly were Cornish versions of Arthurian tales. This is evidenced by the Cornish glosses in

the commentary on Merlin's prophecies written by John of
Cornwall. This was the twelfth-century *Prophecy of Merlin*
(*Prophetiae Merlini*) written in Latin hexameters. John
claimed that it was based on a lost original that was written
in the Cornish language. This is highly unlikely for three
main reasons: firstly, it repeated Geoffrey of Monmouth's
unlikely claim that his own book was based on a lost British
manuscript, almost certainly to enhance the authority of his
own work; secondly, Merlin only became widely famous
due to Geoffrey, and so John's work was clearly dependent on his work and not based on ancient sources; thirdly,
the 'prophecies' were clearly fabricated in order to refer to
events of the first half of the twelfth century in the strug-
gle between Stephen and Matilda over the English crown.
However, the Cornish references suggest that it did also tap
into some, otherwise unrecorded, Cornish Arthurian tales.
Additional comments, in Cornish, written in the margins
of the Latin work provide some of the earliest survivals of
the Cornish language. Furthermore, the association of Tintagel with King Mark of Cornwall in the story of Tristan
and Isolde (see below) may suggest that there was some
independent tradition that fed into both Geoffrey of Monmouth's work and that of the writers of the Tristan tales.

This connection of Arthur with Cornwall was enhanced
by the popularity of the legendary love story of Tristan
and Isolde (or Iseult). This love story survives in a number
of different versions but its core information centred on the
mission of Tristan to Ireland to win Isolde of Ireland as a
bride for his uncle, King Mark of Cornwall. On the return
trip to Cornwall the two accidentally drank a love potion
intended for the bridal couple, fell irreversibly in love and
consummated this before their arrival at Mark's Cornish
court. The rest of the story then followed their trials, dangers and adventures that were set in motion by this series of
events. The end of the story varied in the different medieval
versions. In one, the lovers eventually parted and Tristan

went into exile and eventually married Isolde of Brittany but could not forget his first love. In the prose versions of the story, Tristan was eventually murdered by Mark. In the verse Romances, Tristan was wounded in battle and died of despair when his jealous wife told him that the ship carrying Isolde of Ireland to heal him carried black sails (not the white that signalled she was on board). On hearing of this, Isolde of Ireland died of grief. The two lovers were buried together and a vine sprouted from his grave, a rose from hers, and the two eventually intertwined.[4]

The amount of Cornish material in versions of this tale suggests that it derived from Cornish folklore that pre-dated the work of Geoffrey of Monmouth.[5] Local knowledge certainly seems to have underpinned one version of the story: that of the French writer, Béroul, in his mid twelfth-century Anglo-Norman *Romance of Tristan* (*Roman de Tristan*). He referred to several motifs, such as Tristan's leap and the presence of Isolde's robe in St Samson's chapel, which pointed to pre-existing Cornish legends of some antiquity (perhaps from the tenth century).[6] The presence of an inscribed stone at Castle Dore commemorating 'Drustanus . . . son of Cunomorus' may either refer to an original – and historical – Tristan ('Drustanus' being a form of 'Tristan'). Alternatively, its existence may have encouraged the localization of a story that was originally set elsewhere (see below).

The Tristan legends were not themselves Arthurian but the two themes (the magical love story of Tristan and Isolde, and the mythical King Arthur) became intertwined in the twelfth century. It should, though, be noted that, while the Cornish connection seems plausible, the original story may not have been Cornish, since Tristan's name was originally Pictish in origin and it is possible that it was yet another example of a transplant from the 'Old North' that then, in this case, became localized in Cornwall. The story also contained themes found elsewhere in Germanic and Persian sources, so the whole 'Cornish legend' may actually have been a composite creation, drawing on many mythical tropes and themes (including some Cornish ones) that began in northern Britain. It was then transmitted to Brittany (perhaps via Cornwall) and from there to France, before being reintroduced to Cornish folklore through its medieval popularity in French literature. The medieval story appeared in various forms, including German, Anglo-Norman, French, Scandinavian and English versions (in both verse and prose).

Despite these doubts about the Cornish roots of some legends, there is still clear evidence that Arthur was a highly popular figure in medieval Cornwall and that the Arthur so revered was very much of the mythical form noted elsewhere. A Cornish tradition tenaciously clung to the belief that Arthur was not dead. In 1113, French canons from Laon, fundraising in Cornwall, precipitated a near-riot when they remarked that Arthur was dead. This extremely important piece of information was recorded in passing, close to the event, by Herman of Tournai (also known as Herman of Laon), in 1146.[7]

Later folklore, though, accepted his death and located it at Slaughterbridge, between Camelford and Tintagel, where a sixth-century inscribed stone has been located. The stone, though, has no bearing on Arthur and the location was probably chosen because of the coincidence of the location of the stone and the name of the river Camel, which then became associated with the legendary battle of Camlan. Dozmary Pool, on Bodmin Moor, became the place into which Arthur's sword, Excalibur, was thrown following his death. Bodmin Moor has other sites similarly associated with Arthur. Arthur's Bed is the name of a rock formation (actually the product of weathering), near Trewortha Tor; King Arthur's Hall, near St Breward, is actually a stone-walled prehistoric enclosure; King Arthur's Downs, near Garrow Tor, describes the surrounding area. These are familiar attempts to localize the Arthurian legend by reference to landscape and prehistoric features of a kind familiar from ninth-century Wales and from medieval Scotland. They testify to the popularity of the myth, not the movements of a real person.

Examples of Arthur asleep beneath a hill occur at St Michael's Mount,[8] in addition to the many other examples elsewhere in Britain such as: at Craig-y-Ddinas (Mid Glamorgan, Wales), South Cadbury (Somerset), Sewingshields (Northumberland), Richmond Castle (Yorkshire), Alderly Edge (Cheshire), the Eildon Hills (Borders, Scotland) and Freeborough Hill (Yorkshire) to name a number of the other similar sites. Arthur asleep in a cave was noted as a common reason for caves bearing his name in western Cornwall in the nineteenth century.[9]

A distinctive Cornish tradition claimed that the dying Arthur was transformed into a bird. Interestingly enough, this Cornish belief was actually first preserved in the unlikely setting of a Spanish work of fiction: in *Don Quixote* (published in 1612) Cervantes mentioned an English superstition regarding a raven or crow.[10] Curiously enough, another reference to this belief also came from Spain, where it appeared in Julian del Castillo's *Historia de los Reyes Godos*[11] (*History of the Kings of the Goths*) of 1624. It was then reported, in the nineteenth century, that an eighteenth-century youth was rebuked for shooting at a raven on Marazion Green since a local claimed King Arthur lived in such a bird. Robert Hunt, who investigated this claim in the nineteenth century, found that the bird then associated with Arthur was always the chough and not the raven.[12] Other Cornish traditions concur and the more usually named species is the red-legged member of the crow family, the Cornish chough (family: Corvidae, subspecies: pyrrhocorax). This was reflected in a Welsh alternative name of *bran Arthur* (Arthur-crow) for the chough. In one isolated account, the bird named was the puffin.[13]

The more usual identification of a member of the crow family is more consistent with Welsh traditions about the mythical significance of these birds, and ravens appeared loosely connected to Arthur in the early medieval poem *Y Gododdin* (*The Gododdin*) and – via Owain and his ravens – in the later medieval account found in the *Dream of Rhonabwy* (*Breuddwyd Rhonabwy*). In later folklore, croaking ravens were regarded as heralds of death.[14] It was, though, the particular association of Arthur's death and choughs that prompted the poet R. S. Hawker (1803–75) to write in his poem 'The Wreck':

> And mark yon bird of sable wing,
> Talons and beak all red with blood,
> The spirit of the long lost king
> Pass'd in that shape from Camlan's flood![15]

Cornish giants

The giant of St Michael's Mount – claimed to have been killed by Arthur – also appeared in a Cornish folk tradition as having been killed by Jack the Giant killer,[16] so well-known from English nursery rhymes. In this account, the giant's name was Cormoran and he raided local farms, stealing livestock. This continued until a local farmer's son dug a huge pit and by camouflaging it caused the giant to crash into it, whereupon Jack killed him with one blow. In one tradition the giant-killing took place at Morvah; in another it occurred on the Mount itself and gave rise to a depression still discernible there.

Another tradition concerning Cormoran had him as the rival of another giant, named Tregeagle, on Tren Crom hill, some five miles away. While throwing stones at one another, Cormoran's wife was killed when one struck her on the head. She was buried under Chapel Rock. This rock sits beside the causeway that links St Michael's Mount to the mainland.

The giant Tregeagle was also associated with other Cornish landscape features.[17] He was, it was claimed, responsible for blocking the mouth of the river Camel with sandbanks, thus making life difficult for the fishermen of Padstow; he was also held responsible for accidentally dropping sand to form Loe Bar in the sea near Porthleven. What is interesting is that, alongside the folk tale of the giant Tregeagle, another Cornish tradition referred to a seventeenth-century magistrate or steward[18] named Jan Tregeagle, who was punished for his sinful life by being set impossible eternal tasks such as draining Dozmary Pool, on Bodmin Moor, with a leaking limpet shell, and weaving a rope of sand in Gwenvor Cove. The story went on to say that his howls of frustration mixed with storm winds and that, if he ceased his tasks, he would be dragged to hell by the hell-hounds. Known in Devon as *yeth*-hounds, one of these beasts featured in Sir Arthur Conan Doyle's *The Hound of the Baskervilles* (serialized in *Strand Magazine*, 1901–2). While this was set in Devon, it was probably a survival of the wild-hunt motif found in a number of Celtic areas and the connection with Jan Tregeagle supports this interpretation by giving it a Cornish location to accompany that of Devon. While Jan Tregeagle's story was given an apparent historicity by the tradition setting it in a particular time-frame[19] and even stating that his spirit once appeared when called on in a law court,[20] it is likely that there never was such a person. The characteristics of the story suggest that it originated as an amalgamation (and adaption) of well-known Celtic motifs – probably drawn from a number of mythical traditions – and also found elsewhere: a giant associated with impossible tasks (such as in *Culhwch and Olwen*, although there the giant set the tasks), the wild-hunt (associated with the Scottish Arthur) and giant hunting dogs (notably Arthur's dog Cafall). This is not to say that these original Tregeagle stories were in any way Arthurian; rather, it suggests that many different mythological and legendary tales drew on a common reservoir of ideas. In the case of Jan Tregeagle, the later 'historicization' of the character was not unique; Arthur was treated in a similar fashion, although the two characters had no link or relationship in myth or folklore. Although it is interesting that Dozmary Pool also appeared in a Cornish version of the Excalibur myth, it is likely that this localization of an Arthurian Romance-feature was imposed on a location that already had folkloric associations.[21]

Another giant was named Bolster and he troubled a local saint – Agnes – with his desire for her. So large was he that it was claimed that he could place one foot on the rocky outcrop at Carn Brea (near Camborne) and the other foot on the cliffs at St Agnes, about six miles away. Eventually St Agnes challenged him to prove his love for her by filling up a hole in the ground at Chapel Porth with his own blood. Unbeknown to the giant, the hole led down into the sea. As a result, his blood was unable to fill it and he kept on bleeding until he died.

At Ralph's Cupboard, near Portreath, is a collapsed sea cave; this is not an unusual geological feature on this stretch of the north Cornish coast, which faces the full force of the Atlantic. Local folklore, though, claimed that it was the remains of the storage cupboard of a local giant who attacked ships and stored his stolen loot there.

These giant stories are found across the Celtic world and, in fact, constitute a mythological motif found in many cultures. Larger-than-life beings clearly offered a way of explaining any natural landscape feature.

Cornish 'little people'

Belief in the bogart was found in Cornwall as in Scotland. Here, it was thought that whether a brownie remained a brownie or, instead, turned into a bogart was down to how well they were treated by 'their' family. These beings were also often referred to as *pobel vean* (little people) in Cornish, although the term *piskie* is more familiar. The origin of this latter word is uncertain. An association between these 'little people' and the high, wild interior of Cornwall and Devon indicates an origin in a Celtic culture that once dominated these areas of south-west England. Folklore often described them as dancing through the night in deserted spots or engaging in wrestling matches.

In the West Penwith area they were called *spriggans*. Unlike the *piskies*, the *spriggans* were regarded as malevolent. However, some folk tales insisted that the *spriggans* could be bested, as in the case of an old woman in whose house they met to divide up their stolen treasures. One night the woman recited a charm, causing the *spriggans* to flee, and she was left with their golden treasure.[22] They were also associated with hilltops and burial mounds. This is reminiscent of the Irish fairy *sídhe*, which were also associated with prehistoric burial mounds, although in the Irish case the inhabitants of the *sídhe* were not considered to be enemies of people. The *fogou* (underground chamber) named Pixies' Hall, on the Lizard Peninsula, refers to just such a perceived link with underground prehistoric structures.

The 'little people' called *skillywiddens* were also considered to be mischievous, with a reputation for turning milk sour and leading livestock astray in the wild moorland uplands. However, they too could sometimes be caught, in the hope of discovering the location of their hidden treasures.[23]

A more ambiguous being was the *knocker*. These were thought to be diminutive tin miners, whose knocking preceded pit-falls. Consequently, some miners regarded them as malevolent and intent on destruction, while others considered the knocking a warning and well intentioned. Miners would sometimes leave offerings of food in the mines in the hope of placating the knockers. In some areas of Cornwall they were known as *buccas*.

This ambiguity reflected a common feature of the mixed attitude towards these Otherworld beings noted in a number of Celtic areas. It may well originally have been based on a more developed mythology (now lost) that considered the Otherworld as being occupied by different races of beings in different states of alliance or animosity with each other and with people. In Ireland there was a varied Otherworld occupied by Fomorians, *Firbolg* and the *Tuatha Dé Danann*. The same detail of mythological evidence has not survived from other areas.

Mermaids

Given the impact of the sea on both the Cornish landscape and economy it would be surprising if it did not also feature in the area's mythology. References to mermaids occurred in a number of folk tales and one of these was located at Zennor, on the Penwith Peninsula. Here a mermaid fell in love with a young man named Matthew Trewhella, whom she heard singing in the nearby church. She made her way to the church, the two fell in love and he followed her into the sea at nearby Pendour Cove, never to be seen again. In another version the two married and lived happily in Zennor until, on a fishing trip, Matthew was washed overboard. The mermaid followed him and the two were never seen again. In Zennor church a pew-end carved with a mermaid holding a mirror and comb is sometimes claimed as evidence of the event. It is more likely, though, that the whole story became localized near Zennor because of the existence of the pew-end. In short, the pew-end probably prompted the telling of the story, rather than the story prompting the carving of the pew-end.

It may well be that this is a survival of a more complex story. The juxtaposition of the mermaid and the man singing in church may well suggest that the original story was more threatening and derived from a conflict with Christian conduct. The vanishing into the sea of the human lover may originally have been a more alarming tale reminiscent of the humans drowned by mermaids that featured in some Scottish stories. Here, there were distinctly different Orkney traditions associated with the malevolent Finfolk and the more amenable seal-people (the selkies); on Shetland, though, the ambiguity was more apparent since the shape-shifting Finfolk could also make themselves appear to be more benign seal-people in order to trap humans. It is now difficult to be sure what was the original form of the Cornish story and certainly any threat or loss found in a putative original story has been sanitized in the modern version preserved in a gentle folk tale of mer–human love.

The lost land of Lyonesse
Traditions of mermaids recall undersea kingdoms found in both Irish and Scottish folklore. In Cornwall a particularly noteworthy example was the belief in the lost kingdom of Lyonesse, said to have lain beyond Land's End but inundated by a great storm. This tradition made no mention of the kind of undersea beings referred to in Ireland and Scotland, and Lyonesse appeared clearly human in the tale. However, it may have had its origins in two strands of mythology: one being that of drowned lands found in a number of cultures and the other prompted by a tradition that the sea could cover Otherworlds.

Fertility, healing and the seasons
At Towednack, near St Ives, it was said that one April, when spring was slow in coming, it was here that a local farmer threw a hollow log onto his fire in the presence of his neighbours and, as they watched, a cuckoo flew out. At that moment spring returned. It may be that this story was the remains of an older tradition in which ceremonies were enacted – perhaps involving reverence for the cuckoo – as a bringer of spring. Without more information, it is difficult

to decide.

The ambivalent attitude towards May – on one hand the arrival of summer, on the other hand regarded as an unlucky month – was noted in Cornwall by at least one nineteenth-century collector of folklore. Children born in May were regarded as unlucky and called 'May chets'; kittens born in May were often destroyed. A hot May was associated with an increase in deaths in the community.[24]

With regard to weather, the malevolent 'little people' known as *spriggans* were thought to have been responsible for causing storms and unseasonable weather as part of their antagonistic relationship with human society. In this way, the mythology of the Otherworld intersected with attempts to explain climatic problems in this world.

Echoes of earlier pre-Christian traditions may also have underlain the folklore associated with the Logan-stone at Nancledra. It was claimed that it rocked at midnight and that a sick child placed on it at that time would be cured (but only if the sick child was legitimate). A similar healing tradition was claimed for the Creeping Stone at Madron. Here, the tradition was that if a sick person crawled nine times through a hole in the stone they would be cured. A similar tradition of passing sick children through a hole in a stone was recorded concerning the stone at Men-an-Tol and the Tolvan Stone. These stories may have derived from a time when these stones were regarded as embodying the character of a pagan deity with supposed healing powers. If so, the collapse of pagan religious tradition caused the name of any such deity to be forgotten.[25]

Similarly, stories concerning the many Cornish holy wells associated with Celtic saints almost certainly derived from pre-Christian beliefs that certain springs possessed healing powers or were the residence of a local deity or Otherworld being. The throwing of objects into many of these wells, often accompanied by the tying of strips of cloth to nearby branches,[26] would originally have been offerings to the deity of the spring. Among the many wells where these activities were recorded by nineteenth-century collectors of folklore were Madron Well, near Penzance (where pins were dropped into the water), and Monacuddle Grove, near St Austell (where pins were also dropped and rags hung on branches). These activities at times were accompanied by attempts to foretell the future by studying the movement of the water.[27] As with so many aspects of Cornish mythology, these accounts were only recorded very late, often in the nineteenth century. However, they almost certainly derived from much older pre-Christian activities and beliefs, even though the documentary evidence has not survived categorically to prove this.

20

THE MYTHOLOGY OF THE
ISLE OF MAN

Echoes of earlier mythologies survive among the people of
the Isle of Man, situated in the Irish Sea and thirty-three
miles long and thirteen miles wide. This chapter will examine some of the ways in which Manx folk tales preserve
links to earlier Celtic mythology.

The Isle of Man occupies a far from peripheral location.
Easily accessible from the British mainland and from Ireland it is, in effect, in a maritime crossroads and so played
an important role in early medieval history. The earliest
occupants of the island almost certainly spoke a British language but, from the fifth century AD, this became replaced
by Gaelic. Given the close proximity of Ireland and the
relationship in the post-Roman period between kingdoms
in Ireland and what would later be south-western Scotland,
it is hardly surprising to learn that the Isle of Man came to
lie within an area of expanding Gaelic influence.

In the seventh century the island was conquered by the Northumbrian Anglo-Saxons, and in the ninth century it fell under Norse domination and became part of the Viking age Kingdom of the Isles. Despite this, a combined Norse–Gaelic culture survived on the island, fusing Celtic and Scandinavian cultural traits. In 1266 the island became part of the kingdom of the Scots and in 1399 passed into the feudal control of the English crown. Today, it has the intriguing status of being an internally self-governing British Crown dependency and is not fully part of the United Kingdom.

Culturally, the island is considered one of the six 'Celtic nations' (Brittany, Cornwall, Ireland, Scotland, Wales and the Isle of Man). Whatever Brittonic language was originally spoken on Man, it is Gaelic that survives as the Celtic language of the island. To differentiate it from the other Gaelic languages of Ireland and Scotland it is often termed Manx or Manx-Gaelic by English-speakers. Native speakers refer to it as *Gaelg* or *Gailck*; or differentiate it from other Gaelic languages by calling it *Gaelg Vannin* (Gaelic of Man or Mann). The language derived from Primitive Irish. From the nineteenth century, Manx Gaelic rapidly retreated in the face of English, although a revival of the spoken language began in the twentieth century.

There survives no Manx Gaelic literature from earlier than the nineteenth century, with the exception of some sixteenth-century songs and some religious documents. Consequently, although there are clearly many ancient Celtic aspects to the mythology and folklore of the Isle of Man, there is no direct evidence of it. As a result, the mythology of the island can only be deduced from the evidence collected by students of folklore in the eighteenth and nineteenth centuries and later; and in traditions preserved outside the island. Much of this, not surprisingly given the island's location and linguistic history, is closely related to Irish traditions. In addition, it should be remembered that the mythology of the Isle of Man has also been influenced by Norse culture, although, surprisingly, the Norse language failed to survive despite a number of place names reflecting the presence of Norse speakers.

The island of Manannán son of Lír, god of the sea

The origin of the name of the Isle of Man is linked to the mythology of the island. Greek and Roman accounts of the geography of the British Isles variously named it as *Monapia*, *Monaoida*, *Monarina*, *Manavi* and *Mevania*; in Old Irish it was *Mano* and in Old Welsh *Manau*. All of these point to a name that was originally derived from a Brittonic word that later gave rise to the Welsh *mynydd* (mountain).[1] This was probably because it appeared to rise from the sea as a mountain, set in the water. The same name was also used for the area along the lower river Forth (*Manau Gododdin*). However, despite this prosaic origin of the name, in early medieval Irish literature an alternative etymology was implied that linked the island (and by implication its name) with the Irish deity Manannán, who was identified as the son of Lír. He was called Manawyddan in Welsh and was said in Wales to be the son of Llŷr. Clearly, both Irish and Welsh mythology preserved evidence of belief in this pagan deity and the Irish sources provided an apparent location for his activities in the Irish Sea.

In this localization of mythology, the Isle of Man was described as a strangely exotic and Otherworldly place. Names used for it included *Inis Falga*[2] and *Emain Ablach*.[3] The first name may have meant 'the noble isle', while the second name meant 'Emain of the apples'. This description was one it shared with another Otherworldly island in Welsh mythology: *Ynys Afallach* ('island of Afallach', a mythical being whose name derived from 'apples'), from which came the Arthurian 'Avalon'. This is not to suggest an Arthurian location on the Isle of Man; instead, it simply reveals the Celtic association of apples growing on a mysterious island, with a fairy realm or an afterlife location. In Welsh the concept of *Ynys Afallach* probably originally envisaged an island of apple orchards and only later was a mythical being invented whose name personified this. Later, folklore claimed that the island was originally named '*Ellan Sheaynt*, the Isle of Peace, or the Holy Island' and was a place of sunshine, where apples grew all year round, the horses there were fine and the women were beautiful.[4]

This is all the more puzzling given the close proximity of the Isle of Man to Ireland and the likelihood that it was frequently visited by Irish seafarers. From this basis in hints of Otherworld character came direct associations with Manannán, who appears to have been considered responsible for the travel of the souls of the dead to the afterlife. This certainly influenced the writer of *Cormac's Glossary* (*Sanas Chormaic*), which may date from as early as the tenth century; although the earliest surviving manuscript is found in the so-called *Speckled Book* (*Leabhar Breac*) from *c.*1410. Attributed to Cormac of Cashel (died 908), an Irish bishop and King of Munster, the glossary named the Isle of Man as the home of Manannán. The same claim was found in the Irish manuscript of *The Wooing of Luan* (*Tochmarc Luaine*).[5] The mainly fifteenth-century Irish *Book of Fermoy* (also known as the *Book of Roche*) named Manannán as protector of the island, which he did by shrouding it in sea-mist. Scottish sources corroborated this association. Gaelic poetry, such as that found in the sixteenth-century *Leabhar Deathan Lios Mòir* (*Book of the Dean of Lismore*), implied an association between Manannán and Man.

Later Manx folklore named him as the first ruler of the island, and a powerful wizard,[6] which appears to have been an attempt to humanize a figure who was originally a pagan deity. In Manx tradition he was the eponymous representation of the island and its people.[7] At Midsummer, Manx fishermen (who by this time were officially Christian) made offerings of reeds and yellow flowers in a ceremony designed to gain the Manx fishing fleet his assistance.

It seems clear from this brief survey that the association of Manannán with Man was quite separate to the origin of the name of the island. It is possible that there was an early belief that he lived on this island in the Irish Sea. However, it is also possible that an incorrect etymology sought to derive the name of the island from Manannán and it was this process that caused him to then be localized on the Isle of Man. Corroborative evidence for this lies in the fact that none of the other mythical names for Man (or descriptions of it in Irish poetry) describe a real place. Therefore, it seems reasonable to conclude that originally Manannán was thought to reside in some Otherworld realm (location unknown) but that the similarity between the name of this deity and the island caused this Otherworld spot to be relocated into the Irish Sea as the Isle of Man/Manannán.

Manx giants

The creation of Man itself was linked to a folklore that was almost certainly derived from a much older Celtic mythology. In this tradition, Finn MacCooil (the mythical Irish hero Finn or Fionn mac Cumhaill) was once fighting a red-haired Scottish giant. As the Scottish giant ran away to escape Finn, the latter scooped up a huge pile of earth to throw; it missed and landed in the sea, becoming the Isle of Man. The hole so scooped out became Lough Neagh in Ireland.[8] Another story named Finn's Scottish rival as the giant of *Far Rua*, who was passing from Ireland to Scotland by using The Giant's Causeway when he challenged Finn. Another rival was a slower-witted Manx giant who lived on South Barrille; as with the Scottish giant, he was bested by Finn.[9]

In common with a number of Celtic mythologies that linked geographical features with giants (for example, in

Wales and in Scotland), another Manx folk tale claimed that the two channels of the Sound were created as the result of a battle between the Irish giant Finn MacCooil and a local Manx giant known as the Buggane. The Sound is the narrow sea channel separating Man from the small island known as the Calf of Man. The Sound is itself divided by an even smaller island, known as Kitterland. The sea water passing through these channels is frequently turbulent.[10]

According to this tradition, the two giants fought at Burroo Ned and during the battle the Buggane lifted and threw Finn. When he landed, the impressions made by Finn's two feet were then flooded by the sea. It was these two flooded footprints that became the Little Sound and the Big Sound.[11] In another story it was Finn leaping from Ireland that left footmarks in the stone at *Slieu ynnyd ny, Cassyn* ('mountain of the place of the feet').

The Buggane featured in a number of other Manx folklore accounts including one that claimed that he once, in a rage, blew the roof off St Trinian's church, at Greeba, in the parish of Marown. In Manx folklore it became known as *Keeill Vrisht* (broken church).[12] In reality, the little chantry was built in the fourteenth century (on the site of a thirteenth-century church) and fell into disrepair in the seventeenth century. It was originally called St Ninian's. Clearly, the whole tradition of the Buggane connected to this building was developed after the church had fallen into ruins in an attempt to explain what had caused this. In the folklore the church was described as never having had a roof since all attempts to roof it had failed. This tradition is therefore no older that the seventeenth century but has the appearance of an ancient tale. This is a reminder that folklore recorded no earlier than the seventeenth and eighteenth centuries may not be of any great antiquity, since older traditions were often reworked and reapplied to new circumstances and locations (in this case an attempted explanation of why the church lay in ruins).

In another folk tale a lazy woman was almost drowned in punishment by the Buggane until she cut the string of her apron and escaped. But for that, she would have been hurled into the *Spooyt Vooar*, the large waterfall tumbling into Glen Meay.[13]

Fairies and 'little people'

In common with Celtic mythology across a wide geographical area, fairy-folk – the 'little people' – featured in a number of Manx traditions. One of these was the *fenodyree* or *phynnodderee*, a diminutive hairy creature whose name derived from the Manx-Gaelic words *fynney* ('hairy') and *oashyree* ('leggings'). The name was used both as a proper-name and as the designation of a class of fairy beings. Rather like the Scottish brownie, these were sometimes described as helpful beings who would carry out tasks to assist humans. At Marown the folklore tradition stated that one *fenodyree* assisted a farmer there by mowing his meadow but angrily dug up the grass when criticized by the farmer for not mowing it low enough.

Other folklore claimed that the particular *fenodyree* that frequented Gordon had fiery eyes and was stronger than any man. This same tradition used the *fenodyree* as a way of explaining the origins of landscape features in a way usually associated with giants. This involved him throwing stones at his wife, which formed a red-marked stone at Cleigh Fainey and a large rock in the Lagg river.[14]

Being so hairy, these creatures had no need of clothes. It is of interest that in the 1819 Manx translation of the Old Testament passage, Isaiah 34:14a ('Desert creatures will meet with hyenas, and wild goats will bleat to each other'),[15] the words 'wild goats' were translated as *fenodyree*. If offered clothes, the *fenodyree* would depart, in one folk tale declaring '*Bayrn da'n chone, dy doogh da'n choine*' ('Cap for the head, alas, poor head').[16]

Fairies or *ferrishyn* (a Manx form of the English word)

also appeared in a number of Manx folklore tales recorded in the nineteenth century. They were described in
Manx-Gaelic as the *mooinjer veggey* (little people). Their
clothing was said to be blue or green, with red caps;[17] and
their packs of fairy-hounds were described as being all
the colours of the rainbow. One tradition claimed that the
fenodyree was once one of the *ferrishyn* but was punished
for falling in love with a human girl and neglecting his
fairy-duties. A particular fairy fiddle-player, known as
Hom Mooar, also appeared in some Manx folklore. The
connection between music and fairy-people occurred
in another account in which a man was led by invisible
musicians to a spot where 'little people' were having a
banquet. Looking about him he thought that some of the
faces seemed familiar. When offered a silver cup of drink
he was advised by one of these people not to drink or eat,
or he would be unable to return to his family. Wisely, he
followed this advice and poured the drink on the ground.
Those around him disappeared and he was left holding
the silver cup. This was later used to hold the wine of
Communion in the church at Kirk-Merlugh.[18] Another
tradition, recorded in the early twentieth century, told
of a man passing *Crosh molley mooar*, near Poyll Vill,
when he saw a crowd of finely dressed 'men' and 'women'
(apparently fairy-folk) dancing and merry-making,
although they ignored him.[19]

It was said that at Bay Mooar, a fisherman once followed
the sound of music to a cave, within which (though deserted) could be seen tiny footprints circling a rock,[20] where
only shortly before the *mooinjer veggey* had danced. The
places where the 'little people' danced were, it was believed,
usually under hillsides and they frequently lived specifically under ancient burial mounds.[21] This was a feature
common to a number of Celtic traditions and, as in Scotland, was reminiscent of an original belief being derived
from the Irish mythology of the *Tuatha Dé Danann* living

in *Tír na nÓg*, which was often entered through prehistoric mounds. These Irish underground homes were the fairy *sídhe*.

In modern English these fairy-people were sometimes simply called 'themselves', which suggests an unwillingness to name them directly. And, it was thought, they had to be treated carefully. Fairy Bridge, on the road from Douglas to Castletown, was so named because it was thought lucky to greet the fairies when crossing the bridge (and unlucky not to). Another Fairy Bridge is near Kewaigue. Manx traditions tended to describe the *mooinjer veggey* as mischievous or spiteful, although there were occasions when they could be benevolent.

The negative characteristic of the Manx *mooinjer veggey* showed itself in a habit (known in other fairy-traditions) of stealing human children and replacing them with a sickly lookalike who was a fairy-child. One such exchange was said to have occurred at *Closeny Lheiy*, near Glen Meay. There a woman could not understand why her child became more and more irritable '*nytng nyanging*' (night and day). Eventually, with the assistance of a tailor who made to throw the changeling child on the turf fire, she regained her own child again.[22] It was also thought that, on occasions, they could also kidnap adults. One such kidnapping, it was claimed, was attempted at *Crosh molley mooar* and involved an old man travelling home to the Mull from Port Erin. He was seized and forced to accompany those who took him, until freed by a larger member of the Otherworld company and allowed to escape 'before the wind'.[23] Others were held responsible for firing flint arrowheads that dealt out death without breaking the skin, although a blue mark would be found on the body of the person so killed by these arrows.[24] In order to placate the little people, fires were often left burning in the hearth for them to warm themselves, and food and clean water was left out in country areas. This was almost certainly a survival of a custom that had originated in the veneration of pre-Christian local deities and household guardian-spirits.

Hedgehogs were associated in Manx folklore with the fairy-people and the Manx-Gaelic name for them is *arkan sonney* ('lucky urchin'). The name connects these real creatures with a fairy-beast that was thought to be a hairy pig and which, if caught, would cause a silver coin to appear in the pocket of the person who had caught it. For this reason it was known as the 'lucky piggy'. In some accounts it appeared as a white pig with red eyes that was capable of changing its shape. Another pig that was thought to be itself the product of shape-shifting was the black pig into which the Buggane sometimes turned himself. Whether there was a separate mythology of a magical black pig is less certain but possible since it was also thought that if a man did not wash his face for nine days he would be capable of 'seeing' both the wind and the black pig (though why he should wish to was not explained).[25] There seem to be echoes here of other pig-related mythology found in the magical pigs described in Welsh mythology and also that associated with Cornwall.

It was thought that – mirroring human society – the *mooinjer veggey* fished for herring and that, if the lights of their fishing fleet were seen, a human fishing trip the next night would be successful. It was also claimed that by night it was possible to hear the sound of hammering at a place called *Ooig-ny-Seyir* ('coopers' cave'). It was there that the little people constructed the barrels they used to store the herrings that they caught. Similarly, a fisherman landing one foggy night at *Lag-ny-Keilley*, stumbled on a fishing fleet of the little people that was also coming ashore. One called to another: '*Hraaghyn boght as earish broigh, skeddan dy liooar ec vn mooinjer seihll shoh, cha nel veg ain I* ' ('Poor times and dirty weather, herring enough at the people of this world, nothing at us').[26] This suggests that, even with their magic, the herring-fleets of the *mooinjer veggey* were not guaranteed success.

Creatures of the water

The *cabyll-ushtey* or the *glashtin* was thought to be a kind of water-horse (although also described as a kind of goblin in some accounts), whose name derived from the Old Irish word *glais* ('stream'). This mythological creature clearly formed part of a wider Celtic tradition, since similar creatures were recorded in the folklore of Scotland (the *each uisge* or *kelpie*), Ireland (the *aughisky* or *capall aughisky*, or *each uisce*), Orkney (the *tangie*), the Shetlands (the *shoopiltee* or *searrach uisge*) and in Wales (the *ceffyl dŵfr*). While these creatures were not identical, they clearly formed part of a related set of beliefs. The Manx *glashtin* was at times described as having shape-shifting powers used in attempts to attract or kidnap women. The tell-tale sign of this creature lay in its horse's ears. As an illustration of the way in which folklore accounts could intersect there was a belief that the fairy-fiddler known as *Hom Mooar* was a *glashtin*. The Scottish *glaistig* was also thought to have had long-eared characteristic although it was of the opposite gender, being usually described as a beautiful woman.

It must be admitted, though, that the Manx folklore accounts collected in the nineteenth century do not always agree with regard to this creature. This may have been because there were once thought to have been different species of this being or it may have simply been that different versions of the belief developed from a common original; or quite different creatures were confused in the retelling of the tales to the first recorders of these beliefs. When a tradition found on the Calf of Man recounted that the *glashtin* (in this case described as the *glashan*) might assist farmers[27] (a belief usually associated with the *fenodyree*), it is clear that the oral tradition was capable of mutation and apparent conflation of otherwise separate traditions. The complexity of this mythology is further seen in the accounts of the *glashtin*, which described it as emerging from the sea to breed with Manx ponies. When described as the *cabyll-ushtey*, the nature of the creature was unambiguous, since this name derived from the Manx for 'water-horse'. This latter name was used in accounts of creatures whose activities ranged from the benign to the malevolent, the latter including drowning a man who inadvertently rode on such a beast having mistaken it for a horse.

Another aquatic creature was the water-bull (also known in Scottish mythology), the *tarroo-ushtey*. This, like the equine form of the *glashtin*, was thought to sometimes leave the water in order to breed with its land-living counterparts. In this case, though, it was thought that a cow with which it bred would often give birth to a dead calf, and folklore claimed that farmers would chase off any *tarroo-ushtey* found among their cattle.

Given the proximity of the sea it is no surprise that mermaids appeared in Manx stories just as they did in Scottish and Cornish tales. One, the mermaid of *Gob ny Ooyl*, was clearly attracted to a young man that she saw when he was returning from a fishing trip. In return for apples that he brought to her, she brought good luck to the family.[28] This connection of an Otherworld being to the apples so closely associated with magical places was probably not coincidental and may once have been part of a larger mythology now lost.

Other evidence for a belief in an underwater realm can be found in the claim that off Langness lay a city that was drowned when the giant Finn struck the ground so hard with his club that the sea poured into the hollow. It was in this drowned city that mer-people lived.

Mauthe Doog or Moddey Dhoo

This creature was thought to be a large black dog that haunted Peel Castle.[29] It was described as being as large as a calf and having very large eyes. It was also known as the *Moddey Dhoo* or *Doo*. Sir Walter Scott made use of this creature in the form the 'Manthe Dog' in his 1823 novel

Peveril of the Peak (one of the Waverley series). In the Manx account, one night at Peel Castle a drunken soldier dared the animal – which each night emerged from a dark passage to sleep by the guardroom fire – to accompany him as he took the castle keys, alone, down the dark passage. Horrific cries echoed from the passageway and, when the man returned, he was struck dumb with terror and died three days later. As if to give credence to the story, it was claimed it had occurred in the seventeenth century, in the time of King Charles II.[30] While there were distinct differences, there was still something in this folklore of the death-dealing dog of Peel Castle reminiscent of the *yeth*-hounds of the south-west of England. The folklore may originally have been derived from a tradition much older than the claimed seventeenth-century setting.

21

THE MYTHOLOGY OF BRITTANY

Echoes of earlier mythologies also survived among the people of Brittany. The name of Brittany means literally 'Little Britain' and it occupies the Armorican peninsula in northern France. Jutting out into the Atlantic, its history and culture have long been connected with south-west Britain. According to Welsh traditions (and followed by a number of modern historians) the name points to an historical migration of British people to Armorica in the fifth and sixth centuries. A combination of Anglo-Saxon pressures, economic crisis and political instability in southern Britain, accompanied by a long-standing trading relationship, may have led to this movement. Its scale, though, is a matter of debate. Welsh and Breton traditions claimed that the migration was led by Cynan (Conan in Breton) Meiriadog or Meriodoc (later a saint), who was granted land in this part of Gaul. This version of events appeared in the Breton saint's life, the *Legend of St Goeznovius* (*Legenda Sancti Goeznovii*), written *c.*1019, although a later date is possible. The Welsh tradition claimed that the migration was on the instigation of the ruler renowned in Welsh legend as Macsen Wledig. This claimed connection with Brittany was based on a well-established legend that first appeared in the ninth-century *History of the Britons* (*Historia Brittonum*) and was picked up and developed by the writer of *The Dream of Macsen Wledig* (*Breuddwyd Macsen Wledig*), *c.*1350.

Whatever the exact circumstances that led to any movements across the English Channel, it is clear that close links existed between south-west Britain, particularly Cornwall and Wales, and Armorica since pre-Roman times. This connection with the south-west of Britain has given rise to the names of two Breton regions: *Cornouaille* in the south-west of Brittany, first recorded in records of the ninth century, commemorates Cornwall; and *Domnonée* (in its French form), a name that persisted in use until the eleventh century, in the north of the peninsula, preserved a reference to Dumnonia (an ancient British kingdom in what is now Dorset, Somerset, Devon and Cornwall). The twelfth-century Norman-Welsh writer Gerald of Wales recorded that in his day Breton was more closely related to Cornish than to Welsh and other evidence confirms this conclusion.

It is not surprising that the Celtic legends of Wales and Cornwall influenced those of Brittany and vice versa. As a consequence, there are a number of common features in their shared mythology as one would expect. On the other hand, Breton mythology is not just a version of Celtic-British mythology and possessed its own very distinctive features. However, when it comes to tracing the history of Breton mythology in written form it shares a number of other features with that of Cornwall: there is no early survival of Breton literature; it features in the legends and myths of neighbouring areas; and it is the setting for mythical and legendary events that were record-ed *elsewhere* – while not having its own clear medieval voice. Surviving Breton literature may have a longer his-tory than that of Cornwall, but none exists prior to 1450.[1] This is frustrating because there clearly once was a rich and varied medieval Breton mythological tradition. Gerald of Wales mentioned Breton singers and storytellers and the twelfth-century French writer, Marie de France, used a form of literary device that was associated with Brittany. This was the Breton *lai*, a short, rhyming tale of chivalric love. *Lais* often referred to mythological themes that had a clear Celtic character. Fifteen of these *lais* have survived, including one called *Sir Launfel* that involved the romantic entanglement of an Arthurian warrior with a fairy and the resultant conflict with Guinevere and Arthur.

Many of the Welsh Arthurian tales so popular in France in the twelfth and thirteenth centuries almost certain-ly reached there via the intermediary of Brittany. From the fourteenth century a number of these stories, which derived from Breton *lais*, became popular in England but these had been transmitted there from French sources, rather than having come direct from Breton literature. As a consequence, there are plenty of hints that point to Bre-ton-located myths and legends, although the most detailed (and definitely) 'native' traditions were not recorded until the nineteenth century, when the oral folklore of rural Brittany was first written down. This leaves us with a dilemma. Should we only examine the traditions that are definitely indigenous and ignore those that refer to Brit-tany but were developed elsewhere? This is a very reason-able position and has influenced the selection of material in other presentations of Breton mythology.[2] It is also the one largely followed in this brief overview but – because the occurrence of Brittany in literature devised elsewhere is so strong – there will also be some references made to this body of evidence too.

Brittany's early medieval structure of petty-kingdoms eventually developed into a duchy that, although at times overshadowed by neighbouring Normandy and the increasingly influential kingdom of France, remained an independent political unit until 1532. Today, Brittany is part of modern France and divided into (four) *départements* in common with the rest of French local government. In the Breton language – which is still spoken by perhaps as many as 200,000 people – the region is called *Breizh*. Its distinctive history and culture is today celebrated in the black and white Breton flag (the *Gwenn Ha Du*), the *triskell* symbol and the initials BZH (for *Breizh*) to be seen on cars. A wide range of cultural events emphasize its membership of the pan-Celtic community. As mentioned, Brittany is today considered one of the six 'Celtic nations'.

This chapter will examine some of the ways in which Breton folk tales preserved links to earlier Celtic mythology. In common with much Celtic mythology these tales contained few references to beings actually described as gods or goddesses. However, by drawing parallels with other Celtic myths it seems clear that many of these mythological characters were either once regarded as deities, or represented classes of beings that were once regarded as Otherworld spiritual creatures. Clearly, the conversion to Christianity had stripped these earlier cultures of both their potency and their specific belief system. What was left was a set of mixed beliefs in Otherworld creatures, enchantments and magic that occupied a place within rural society on the edges of sincerely held Christian faith. As in the other Celtic regions it would be clearly wrong to regard this as the survival of paganism beneath a veneer of Christianity. On the contrary, the Christian conversion produced a deep-rooted faith that still survives in Breton Catholicism and that reduced older religions (and their deities) to fairies and enchanters whose power was no match for Christian spiritual supremacy. Consequently, we find these once-rival beings being described in highly negative tones or not having their specific status described at all.

As we have already seen, Breton mythology survives in a number of sources. One at least dates from the Roman period; others such as the Arthurian (and Arthur-related) tales are medieval although much adapted to suit French tastes; many more were recorded by folklorists in the eighteenth and nineteenth centuries, and represented the beliefs and superstitions of country people. The *Bards of Brittany* (*Barzaz Breiz*), for example, dates from 1839 and was the work of Théodore Hersart de la Villemarqué (1815–96). Growing up at Plessix, in Nizon, near Pont-Aven, Hersart was half-Breton and collected traditional legends, folk tales and music. Other collectors of such folk tales include François-Marie Luzel (1821–95), who published *Popular Tales of Lower Brittany* (*Contes Populaires de Basse-Bretagne*) in 1879. While questions have been raised about the authenticity of some aspects of nineteenth-century folklore collecting, these stories in the main clearly represented the traditions of the Breton countryside.

Enchanted islands

Geoffrey of Monmouth's twelfth-century description of Avalon, in the *History of the Kings of Britain* (*Historia Regum Britanniae*), as an island ruled over by nine magical virgins was reminiscent of the stories told of the nine virgin enchantresses of the island of *Sena*, said to have lain off the coast of Brittany. They were skilled in magic, medicine, divination and shape-shifting – as recorded most fully by the Roman writer, Pomponius Mela (*c.* AD 41–50). The story is also reminiscent of the nine maidens who resided in an overseas fortress and had in their charge the cauldron of the Chief of *Annwfn* (the Otherworld) in the early medieval Welsh poem *The Spoils of Annwfn* (*Preiddeu Annwfn*). It seems that either Geoffrey and the anonymous writer of

The Spoils of Annwfn both drew on an earlier myth that was located off the Breton coast or that all three writers (including the Roman one) recorded a widespread myth of enchanted islands that was known across a number of Celtic cultures.

Lost lands

As well as having enchanted islands, Brittany was reputed to have had lands lost to the sea. Most famous of these was the lost city of *Ys* (also spelled *Is* and *Kêr-Is* in Breton), usually located in Douarnenez Bay. The fate of this city was recalled in a story entitled *City of Ys* (*Kêr Ys*). According to one version of the story the city of *Ys* was sunk in sin and this was largely due to the lustful influence of Dahut (or Ahés or Ahé), the daughter of Gradlon (*Gralon* in Breton), the King of Cornouaille (*Kerne* in Breton). Dahut's mother was a mer-woman, which clearly emphasized the marine theme so central to the myth. After much negative impact on the city, Dahut finally gained possession of the key that opened the dyke protecting the city from the sea. This dyke had earlier been constructed by a good king named Meur the Great. In one version of the story, she was tricked into giving it to the devil; in another, older, version it was Dahut herself who opened the dyke alongside her lover, being under the influence of alcohol. Once opened, the sea crashed into the city and drowned it. Only Dahut and Gradlon were able to make their escape, riding a magical horse named *Morvarc'h* ('horse of the sea'). St Winwaloe – who had long opposed the sinful actions of Dahut – ordered Gradlon to push her from the horse. Eventually he did so and she was claimed by the sea, becoming a *morgen* (mermaid). In this she continued a role that appeared earlier in one version of the story which claimed that, while ruling *Ys*, she had made it a place to which passing ships were lured, capsized and robbed. This clearly was part of a tradition concerning the dangerous activities of mer-people found in a number of Celtic (and non-Celtic) cultures.

In another version of the story, Dahut was so angry at the presence of churches in the city that her father had built that she turned for advice to the pagan sisterhood living on the Isle of Sein.[3] This part of the tradition was almost certainly derived from the ancient account of an island of priestesses found in the writings of Pomponius Mela. These conjured the *korrigans* (see below) who both sexually corrupted innocent Christians and built a new castle for Dahut. In yet another and later version, preserved in ballads, Gradlon himself was corrupt and willingly gave the key of the dyke to Dahut.[4]

It is possible that in the original story Dahut was made to represent the paganism of Brittany in the conversion period and Gradlon those who responded positively to the Christian message. However, the tradition was complex and contradictory, and in other stories Gradlon was associated with the last Breton druid. The story of *Ys* was popularized in the nineteenth century through the publication and dissemination of *Barzaz Breiz*. The holy man who advised Gradlon was sometimes named as St Corentin. The story of *Ys* first appeared in the late fifteenth century, in *Compilation of the Chronicles and Histories of the Bretons* (*Compillation des cronicques et ystoires des Bretons*), written by Pierre Le Baud, who served as the chaplain to Anne, Duchess of Brittany.

The story of the inundation of *Ys* is similar to the motif of a lost city found in a number of Celtic regions (and, indeed, elsewhere). There are, for example, parallels with a Welsh account of the drowning of *Cantref Gwaelod* (said to lie beneath Cardigan Bay, between Ramsey Island and Bardsey Island). The story of *Ys* inspired Debussy's piano prelude '*La Cathédrale engloutie*' ('The Sunken Cathedral') of 1910.[5]

Ankou, the collector of the dead

In Breton mythology, Ankou was the one who carried the
dead on their journey in his cart (the *Karrig an Ankou*).
In some accounts the cart was pulled by two horses: one
young and fit and the other thin and old; in other accounts
the cart was pulled by four black horses. Ankou was
thought to wear a wide-brimmed hat and a long coat. In
some accounts his cart was followed by two skeletal figures who threw the souls of the dead into his cart. This
tradition certainly sounded as if it derived from a pagan
tradition since there was something Charon-like in the
accounts (although they involved a cart rather than a boat).
It is likely that Ankou was originally a chthonic deity
transferring the dead to the Underworld. When accounts
described him as being the first child of Adam and Eve
this represented a Christianization of the original mythology. And, since it was through the sin of Adam that death
entered the world, this further emphasized the role associated with Ankou (who, of course, had no parallel in Christian beliefs).

In one folk tale Ankou was called on to punish twin
brothers who had tormented an old beggar. When one
brother died he was forced into a kind of purgatory in the
cold waters of the local millpond and was only relieved
of it when his twin agreed to accompany him there and
share his suffering. This resulted in the first brother being
freed to enter the Otherworld but it led to the death of the
second brother who was then forced to endure the dark,
cold waters alone.[6] This association of Ankou with water
as the abode of the *anaon* (Breton for spirits of the dead)
suggests that the story is of some antiquity since the idea of
water as a portal to the Otherworld appeared in a number
of Celtic myths, and other evidence too shows that Celtic
peoples associated water with the presence of spirits and
deities.

The 'little people' of Brittany

Breton fairy-people featured in a similar set of Otherworld myths to those found in Ireland, Wales, Scotland, Cornwall and the Isle of Man. In Brittany these creatures were described by a number of names.

The *korrigans* were considered to be princesses who had opposed the Christian conversion of Brittany. In other accounts they were described as more dwarf-like. Diminutive stature was apparent in the name: *korr* meant 'dwarf', *ig* was an additional diminutive and the suffix *an* was yet another diminutive (though in the form usually used to make a pet-name). This latter element may suggest that originally they were not regarded negatively.

Being reduced from their original stature as a judgement on their opposition to the Church, they were enemies of Christian beliefs and places of worship. They were afraid of the sound of bells calling faithful parishioners to church and would run away if they were rung. It was thought that they had originally lived in springs and wells but had been driven from these by the power of the Virgin Mary. Despite their beauty, they were deadly and anyone who chanced on them combing their long hair or counting their treasure would die. Death would also occur if a *korrigan* breathed on a person. Men who saw them would be entranced by them but would die when they inevitably vanished. Their red, flashing eyes marked them out as Otherworld beings. They sometimes stole human babies and on All Souls' Night (31 October), they were thought to appear near prehistoric standing-stones, waiting for victims.

This highly negative set of beliefs was in contrast to the more favourable accounts regarding fairies found in Celtic folklore in some other regions. Nevertheless, even in other areas the belief in fairy-people as ambivalent towards humans or openly hostile was also found. One fairy-woman with long blonde hair was specifically named as Mélusine, although this might not have been a reference to a *korrigan* since she appeared carved in Saint-Sulpice Church, located at Fougères, which suggests acceptability.

It seems clear that these fairies were once pre-Christian local water deities or local spirits. The Breton belief that many springs, chateaux and ruined buildings were home to one of *les Fées* ('fairies') corroborates this interpretation. Similarly, the link between watery areas and a being named *Ar Helern* reinforced the link with water-sources. The reference to their association with standing stones again linked them to pre-Christian beliefs and activities. This was common across much of Europe as Roman-era altars made frequent references to the *genius loci* (the protective spirit of a place); many by names suggesting very localized beliefs or by no name at all. Belief in such beings was disrupted and condemned following Christian conversion; hence the belief that they were antagonistic to the Christian faith and were to be regarded as enemies.

Similar creatures – though more mischievous than deadly – were *les Lutins*. Differently described in different regions of Brittany, it is possible that this varied class of Otherworld creatures was actually a catch-all phrase devised to include a disparate group of pre-Christian deities and magical beings. At Plusquellec the local representative of *les Lutins* was an old and bearded man who frightened children; elsewhere it was recorded that the form was that of a dog; other areas described their variants as goats, horses and chickens. They were regarded as haunting byways and crossroads, which clearly implied a threat to lone travellers.

A similar range of descriptions were associated with the *Bugel-Noz*, the 'shepherd of the night'. In some areas they masqueraded as choirboys; in other areas they stole food from country cottages; in yet others they cried at night like little children; a variant called the *Buitel-Noz* was reputed to attack people.

In a tradition similar to the Irish beliefs in the 'Washer at the Ford', the *Lavandières de la Nuit* (also known as the *kannerezed noz*) washed shrouds. If a traveller encountered one at night, they would soon discover that the shroud was their own and would die at the hands of this malevolent being.

The *Vieilles Fées* ('old fairies') were dangerous creatures that could only be driven from their habitation by placing the bodies of magpies around the spot. Clearly, many of the Breton fairy-folk were malevolent and seemed to have been more so than in other Celtic cultures. The night-dancing *korils*, for example, were reputed to have been able to entrance any mortal who inadvertently chanced on them and forced the unfortunate to dance all night with them.[7]

Some fairy-people were associated with prehistoric standing-stones, for which Brittany is renowned. One, named Margot, was in some traditions seen as both an individual queenly figure and a class of beings found at different stones. This belief in a being that was also a multiplicity of female spirits was also known in Irish mythology. The belief was also reflected in the threefold *deae matres* (divine mothers) and the *genii cucullati* (hooded spirits) found on Roman-era inscriptions in Britain and across Europe.

The origin of the Gulf of Morbihan

This inland sea is a striking feature of the south-east coast of Brittany. Studded with islands, it was claimed to have been formed from the tears of fairy-people. These tears were shed when they were driven out of the enchanted forest of *Brocéliande*. At the same time, the fairies threw their garlands of flowers into the sea and each flower was transformed into an individual island. In total there are some 368 islands in Morbihan. Two flowers were cast out to sea and became the islands of Houat and Hoedic; the one cast by the queen of the fairies became the Isle of Beauty.

The enchanted forest of *Brocéliande* and Arthurian connections

The myth associated with the creation of the Gulf of Morbihan referred to an enchanted forest, once thought to be located near Rennes. This was the forest that is now called Paimpont. However, it is difficult to determine how much this represented an ancient Breton tradition of the expulsion of the fairy-people and how much it was, instead, a later response to medieval Arthurian stories that were actually devised elsewhere but set in Brittany.

What is clear is that in French Arthurian tales it was believed that there was an enchanted forest in Brittany. In the sequels to the Old French *Merlin* it was the place where Merlin was imprisoned by Niniane the enchantress. The magical forest also appeared in other medieval French stories such as: *Tournament Antichrist* (*Tournoiement Anticrist*), *Claris and Laris* (*Claris et Laris*) and *Brown of the Mountain* (*Brun de la Montaigne*). Similarly, it was mentioned in a German Romance, *Garel of the Flower Valley* (*Garel von dem blühenden Tal*).[8]

The overall evidence does suggest, therefore, that there was a strong medieval Breton tradition of enchantment associated with this area. Although only recorded elsewhere – such as in Chrétien de Troyes's *Yvain* and in references made by Gerald of Wales – it was renowned as the location of the fountain of Bérenton, which was thought to be a storm-making spring. The Norman writer Wace, in his *Romance of Rollo* (*Roman de Rou*) of 1160–74, wrote how he visited *Brocéliande* to see the marvels spoken of by the Bretons but found none.[9] He self-deprecatingly described his disappointment in this Breton place of marvels: 'A fool I went, a fool I returned.'[10]

The link between Merlin and the forest of *Brocéliande* reminds us that there is a well-rooted Arthurian tradition in Brittany but it is mostly evidenced from references elsewhere or later than the Middle Ages. That it existed before this is clear from the English writer Henry of Hunting-don (died *c.*1157), who referred to the existence of Breton legends concerning Arthur's immortality and promised return in his *History of the English* (*Historia Anglorum*). The twelfth-century writer Geoffrey of Monmouth appeared very favourable to the Bretons and probably derived at least some of his Arthurian material from there, although it is difficult to identify exactly what strands were Breton. When French Romances later set scenes in Brittany they probably did so because Arthurian legends had been communicated to them from there and they made Brittany the chief residence of the Arthurian knights.[11] So, Chrétien de Troyes's *Cligés* (*c.*1180) stated that Arthur held court in Brittany and the German writer Wolfram von Eschenbach's *Parzival* (*c.*1210) claimed this was at Nantes. Brittany also featured in the Tristan legend and may have supplied some of the distinctive features in that story. The Norman writer, Wace, who first mentioned the Round Table in his *Romance of Brutus* (*Roman de Brut*) of 1155, claimed that he first heard of it from Breton storytellers; he also referred to the 'Breton hope' in the return of Arthur from the Isle of Avalon.[12]

Breton mermaids – *Les Sirènes*

Borrowing from both Classical and Celtic traditions, the mermaids of Brittany were regarded as highly dangerous. Usually described as *morgen* or *mari-morgan*, they were thought to lure men to their deaths, as a result of their beauty or because they revealed a glimpse of fabulous cities beneath the waves. In either case, once attracted, a man was drawn beneath the waves and drowned.

Arthurian traditions referred to a threatening female character named Morgan le Fay and it is possible that she was based on these Breton myths of highly dangerous water-spirits. Other – and similar creatures – were called the *morwreg*, the daughters of the sea, and had bright, silver fishtails.

N'oun Doaré or 'I don't know'

In this story a nobleman, Bras, the Marquis of Coat-Squiriou was returning home from Morlaix when he came upon a child beside the road. To every question asked (such as 'Why are you here?' and 'What is your name?') the child answered, *'N'oun Doaré'* ('I don't know'). For this reason he was named N'oun Doaré. The nobleman raised the child in his house, had him educated by a druid at Carhaix and eventually made him his heir. Seeking to equip him suitably, Bras was astonished when N'oun Doaré turned down the offer of a fine sword in favour of an old and rusty one, and a fine horse in favour of an old, broken-down one. But the sword proved to be invincible and the horse could transport him anywhere he wished to go. It turned out that the horse could also speak. Having found a magical crown, N'oun Doaré went to Vannes where it was revealed that the crown belonged to Aour, the Princess of the Golden-Ram, whom he was to seek out as a bride for the King of Vannes. On the way he saved a fish (which turned out to be the King of the Fish), a bird (which turned out to be the King of the Birds) and a snake-man (who turned out to be a demon-king).

On reaching the castle of Aour, N'oun Doaré was advised by his horse to kill those acting as gatekeepers (since they meant him harm) and to enter only on the express instructions of the princess. This all occurred and N'oun Doaré eventually persuaded the princess to come and see the dances his horse could perform. Having tricked her to mount the horse, N'oun Doaré used the horse's magical ability to transport the princess back to Vannes. There the princess (who was not happy at this turn of events) was presented to the ruler of Vannes. N'oun Doaré was then given yet another task: retrieving the princess's ring that had been left in a box in the castle. He enlisted the King of the Birds and a wren performed this task for him. That it was a wren may have had significance beyond the diminutive size of the bird since the wren appeared in a number of Celtic myths as a significant bird.

Two other obstacles to marriage were then put forward by the princess and each was overcome. Her demand that her castle be transported to Vannes was accomplished by the demon-king at N'oun Doaré's request; her demand that the lost key to her castle be located was accomplished by the King of the Fish, again at the request of N'oun Doaré. Finally, N'oun Doaré caused the princess formally to invite all present into her castle. When this occurred, N'oun Doaré's mare ate the oats found there and the castle vanished. The haughty and demanding Princess of the Golden-Ram suddenly became amenable and even more beautiful. The mare was transformed into another beautiful woman – her sister, who was named Ruz-glaou. It turned out that both had been cursed by a druid who had also sent into exile the boy-child destined to marry one of them – none other than N'oun Doaré. Aour, the Princess of the Golden-Ram, married the King of Vannes and Ruz-glaou married N'oun Doaré.[13]

In some versions of the story it was the King of Paris, rather than of Vannes, who gained the hand of Aour and the mare who was transformed back to a woman was the daughter of the King of Tartary. The reference to the sword being made by a smith-deity named Govan[14] also indicated threads of the story that extended into antiquity, since Goibhniu was named as the Irish god of smithing and the making of weapons, in Irish medieval sources.

Other Breton folk tales also featured quests for a golden-haired princess and were recorded in the nineteenth century. These were *Princis Velandinenn* and *The Princess of the Shining Star*.[15] These stories show evidence of ancient themes involving shape-shifting, talking animals and magical weapons found in a number of Celtic myths. That of *The Princess of the Shining Star* (*Prinsez a Sterenn*) involved a miller who – on discovering a duck that

changed into a woman while he was out hunting – freed
her from the enchantment of three evil wizards from the
Otherworld. He did this by spending three nights in the
ruined castle in which the evil wizards lived. There, he was
tortured but revived by the magic ointment of the duck-
princess. Defeated, the evil wizards left but so did the princess – promising she would return in a year. Just before the
year ended, the miller made the mistake of buying three
apples from an old woman. She was the mother of the three
wizards and took revenge on the miller by using a spell
that caused him to eat one of the sleep-inducing apples
each day before the princess came for him. Unable to take
a sleeping man into her magical carriage, she was forced to
leave. Pursuing her, the awoken miller overcame the threat
of three terrible brothers by persuading their mother to
assist him and eventually arrived in the land of the princess just before her wedding to the prince of *Hent Sant
Jakez* (the Milky Way). By showing gifts that the princess
had left behind, he signalled his arrival and eventually was
revealed, and she married him instead of his rival.

This story, with its shape-shifting, trials to free a princess and eventual union with a star-princess suggests an
ancient mythology connected to a star-deity and a mortal
who gained her hand through endurance. It could even
have once involved ideas relating to a mating of the star-
deity with the land (the miller). It has been suggested that
the witch who poisoned apples may have influenced tales
as famous as Snow White[16] or the story may simply have
drawn on similar mythological motifs found across a
number of different folk tales.

The saga of Koadalan
This complex tale involved the hero Koadalan, who entered
a nobleman's service, being given the conditions that he
must always keep a fire under the pot, beat a mare with
a holly stick and never open two prohibited doors in the

castle. Lighting the fire, he heard people moan in pain, and while beating the mare she begged him for mercy and his pity was rewarded by being told to go through the two forbidden doors where he learned magic from the books therein. He also washed in the castle fountain and became a handsome prince. After all this, he fled with the mare, pursued by his master in the form of a black dog. Wounded, the mare ordered him to cut her open to reveal a beautiful princess, who advised him he would marry an even more beautiful woman. Koadalan travelled to Spain where he used magic to gain access to the imprisoned princess there. She became pregnant, he married her and later became King of Spain. While travelling on a magical journey on the back of an eagle, they were imprisoned by a magician who desired the princess; Koadalan was imprisoned down a well but rescued when he called for his mare-princess.

He returned to his original home where he built a great castle for his parents. Later, he told his father to go to market and sell first a bullock and then a horse, but not the rope-bridle. The second time the father got drunk and sold the rope, too. This time the previous would-be buyers of the rope (three devils) gained ownership of the bridle and the horse – who was none other than Koadalan himself. He attempted to escape them in the form of an eel, a dove and a gold ring, and finally succeeded when the ring was thrown into a fire that burned up the devils who pursued him into the flames.

Later, seeking to cheat death, Koadalan gave instructions for his body to be chopped up and placed beneath hot manure in a pit, and the milk of a nursing mother was to be sprinkled on it twice a day for six months. But, three days before the end of the allotted time, she fell asleep and Koadalan could not be restored to life.

This strange tale had some parallels with the Welsh traditions concerning the horse-maiden Rhiannon in *Pwyll, Prince of Dyfed* (*Pwyll Pendevic Dyfed*) but remains enigmatic. Koadalan's name meant 'Wood-Allan' from the Breton word *koad* (wood) combined with a male personal name, so he may originally have been some kind of woodland deity engaged in a rebirth mythology that also involved a shape-shifting woman. It is not at all clear.[17]

The ruler of the Land of Silver

This story told of the predicament of a young girl, Litavis, who was married to Avoez, lord of Briezh Izel, as the price for sparing her father from being driven from his home in debt. For seven long years she was locked in a tower that was guarded by Avoez and his sister, Moravik. Finally, her distress was rewarded when a champion in the form of a hawk flew through her window, changed into a man and declared himself to be Eudemarec of *Bro Arc'hant* (land of silver). Although still a prisoner, Litavis became his lover. On discovering this, Avoez and Moravik set a trap that mortally wounded the hawk and he flew off, bleeding. Litavis escaped and followed the spots of blood. On the way she was guided by *Bugel-Noz*, the 'shepherd of the night', one of the fairy-people. She closed her ears to the captivating voices of the mermaids known as the *mari-morgan* and was protected by magic from being captured by the *korrigans* who were dancing at a stone circle. Along the way, her guide changed from the *Bugel-Noz* to yet another fairy creature and, finally, she wandered on alone. She followed the blood spots through a door in a hillside and eventually reached a silver city. There her lover was dying and he persuaded her to leave the city and return to her tower to prevent her from being blamed for his death. But, in future, she would bear his son who would avenge him. She did so and, in time, gave birth to a boy she named Ywenec. She hid a silver sword that Eudemarec of *Bro Arc'hant* had given her during her brief time in the silver city. Eventually Avoez took Litavis on a journey that involved resting by the tomb of an unknown king. This was the tomb of

Eudemarec of *Bro Arc'hant*. At this place, Litavis gave the silver sword to their son, Ywenec. Then she died and was reunited with Eudemarec. Ywenec killed Avoez with the silver sword and went on to discover and become the ruler of *Bro Arc'hant*. Moravik fled by sea, her ship sank and she was dragged beneath the waves by the *mari-morgan*.

With the interweaving of themes of a quest for a princess, shape-shifting, magic potions, a ruler of a land beneath a hill, fairy creatures, underwater realms and a quest for the rightful recognition of an heir to a kingdom, the story contains many of the themes found across Celtic mythology. It is a fitting place to close this brief examination of the mythology of Brittany and of the Celtic communities generally.

NOTES

Introduction

1. Hutton, R., *The Pagan Religions of the Ancient British Isles* (Basil Blackwell Ltd, 1991). See Chapter 8, 'Legacy of Shadows', especially 284–308.

1. Who Are and Were the Celts?

1. A short article on Breton history and nationhood by Paul Kavanagh, 'Wha's Like Us? Brittany', appeared in July 2011 on the website newsnetscotland.com. See www.newsnetscotland com/index.php/affairs-scotland/2690-whas-like-us-brittany. html.
2. See Harding, D. W., *The Archaeology of Celtic Art* (Routledge, 2007), 4.
3. Cunliffe, B., *The Ancient Celts* (Oxford University Press, 1997).
4. MacCana, P., *Celtic Mythology* (Hamlyn, 1970), 11.
5. Harding, D. W., op. cit., 3–4.
6. See Haywood, J., *The Historical Atlas of the Celtic World* (Thames & Hudson, 2001), 30–37.
7. Collis, J., *The Celts: Origins, Myths and Inventions* (Tempus, 2003), 195.

8. Harding, D. W., op. cit., 5.

9. For an accessible overview of the relationship between Iron Age Celtic identity and modern British and Irish populations, see James, S., *The Atlantic Celts: Ancient People or Modern Invention?* (British Museum Press, 1999).

10. A very helpful overview of this issue and different views on it – and one that has influenced this set of definitions here – is found in Csapo, E., *Theories of Mythology* (Wiley, 2005), 1–3.

2. The Gods and Religion of the Celts: The European picture

1. See Ross, A., *The Pagan Celts* (Barnes & Noble, 1986).

2. Leeming, D. A., K. Madden and S. Marlan, *Encyclopedia of Psychology and Religion, Volume 2* (Springer, 2009), 129.

3. See Stead, I., *The Gauls: Celtic Antiquities from France* (British Museum Publications, 1981).

4. Bonnefoy, Y., *American, African, and Old European Mythologies* (University of Chicago Press, 1993), 225.

5. Doniger, W., et al., *Merriam-Webster's Encyclopedia of World Religions* (Merriam-Webster, 1999), 669.

6. Green, M. J., *Symbol and Image in Celtic Religious Art* (Routledge, 1989), 4.

7. Green, M. J., *Dictionary of Celtic Myth and Legend* (Thames & Hudson, 1992), 159–60.

8. Green, M. J., *The Gods of the Celts* (Allan Sutton, 1986), 66.

9. MacCana, P., *Celtic Mythology* (Hamlyn, 1970), 32.

10. See MacKillop, J., *Myths and Legends of the Celts* (Penguin, 2005), 39, for continental references to Uxellinus.

11. Green, M. J., 1989, op. cit., 107.

12. Ibid., 108.

13. MacKinnon, D. and E. C. Carmichael Watson, *The Celtic Review, Volumes 3–4* (Kraus Reprint, 1975), 41.

14. Jacques, D. and T. Phillips, 'Vespasian's Camp: Cradle of Stonehenge?', *Current Archaeology*, 271 (October 2012), 32–3.

15. Lacy, N. J. (ed.), *The Arthurian Encyclopedia* (Boydell Press, 1988), 94.

16. Green, M. J., 1989, op. cit., 109–10.

17. Bonnefoy, Y., op. cit., 225.

18. Price, S. and P. Thonemann, *The Birth of Classical Europe: A History from Troy to Augustine* (Allen Lane, 2010), 275–6.
19. Maier, B., *Dictionary of Celtic Religion and Culture* (Boydell Press, 1997), 96.
20. Ibid., 97.

3. The Gods and Religion of the Celts: The British Picture

1. Paice MacLeod, S., *Celtic Myth and Religion* (McFarland, 2012), 44.
2. Green, M. J., *Symbol and Image in Celtic Religious Art* (Routledge, 1989), 112.
3. Ibid., 114.
4. *Current Archaeology*, 271 (October 2012), 7.
5. Green, M. J., *The Gods of the Celts* (Allan Sutton, 1986), 66.
6. Clegg, R. and M. Richards, *The Spirit of Hadrian's Wall* (Cicerone Press, 2008), 177.
7. Rivet, A. L. F. and C. Smith, *The Place-names of Roman Britain* (Batsford, 1979), 402.
8. Ekwall, E., *The Concise Oxford Dictionary of English Place-names* (4th edn, Oxford University Press, 1960), 291.
9. Jacques, D. and T. Phillips, 'Vespasian's Camp: Cradle of Stonehenge?', *Current Archaeology*, 271 (Oct. 2012), 32–3.
10. Heaney, M. (ed.), *Over Nine Waves: A Book of Irish Legends* (Macmillan, 1995), 39.
11. Monaghan, P., *The Encyclopedia of Celtic Mythology and Folklore* (Facts On File, 2004), 303.
12. MacCana, P., *Celtic Mythology* (Hamlyn, 1970), 47.
13. Hull, V., 'Aided Meidbe: The Violent Death of Medb', *Speculum* (Medieval Academy of America), 13: 1 (January 1938), 52–61.
14. www.ucc.ie/celt/published/G503002/index.html.
15. Paice MacLeod, S., op. cit., 44.
16. Ibid., 45.
17. Green, M. J., *The Gods of Roman Britain* (Osprey, 2008), 65.
18. All three items being bronze cookware bearing the names of forts; they were clearly made as Roman souvenirs.
19. See MacKillop, J., *Myths and Legends of the Celts* (Penguin, 2005), 39, for continental references to Uxellinus.
20. Museum of Archaeology and Anthropology, University of Cambridge; Artefact (D 1970.2).

21. Henig, M., *Religion in Roman Britain* (Batsford, 1984), 203.

4. Festivals and Celebrations across the Year

1. Trevelyan, M., *Folk-Lore and Folk-Stories of Wales* (Kessinger, 1909), 38.
2. Hutton, R., *The Stations of the Sun* (Oxford University Press, 1996), 6.
3. Ibid., 8.
4. *Encyclopedia of Observances, Holidays and Celebrations* (Mobile Reference, 2007).
5. Macleon Banks, M., *British Calendar Customs: Scotland*, (Folklore Society William Glaisher, 1937), vol. II, 35–7.
6. Hutton, R., op. cit., 79.
7. For the context of its compilation see Charles-Edwards, T. M., *Early Christian Ireland* (Cambridge University Press, 2004), 164.
8. Hutton, R., op. cit., 97.
9. *Chambers English Dictionary* (W. & R. Chambers, 1990), 1711.
10. Atwood Lawrence, E., *Hunting the Wren: Transformation of Bird to Symbol* (University of Tennessee Press, 1997), 26.
11. Davies, S. (trans.), *The Mabinogion* (Oxford University Press, 2007), 56.
12. Hutton, R., op. cit., 134.
13. For an examination of the nature of the cult of this saint, see Cathain, S., *The Festival of Brigid, Celtic Goddess and Holy Woman* (DBA, 1995).
14. Hutton, R., op. cit., 135.
15. For a succinct overview of discussions concerning the origins of St Brigid, see McKenna, C., 'Brigid of Ireland', in P. G. Jestice (ed.), *Holy People of the World: A Cross-Cultural Encyclopedia* (ABC-CLIO, 2004), vol. 1, 140–1.
16. Hutton, R., op. cit., 136–7.
17. Martin, M., *A Description of the Western Isles of Scotland* (1703), 119.
18. Allardyce, A., *Scotland and Scotsmen in the Eighteenth Century* (1888), vol. II, 447.
19. Carmichael A., *Carmina Gadelica* (1900), vol. I, 167–73.
20. Koch, J. T., *Celtic Culture: A Historical Encyclopedia*, 5 vols (ABC-CLIO, 2006), vol. 1, 195.

21. Allardyce, A., op. cit., vol. II, 439–45, quoting John Ramsay.
22. Hutton, R., op. cit., 223–4.
23. *Chambers's Etymological Dictionary of the English Language* (Elibron Classics, 2001), 440.
24. Hutton, R., op. cit., 225.
25. MacNeill, M., *The Festival of Lughnasa* (Oxford University Press, 1962), 426.
26. Gantz, J., *Early Irish Myths and Sagas* (Penguin Classics, 1981), 12–13.
27. See Hutton, R., op. cit., 362.
28. Hall, J., *Cambridge Medieval Celtic Studies* (University of Cambridge, Department of Anglo-Saxon, Norse and Celtic), 6 (1983), 75.
29. For a persuasive presentation of this argument see Hutton, R., op. cit., 364–5.

5: Irish Origin Myths: Irish Gods before the Gods

1. Berresford Ellis, P., *The Mammoth Book of Celtic Myths and Legends* (Robinson, 2002), 17.
2. See the *Anglo-Saxon Chronicle* genealogy for the West Saxon king Æthelwulf, under the entry for the year 855, in D. Whitelock (ed.), *English Historical Documents, Volume I, c.500–1042* (Eyre Methuen, 1979), 190.
3. Interestingly, the most recent research does indeed suggest, from the genetic evidence, that the British Isles were originally populated from northern Iberia via the Atlantic sea lanes. Cunliffe, B., *Britain Begins* (Oxford University Press, 2012).
4. Monaghan, P., *The Encyclopedia of Celtic Mythology and Folklore* (Facts On File, 2004), 353.
5. Cahill, M. A., *Paradise Rediscovered: The Roots of Civilisation*, 2 vols (Glass House, 2012), vol. 1, 240.
6. Green, M. J., *Dictionary of Celtic Myth and Legend* (Thames & Hudson, 1992), 99.
7. Monaghan, P., op. cit., 353.
8. On the relationship between British accounts of their own origins and Bede's work in the context of the Old Testament, see Higham, N., *An English Empire: Bede and the Early Anglo-Saxon Kings* (Manchester University Press, 1995), 18–21.
9. Berresford Ellis, P., op. cit., 17.

10. Hence his name: Nuada Airgedlámh (Nuada of the Silver Hand).
11. The term 'evil-eye' is found in many different cultures and languages including: Greek *matiasma*, Hebrew *ayin hara*, Sanskrit *drishti dosha*.

6. Irish Origin Myths: The People of the Goddess Dana

1. For an overview of the motives of its compilers, see Paice MacLeod, S., *Celtic Myth and Religion* (McFarland, 2012), 125.
2. Pu, M., *Rethinking Ghosts in World Religions* (Brill, 2009), 149.
3. Woodard, R. D., *Indo-European Sacred Space: Vedic and Roman Cult* (University of Illinois, 2006), 62.
4. For a study of the evidence for early medieval traditions concerning the origins of Irish lore, see Ó Hógáin, D., *The Sacred Isle: Belief and Religion in Pre-Christian Ireland* (Boydell Press, 1999).
5. Hutton, R., *The Pagan Religions of the Ancient British Isles* (Basil Blackwell, 1991), 285.
6. Cotterell, A., *The Encyclopedia of Mythology* (Lorenz, 1999), 170.
7. For an examination of whether Ogham script was an Irish invention or an adaption of Norse runes, see Danver, S. L., *Popular Controversies in World History* (ABC-CLIO, 2011), 50–61.
8. Adams Leeming, D., *The Oxford Companion to World Mythology* (Oxford University Press, 2005), 270.
9. Ellis Davidson, H. R., *Myths and Symbols in Pagan Europe: Early Scandinavian and Celtic Religions* (Manchester University Press, 1988), 97.
10. MacBain, A., *Celtic Mythology and Religion* (Cosimo, 2005), 127.
11. Regarding this matter of goddesses thought to have been linked to the land, see Monaghan, P., *The Encyclopedia of Celtic Mythology and Folklore* (Facts On File, 2004), 424.
12. MacCana, P., *Celtic Mythology* (Hamlyn, 1970), 72–3.
13. Cotterell, A., op. cit., 106.

7. Irish Origin Myths: The Daghda and his Children

1. MacCana, P., *Celtic Mythology* (Hamlyn, 1970), 66.

2. Wilkinson, P. and N. Philip, *Mythology* (Dorling Kindersley, 2007), 100.

3. MacCana, P., op. cit., 66.

4. Brezina, C., *Celtic Mythology* (Rosen, 2008), 30.

5. A characteristic described in the sixteenth-century text, *The Battle of Magh Tuireadh* (*Cath Maige Tuired*).

6. MacCana, P., op. cit., 66.

7. Cotterell, A., *The Encyclopedia of Mythology* (Lorenz, 1999), 121.

8. See Paice MacLeod, S., *Celtic Myth and Religion* (McFarland, 2012), 54–5.

9. Koch, J. T., *Celtic Culture: A Historical Encyclopedia*, 5 vols (ABC-CLIO, 2006), vol. 1, 220.

10. Monaghan, P., *The Encyclopedia of Celtic Mythology and Folklore* (Facts On File, 2004), 51.

11. *Expugnatio Hibernica*, I: 33.

8. Irish Origin Myths: The Coming of the Milesians

1. Lennon, J., *Irish Orientalism: A Literary and Intellectual History* (Syracuse University Press, 2004), 25.

2. Bede, *A History of the English Church and People*, trans. L. Sherley-Price (Penguin, 1968), 38–9.

3. A name clearly invented in order to explain the ethnic name 'Gael'. See Lennon, J., op. cit., 25.

4. MacKillop, J., *Myths and Legends of the Celts* (Penguin, 2005), 145.

5. Acts 20:15–38.

6. For an overview of the motives of the compilers of the *Book of Invasions*, see Paice MacLeod, S., *Celtic Myth and Religion* (McFarland, 2012), 125.

7. Higham, N. J., *King Arthur: Myth-Making and History* (Routledge, 2002), 141.

8. Koch, J. T., *Celtic Culture: A Historical Encyclopedia*, 5 vols (ABC-CLIO, 2006), vol. 2, 710.

9. MacKillop, J., op. cit., 145.

10. Koch, J. T., op. cit., 711.

11. This issue is explored in Bradley, R., *Rock Art and the Prehistory of Atlantic Europe: Signing the Land* (Routledge, 1997), 37. See also evidence for this distribution in Chippindale, C.

and P. S. C. Taçon, *The Archaeology of Rock-Art* (Cambridge University Press, 1998).

12. See Merrills, A. H., *History and Geography in Late Antiquity* (Cambridge University Press, 2005), 287.

13. Green, M. J., *Dictionary of Celtic Myth and Legend* (Thames & Hudson, 1992), 190.

14. Pu, M., *Rethinking Ghosts in World Religions* (Brill, 2009), 149–50.

15. Grimal, P. (ed.), *Larousse World Mythology* (Hamlyn, 1971), 353.

16. Monaghan, P., *The Encyclopedia of Celtic Mythology and Folklore* (Facts On File, 2004), 176.

9. Magic and Shape-shifters in the Irish Mythological Cycle

1. O'Donovan, J. (trans.) and W. Stokes (ed.), *Sanas Chormaic: Cormac's Glossary* (O. T. Cutter for the Irish Archaeological and Celtic Society, 1868), 159.

2. Carson, C., *The Táin, A New Translation of the Táin Bó Cúailnge* (Penguin, 2007), 92.

3. MacKillop, J., *Myths and Legends of the Celts* (Penguin, 2005), 166.

4. Cotterell, A., *The Encyclopedia of Mythology* (Lorenz, 1999), 129.

5. DeLaney, F., *Legends of the Celts* (HarperCollins, 2008), 59–60.

6. Ibid., 59.

7. Gandolfi, C. and J. Gershman, *Tales & Songs of Ireland* (Peter Pauper Press, 2002), 32.

8. Ashe, G., *Mythology of the British Isles* (Methuen, 1990), 86.

9. Green, M. J., *Dictionary of Celtic Myth and Legend* (Thames & Hudson, 1992), 133.

10. MacKillop, J., op. cit., 163.

11. Spence, L., *The Minor Traditions of British Mythology* (Ayer, 1948), 25.

12. Grimal, P. (ed.), *Larousse World Mythology* (Hamlyn, 1971), 349.

13. Cotterell, A., op. cit., 146.

14. Llywelyn, M., *Finn Mac Cool* (Mandarin, 1995), 22.

15. MacNeill, J. and G. Murphy, *Duanaire Finn: The Book of the Lays of Fionn, pt. 1, Volume 28* (Irish Texts Society, 1908), 119.
16. Matson, G. and J. Roberts, *Celtic Mythology A to Z* (Infobase, 2010), 2.
17. Monaghan, P., *The Encyclopedia of Celtic Mythology and Folklore* (Facts On File, 2004), 7.
18. Heaney, M., *Over Nine Waves: A Book of Irish Legends* (Macmillan, 1995), 162.
19. Cotterell, A., op. cit., 163.
20. Monaghan, P., op. cit., 404.
21. Raglan, F. R. S., *The Hero: A Study in Tradition, Myth and Drama* (Dover, 2003 [1936]), 262.
22. www.maryjones.us/ctexts/deatheochaid.html.
23. Brannigan, M., *TirNaNog* (Lulu.com, 2005), 209.

10. Cú Chulainn, the Hound of Ulster and the Ulster Cycle

1. The four collections of stories being: the Mythological Cycle, with its stories of the origins of Ireland; the Ulster Cycle; the Fenian Cycle; and the Historical Cycle, or the Cycles of the Kings.
2. MacCana, P., *Celtic Mythology* (Hamlyn, 1970), 17.
3. Ibid., 97.
4. Carson, C., *The Táin, A New Translation of the Táin Bó Cúailnge* (Penguin, 2007), 58.
5. Ibid., 69.
6. See Maier, B., *Dictionary of Celtic Religion and Culture* (Boydell Press, 1997), 209.
7. Kinsella, T., *The Táin: From the Irish Epic Táin Bó Cúailnge* (Oxford University Press, 1969), 257, n. 6.
8. Carson, C., op. cit., 91–2.
9. Kinsella, T., op. cit., 257, n. 6.
10. Carson, C., op. cit., 91–2.
11. Ibid., 109.
12. Findon, J., *A Woman's Words: Emer and Female Speech in the Ulster Cycle* (University of Toronto Press, 1997), 91–2.
13. Kinsella, T., op. cit., 257, n. 8.

11. Finn mac Cumhaill and the Warriors of the *Fianna*

1. For an examination of the role and character of Finn within the tales, see MacKillop, J., *Fionn Mac Cumhaill: Celtic Myth in English Literature* (Syracuse University Press, 1986), 3–9.

2. Monaghan, P., *The Encyclopedia of Celtic Mythology and Folklore* (Facts On File, 2004), 185–6.

3. France, P., *The Oxford Guide to Literature in English Translation* (Oxford University Press, 2001), 176–7, provides a succinct overview of the Fenian Cycle.

4. For more on this rivalry, see Burns, B. and I. Oleynikov, *The King with Horse's Ears and Other Irish Folktales* (Sterling, 2009), 21.

5. Coates, P. A., *Salmon* (Reaktion, 2006), 154.

6. Heaney, M., *Over Nine Waves: A Book of Irish Legends* (Macmillan, 1995), 164–6, provides a detailed retelling of the way in which Finn became leader of the *fianna*.

7. Green, M. J., *Dictionary of Celtic Myth and Legend* (Thames & Hudson, 1992), 108.

8. www.ucc.ie/celt/online/G303003/text001.html.

9. Bodleian codex Laud 610, folio 122b, 2 and British Museum MS Egerton 92, folio 6a, 1, according to: www.medievalsourcesbibliography.org/sources/2146115692.

10. www.ucc.ie/celt/online/G303003/text001.html.

11. Cotterell, A., *The Encyclopedia of Mythology* (Lorenz, 1999), 131.

12. For an examination of aspects of the Fenian movement in the United States, see Steward, P. and B. McGovern, *The Fenians: Irish Rebellion in the North Atlantic World, 1858–1876* (University of Tennessee Press, 2013); Snay, M., *Fenians, Freedmen, and Southern Whites: Race and Nationality in the Era of Reconstruction* (Louisiana State University Press, 2007).

13. Green, M. J., op. cit., 98–9.

14. Monaghan, P., op. cit., 190.

15. MacKillop, J., *Myths and Legends of the Celts* (Penguin, 2005), 229–34, provides an overview of the folklore development of the character and adventures of Finn.

16. MacKillop, J., op. cit., 115.

12. The Cycles of the Kings: Tales of the Traditional Kings of Ireland

1. www.maryjones.us/jce/cyclekings.html.
2. Dillon, M., *The Cycles of the Kings* (Oxford University Press, 1946).
3. Bruford, A., *Gaelic Folk-Tales and Medieval Romances* (Folklore of Ireland Society, 1969).
4. So called because Brian was of the *Dál Cais* (or *Dál gCais*), also known as the *Dalcassians*, one of the royal free tribes of Munster.
5. Cross, T. P. and C. H. Slover, *Ancient Irish Tales* (Henry Holt, 1936).
6. Joyce, T., *The Poems of Sweeny, Peregrine: A Working of the Corrupt Irish Text* (New Writers' Press, 1976).
7. Heaney, S., *Sweeney Astray: A Version from the Irish* (Field Day Theatre, 1983).
8. MacKillop, J., *Myths and Legends of the Celts* (Penguin, 2005), 245.
9. Twadell Shipley, J., *The Origins of English Words: A Discursive Dictionary of Indo-European Roots* (Johns Hopkins University Press, 1984), 194. In Modern Irish the word is *leipreachán* and it derives from *luchorpán* (plural *luchorpáin*).
10. Dunn, J., 'The Brendan Problem', *Catholic Historical Review* (Catholic University of America Press, 1921), vol. 6, 439.
11. Genesis 9:25 (New International Version, Hodder & Stoughton, 1979).
12. Koch, J. T., *Celtic Culture: A Historical Encyclopedia*, 5 vols (ABC-CLIO, 2006), vol. 3, 1199–200.
13. Ibid., 1200.
14. Lehane, B., *Early Celtic Christianity* (Continuum International, 1968), 37.
15. Monaghan, P., *The Encyclopedia of Celtic Mythology and Folklore* (Facts On File, 2004), 357.
16. www.maryjones.us/ctexts/crimthann.html.

13. Myth, Legend and History in the Post-Roman Twilight: Arthur, King of Britain

1. Alcock, L., *Arthur's Britain* (Allen Lane, 1971).
2. Ashe, G. (ed.), *The Quest for Arthur's Britain* (Granada, 1971).

3. Morris, J., *The Age of Arthur* (Weidenfeld & Nicolson, 1973).

4. Ashe, G., *The Discovery of King Arthur* (Guild, 1985); a theory first proposed in 1981.

5. Barber, R., *The Figure of Arthur* (D. S. Brewer, 1972).

6. Dumville, D. N., 'Sub-Roman Britain: History and Legend', *History*, 62 (1977), 173–92.

7. Sims-Williams, P., 'Gildas and the Anglo-Saxons', *Cambridge Medieval Celtic Studies* (University of Cambridge, Department of Anglo-Saxon, Norse and Celtic), 6 (1983), 1–30.

8. Yorke, B., 'Fact or Fiction? The Written Evidence for the Fifth and Sixth Centuries AD', *Anglo-Saxon Studies in Archaeology and History*, 6 (1993), 45–50.

9. Higham, N. J., *King Arthur: Myth-Making and History* (Routledge, 2002), 3.

10. Barber, R., op. cit., 59–60.

11. Higham, N. J., op. cit., 118.

12. An attribution dismissed as a late forgery in Dumville, D. N., 'Some Aspects of the Chronology of the Historia Brittonum', *Bulletin of the Board of Celtic Studies*, 25 (1974), 439–45.

13. Padel, O. J., *Arthur in Medieval Welsh Literature* (University of Wales Press, 2000), 6.

14. Higham, N. J., op. cit., 146.

15. Ibid., 165.

16. Halsall, G., *Worlds of Arthur* (Oxford University Press, 2013), 168–73.

17. Higham, N. J., op. cit., 136.

18. Alcock, L., op. cit., 57.

19. Ibid.

20. Charles-Edwards, T., 'The Arthur of History', in R. Bromwich, A. O. H. Jarman and B. F. Roberts (eds), *The Arthur of the Welsh* (University of Wales Press, 1991), 25.

21. Higham, N. J., op. cit., 95.

22. Llyfrgell Genedlaethol Cymru/The National Library of Wales, Aberystwyth, Wales, www.llgc.org.uk /index. php?id=blackbookofcarmarthen.

23. Barber, R., op. cit., 68.

24. Sims-Williams, P., 'The Early Welsh Arthurian Poems', in R. Bromwich, A. O. H. Jarman and B. F. Roberts (eds), *The Arthur of the Welsh* (University of Wales Press, 1991), 49.

25. Barber, R., op. cit., 70.

26. See Padel, O. J., op. cit., 51, 56.

27. Ibid., 40.

28. Korrel, P., *An Arthurian Triangle: A Study of the Origin, Development, and Characterization of Arthur, Guinevere, and Modred* (Brill, 1984), 49.

29. Bryden, I., *Reinventing King Arthur: The Arthurian Legends in Victorian Culture* (Ashgate, 2005), 10. The connection of Arthur with Glastonbury was further reinforced when Gerald of Wales, in *On the Instruction of Princes* (*Liber de Principis Instructione*), *c.*1195, stated that Glastonbury was the site of Avalon, where the dying Arthur had been taken. He even claimed that Arthur's body had recently been exhumed there. Before this, Avalon was presented as a vague Otherworld place without specific geographical location. He also claimed that its English name was a translation of a Welsh original ('glassy isle') and meant 'fort of glass'.

30. Sims-Williams, P., 'The Early Welsh Arthurian Poems', op. cit., 60–1.

31. Lacy, N. J. (ed.), *The Arthurian Encyclopedia* (Boydell Press, 1988), 209–10, 214, 382–5.

14. Welsh Mythological Heroes of the *Mabinogi*

1. An excellent modern translation, accompanied by explanatory notes, is Davies, S. (trans.), *The Mabinogion* (Oxford University Press, 2007).

2. www.bbc.co.uk/wales/history/sites/themes/society/myths_mabinogion.shtml.

3. Davies, S., op. cit., x.

4. For an examination of the works of Chrétien, see Staines, D., *The Complete Romances of Chrétien de Troyes* (Indiana University Press, 1990).

5. Davies, S., op. cit., 4.

6. Monaghan, P., *The Encyclopedia of Celtic Mythology and Folklore* (Facts On File, 2004), 112.

7. Ibid., 237.

8. Miles-Watson, J., *Welsh Mythology: A Neostructuralist Analysis* (Cambria Press, 2009), 50.

9. Davies, S., op. cit., 8.
10. For an examination of the significance of this mound in more than one story, see Green, M. J., *Celtic World* (Routledge, 1995), 789.
11. Concerning the uncertainty of the actual location, see Bollard, J. K., *The Mabinogi: Legend and Landscape of Wales* (Gomer Press, 2006), 24.
12. For a comparison of the roles of Gwawl and Hafgan, see Miles-Watson, J., op. cit., 53.
13. Davies, S., op. cit., 23.
14. Leeming, D., *The Oxford Companion to World Mythology* (Oxford University Press, 2005), 54–5.
15. Green, M. J., op. cit., 789.
16. www.archeurope.com/index.php?page=gundestrup-cauldron.
17. Jenkins, D. (ed. and trans.), *The Law of Hywel Dda* (Gomer Press, 1986), 6.
18. Davies, S., op. cit., 46.
19. Leeming, D., *From Olympus to Camelot: The World of European Mythology* (Oxford University Press, 2003), 91.

15. Where Myth Meets History: Legendary Welsh Stories

1. Slotkin, E., 'The Fabula, Story and Text of Breuddwyd Rhonabwy', *Cambridge Medieval Celtic Studies* (University of Cambridge, Department of Anglo-Saxon, Norse and Celtic), 18 (1989), 98.
2. Reno, F. D., *The Historic King Arthur: Authenticating the Celtic Hero of Post-Roman Britain* (McFarland, 2007), 317. See also: Gantz, J., *The Mabinogion* (Penguin, 1976), 114.
3. Bollard, J. K., *The Mabinogi: Legend and Landscape of Wales* (Gomer Press, 2006), 76.
4. Monaghan, P., *The Encyclopedia of Celtic Mythology and Folklore* (Facts On File, 2004), 39.
5. http://projecteliseg.org/wp-content/themes/thematic/reading/rethinking-the-pillar.pdf. This contains a detailed analysis of the pillar and its inscription: Edwards, N., 'Rethinking the Pillar of Eliseg', *Antiquaries Journal*, 89 (2009).
6. www.dafyddiwan.com/english/index.html. Words by Dafydd Iwan, copyright Cyhoeddiadau Sain.

7. See Higham, N., *The English Conquest: Gildas and Britain in the Fifth Century* (Manchester University Press, 1994).
8. Padel, O. J., *Arthur in Medieval Welsh Literature* (University of Wales Press, 2000), 16–17.
9. Davies, S., 'Performing Culhwch ac Olwen', in C. Lloyd-Morgan, *Arthurian Literature XXI: Celtic Arthurian Material* (D. S. Brewer, 2004), 50.
10. Gerritsen, W. P., A. G. Van Melle and T. Guest, *A Dictionary of Medieval Heroes: Characters in Medieval Narrative Traditions and Their Afterlife in Literature, Theatre and the Visual Arts* (Boydell Press, 2000), 91.
11. Davies, S. (trans.), *The Mabinogion* (Oxford University Press, 2007), 195–200.
12. Ibid., xxiii.
13. Tristram, H. L. C., *The Celtic Languages in Contact* (Universitätsverlag Potsdam, 2007), 15.
14. Davies, S., op. cit., 189.
15. Ibid., 217.

16. Where Welsh Myth Meets 'Romance'

1. http://medievalwriting.50megs.com/word/romance.htm.
2. Davies, S. (trans.), *The Mabinogion* (Oxford University Press, 2007), xi.
3. Ibid., xxiv.
4. Lacy, N. J. (ed.), *The Arthurian Encyclopedia* (Boydell Press, 1988), 257–8.
5. Lovecy, I., 'Historia Peredur ab Efrawg', in R. Bromwich, A. O. H. Jarman and B. F. Roberts (eds), *The Arthur of the Welsh* (University of Wales Press, 1991), 176.
6. Ibid., 180.
7. Middleton, R., 'Chwedl Geraint ab Erbin', in R. Bromwich, A. O. H. Jarman and B. F. Roberts (eds), *The Arthur of the Welsh* (University of Wales Press, 1991), 151.
8. Lacy, N. J. (ed.), op. cit., 215.
9. Davies, S., op. cit., 258.
10. Middleton, R., op. cit., 148.
11. Bitel, L. M., *Land of Women: Tales of Sex and Gender from Early Ireland* (Cornell University Press, 1996), 214. Although there have been suggestions that this should not be overstressed

– for example, Dooley, A., *Playing the Hero: Reading the Irish Saga Táin Bó Cúailnge* (University of Toronto Press, 2006), 224–5 – it is the usual interpretation of her role within Irish mythology.

12. Davies, S., op. cit., 138.
13. Thomson, R. L., 'Owain: Chwedl Iarlles y Ffynnon', in R. Bromwich, A. O. H. Jarman and B. F. Roberts (eds), *The Arthur of the Welsh* (University of Wales Press, 1991), 160, 164, 166.
14. Ibid., 160.

17. Heroes and Villains of the Welsh Triads

1. Le Saux, F. H. M., *Layamon's Brut: The Poem and its Sources* (Boydell & Brewer, 1989), 146.
2. The classic scholarly account of the triads is: Bromwich, R., *Trioedd Ynys Prydein: The Triads of the Island of Britain* (3rd rev. edn, University of Wales Press, 2006). An accessible online presentation (by Mary Jones) of the triads in the *Red Book of Hergest* can be found at: www.ancienttexts.org/library/celtic/ctexts/triads1.html. This is based on: Rhys, J. and J. G. Evans (eds), *The Text of the Mabinogion and Other Welsh Tales from the Red Book of Hergest* (Series of Welsh Texts 1, J. G. Evans, 1887). A selection of triads (in both Welsh and English translations) that have been translated by Siân Echard can be found, accompanied by a short introduction, at: http://faculty.arts.ubc.ca/sechard/492triad.htm. These last two sources have been used in the exploration of the triads in this chapter.
3. Le Saux, F. H. M., op. cit., 146–7.
4. An outline of the dating of these manuscripts by Rachel Bromwich and others can be found in Reno, F. D., *The Historic King Arthur: Authenticating the Celtic Hero of Post-Roman Britain* (McFarland, 2007), 194.
5. Snyder, C. A., *The Britons* (Wiley, 2003), 263.
6. Lacy, N. J., *A History of Arthurian Scholarship* (Boydell & Brewer, 2006), 82.
7. Snyder, C. A., op. cit., 263.
8. Ibid.
9. Le Saux, F. H. M., op. cit., 146.
10. Quoted in Reno, F. D., op. cit., 194.
11. Echard, S., op. cit.

12. Jones, M., op. cit.; Rhys, J. and J. G. Evans, op. cit.
13. Leeming, D., *From Olympus to Camelot: The World of European Mythology* (Oxford University Press, 2003), 91.
14. Echard, S., op. cit.
15. Barber, R., *The Figure of Arthur* (D. S. Brewer, 1972), 71.
16. Ashe, G., *A Guidebook to Arthurian Britain* (Longman, 1980), 6.
17. Barber, R., op. cit., 71.
18. Jones, M., op. cit.; Rhys, J. and J. G. Evans, op. cit.
19. First given this family relationship by Geoffrey of Monmouth in his *History of the Kings of Britain* (*Historia Regum Britanniae*), c.1136.
20. Jones, M., op. cit.; Rhys, J. and J. G. Evans, op. cit.
21. Bromwich, R., *Trioedd Ynys Prydein: The Triads of the Island of Britain* (University of Wales Press, 1961), 341.
22. Clancy, T., 'A Fragmentary Literature: Narrative and Lyric from the Early Middle Ages', in I. Brown, T. Clancy, S. Manning and M. Pittock (eds), *The Edinburgh History of Scottish Literature, Volume One: From Columba to the Union (Until 1707)* (Edinburgh University Press, 2007), 127.
23. Stenton, F. M., *Anglo-Saxon England* (Oxford University Press, 1971), 64.

18. The Mythology of the North

1. See Snow, D. R., 'Scotland's Irish Origins', *Archaeology*, 54: 4 (July/August 2001). As with so much in this period of history, this view has not gone unchallenged. At the same time as it was being restated, Glasgow University's Ewan Campbell argued that the account of Irish settlement of Argyll was actually based on elite-origin myths and that archaeological evidence was lacking for Irish settlement. If anything, he suggested, the movement was the other way. See *Glasgow Herald*, 11 June 2001. What is clear, however, is that Scotland and north-east Ireland have strong connections, whether the accounts of the foundation of Dál Riata were based on fact or on political spin.
2. Fraser, J. E., *From Caledonia to Pictland: Scotland to 795* (Edinburgh University Press, 2009), 144–9.
3. For an overview of this discussion of the Picts' linguistic origins, see Nicolaisen, W., 'Pictish', in K. Brown and S. Ogilvie, *Concise Encyclopedia of Languages of the World* (Elsevier, 2009),

855–6; Dunbavin, P., *Picts and Ancient Britons: An Exploration of Pictish Origins* (Third Millennium, 1998), 15–18.

4. Dunbavin, P., op. cit., 15.

5. Lynch, M., *Scotland, A New History* (Pimlico, 1992), 15.

6. Fouracre, P. (ed.), *The New Cambridge Medieval History: Volume 1: c.500–c.700* (Cambridge University Press, 2005), 232.

7. Fraser, J. E., op. cit., 53.

8. Robinson, M. (ed.), *Concise Scots Dictionary* (Edinburgh University Press, 2005), 336.

9. Eberhart, G. M., *Mysterious Creatures: A Guide to Cryptozoology* (ABC-CLIO, 2002), 580.

10. Ibid.

11. Adomnán, *Life of St Columba*, trans. R. Sharpe (Penguin Classics, 1995).

12. Ferguson, R., *Chasing the Wild Goose: The Story of the Iona Community* (Wild Goose, 2001), 25–6.

13. See Bradley, I. C., *Celtic Christianity: Making Myths and Chasing Dreams* (Edinburgh University Press, 1999), 20.

14. Monaghan, P., *The Encyclopedia of Celtic Mythology and Folklore* (Facts On File, 2004), 53.

15. MacKenzie, D. A., *Scottish Wonder Tales from Myth and Legend* (Dover, 1997; an unabridged republication of *Wonder Tales From Scottish Myth and Legend*, Frederick A. Stokes, 1917).

16. Ibid., 10–11.

17. Ibid., 22–30.

18. Monaghan, P., op. cit., 166.

19. MacKenzie, D. A., op. cit., 17.

20. Ibid., 19.

21. Ibid., 11–12.

22. www.orkneyjar.com/folklore/finfolk/mermaid.html.

23. www.orkneyjar.com/folklore/selkiefolk/index.html.

24. MacKenzie, D. A., op. cit., 16.

25. Monaghan, P., op. cit., 53.

26. www.girlguiding.org.uk/about_us/key_information/history.aspx.

27. Monaghan, P., op. cit., 62.

28. Avant, G. R., *A Mythological Reference* (Author House, 2005), 471.

29. Robinson, M. (ed.), *Chambers 21st Century Dictionary* (Allied, 2006), 742.
30. MacKenzie, D. A., op. cit., 12.
31. Wood, J., 'The Arthurian Legend in Scotland and Cornwall', in H. Fulton (ed.), *A Companion to Arthurian Literature* (Wiley, 2012), 103–4.
32. Ibid., 108.
33. Gillies, W., 'Arthur in Gaelic Tradition, Part II: Romances and Learned Lore', *Cambridge Medieval Celtic Studies* (University of Cambridge, Department of Anglo-Saxon, Norse and Celtic), 3 (1982), 41–75.
34. For a detailed examination of these sites in the landscape, see Ashe, G., *A Guidebook to Arthurian Britain* (Longman, 1980).
35. Chambers, E. K., *Arthur of Britain* (Sidgwick & Jackson, 1927), 228.
36. Potter, B., *The Tale of Squirrel Nutkin* (Frederick Warne, 1987 [1903]), 50.

19. The Mythology of the 'West Welsh': Cornish Myths and Legends

1. Fouracre, P. (ed.), *The New Cambridge Medieval History: Volume 1: c.500–c.700* (Cambridge University Press, 2005), 232.
2. Bradbury, J., *The Routledge Companion to Medieval Warfare* (Routledge, 2004), 4.
3. Wood, J., 'The Arthurian Legend in Scotland and Cornwall', in H. Fulton (ed.), *A Companion to Arthurian Literature* (Wiley, 2012), 109–10.
4. For a detailed description of the tale and its history, see Lacy, N. J. (ed.), *The Arthurian Encyclopedia* (Boydell Press, 1988), 575–8.
5. Wood, J., op. cit., 110.
6. Ibid.
7. Benton, J. F., *Self and Society in Medieval France: The Memoirs of Abbot Guibert of Nogent* (University of Toronto Press, 1984), 191, n. 1; Barber, R., *King Arthur Hero and Legend* (Boydell Press, 1986), 16.
8. Simpson, R., *Camelot Regained* (D. S. Brewer, 1990), 93.

9. Hunt, R., *Popular Romances of the West of England: The Drolls, Traditions and Superstitions of Old Cornwall* (Felinfach, 1865; repr. Chatto & Windus, 1923, and Forgotten Books, 2008), vol. II, 186.

10. For example, in *Don Quixote*, I, ii, 5. English translations from the Spanish have varied in their identification of the bird mentioned as being either a raven or a crow.

11. Loomis, R. S., 'Arthurian Tradition and Folklore', *Folklore*, 69 (1958), 16–17.

12. Hunt, R., op. cit., 309.

13. Chambers, E. K., *Arthur of Britain* (Sidgwick & Jackson, 1927), 229.

14. Hunt, R., op. cit., 238–9.

15. www.robertstephenhawker.co.uk/?page_id=2011.

16. Jones, R., *Myths and Legends of Britain and Ireland* (New Holland, 2006), 17.

17. Naylor, R. and J. Naylor, *From John O' Groats to Land's End* (Echo Library, 2007), 489–90.

18. Hope, R. C., *Legendary Lore of the Holy Wells of England Including Rivers, Lakes, Fountains and Springs* (Kessinger, 2003 [1893]), 29.

19. Ashe, G., *The Landscape of King Arthur* (Webb & Bower, 1987), 145.

20. Whitlock, R., *In Search of Lost Gods: A Guide to British Folklore* (Phaidon, 1979), 47.

21. Lacy, N. J. (ed.), op. cit., 557.

22. Hunt, R., op. cit., 113–14.

23. Ibid., 450–1.

24. Ibid., 237.

25. The matter may have been even more complex with the healing stories invented relatively recently in order to attempt to explain the significance of the stones. The one at Men-an-Tol was probably formed from a restructured Neolithic tomb and the hole in the Tolvan Stone may have been enlarged in relatively recent times. See Hutton, R., *The Pagan Religions of the Ancient British Isles* (Basil Blackwell, 1991), 294–5.

26. Hunt, R., op. cit., 49.

27. Ibid.

20. The Mythology of the Isle of Man

1. Koch, J. T. and A. Minard, *The Celts: History, Life, and Culture* (ABC-CLIO, 2012), 310.
2. Or *Fir Fálgae*.
3. Koch, J. T. and A. Minard, op. cit., 311.
4. Morrison, S., *Manx Fairy Tales* (David Nutt, 1911), 16. For a very useful version of this work, see www.isle-of-man.com/manxnotebook/fulltext/sm1911/index.htm.
5. Koch, J. T. and A. Minard, op. cit., 311.
6. Morrison, S., op. cit., 171.
7. Moore, A. W., *The Folklore of the Isle of Man* (David Nutt, 1891), 1. For a very useful version of this work, see www.isle-ofman.com/manxnotebook/fulltext/folklore/index.htm.
8. Morrison, S., op. cit., 16.
9. Roeder, C. (ed.), *Manx Notes & Queries* (S. K. Broadbent, 1904), n. 216.
10. www.kayak.im/sound.php.
11. www.gov.im/mnh/heritage/countryside/sound/mythslegends.xml.
12. Morrison, S., op. cit., 153.
13. Ibid., 8.
14. Ibid., 48.
15. Isaiah 34:14a, New International Version (Hodder & Stoughton, 1979).
16. Campbell, J. F., *Popular Tales of the West Highlands* (Edmonston and Douglas, 1860), lv.
17. Moore, A. W., op. cit., 33.
18. Waldron, G., *A Description of the Isle of Man* (1731), 39.
19. Roeder, C. (ed.), op. cit., n. 189.
20. Morrison, S., op. cit., 93.
21. Moore, A. W., op. cit., 33.
22. Morrison, S., op. cit., 85.
23. Roeder, C. (ed.), op. cit., n. 189.
24. Moore, A. W., op. cit., 33.
25. Roeder, C. (ed.), op. cit., n. 13, n. 14.
26. Morrison, S., op. cit., 93.
27. Campbell, J. F., op. cit., liii–lv
28. Morrison, S., op. cit., 71.
29. Waldron, G., op. cit., 14–15.

30. Morrison, S., op. cit., 129. This story was recorded earlier in Waldron, G., op. cit.

21. The Mythology of Brittany

1. MacKillop, J., *Myths and Legends of the Celts* (Penguin, 2005), 298.
2. Berresford Ellis, P., *The Mammoth Book of Celtic Myths and Legends* (Robinson, 2002). For a persuasive explanation for this point of view see 510.
3. MacKillop, J., op. cit., 300.
4. Ibid., 301.
5. Hutcheson, E., *The Literature of the Piano* (Knopf, 1981), 314.
6. Retold in Berresford Ellis, P., op. cit., 545–51.
7. Kennedy, P., *Legendary Fictions of the Irish Celts* (Macmillan, 1891), 86.
8. Lacy, N. J. (ed.), *The Arthurian Encyclopedia* (Boydell Press, 1988), 67.
9. Ibid.
10. Moorman, C. and R. Moorman, *An Arthurian Dictionary* (University Press of Mississippi, 1978), 24.
11. Ibid.
12. Lacy, N. J. (ed.), op. cit., 615–16.
13. This story is retold in Berresford Ellis, P., op. cit., 522–44.
14. Ibid., 543.
15. See Bryce, D., *Celtic Folk Tales from Armorica* (Llanerch, 1985).
16. Buck Baker, W., *Celtic Mythological Influences on American Theatre 1750–1875: Chwedioniaeth Geltaidd Dylanwad Ar Chwaraedy Americanaidd 1750–1875* (University Press of America, 1994), 36.
17. See Luzel, F. M., 'Koadalan', *Revue Celtique*, 1 (1870–1), 106–31; Bryce, D., op. cit., 70–84.

SELECT BIBLIOGRAPHY

Adams Leeming, D., *The Oxford Companion to World Mythology* (Oxford University Press, 2005).

Archibald, E. and A. Putter (eds), *The Cambridge Companion to the Arthurian Legend* (Cambridge University Press, 2009).

Ashe, G., *A Guidebook to Arthurian Britain* (Longman, 1980).

——, *The Discovery of King Arthur* (Guild, 1985).

——, *The Landscape of King Arthur* (Webb & Bower, 1987).

——, *Mythology of the British Isles* (Methuen, 1990).

——, (ed.), *The Quest for Arthur's Britain* (Granada, 1971).

Avant, G. R., *A Mythological Reference* (Author House, 2005).

Barber, R., *The Figure of Arthur* (D. S. Brewer, 1972).

——, *King Arthur Hero and Legend* (Boydell Press, 1986).

Berresford Ellis, P., *The Mammoth Book of Celtic Myths and Legends* (Robinson, 2002).

Bollard, J. K., *The Mabinogi: Legend and Landscape of Wales* (Gomer Press, 2006).

Bonnefoy, Y., *American, African, and Old European Mythologies* (University of Chicago Press, 1993).

Bradley, I. C., *Celtic Christianity: Making Myths and Chasing Dreams* (Edinburgh University Press, 1999).

Brezina, C., *Celtic Mythology* (Rosen, 2008).

Bromwich, R., A. O. H. Jarman and B. F. Roberts (eds), *The Arthur of the Welsh* (University of Wales Press, 1991).

Cahill, M. A., *Paradise Rediscovered: The Roots of Civilisation, Vol. 1* (Glass House, 2012).

Carson, C. (trans.), *The Táin, A New Translation of the Táin Bó Cúailnge* (Penguin, 2007).

Charles-Edwards, T. M., *Early Christian Ireland* (Cambridge University Press, 2004).

Collis, J., *The Celts: Origins, Myths and Inventions* (Tempus, 2003).

Cotterell, A., *The Encyclopedia of Mythology* (Lorenz, 1999).

— —, *Mythology of the Celts: Myths and Legends of the Celtic World* (Southwater, 2007).

Csapo, E., *Theories of Mythology* (Wiley, 2005).

Cunliffe, B., *The Ancient Celts* (Oxford University Press, 1997).

Davies, S. (trans.), *The Mabinogion* (Oxford University Press, 2007).

DeLaney, F., *Legends of the Celts* (HarperCollins, 2008).

Doniger, W., et al., *Merriam-Webster's Encyclopedia of World Religions* (Merriam-Webster, 1999).

Eberhart, G. M., *Mysterious Creatures: A Guide to Cryptozoology* (ABC-CLIO, 2002).

Ellis Davidson, H. R., *Myths and Symbols in Pagan Europe: Early Scandinavian and Celtic Religions* (Manchester University Press, 1988).

Findon, J., *A Woman's Words: Emer and Female Speech in the Ulster Cycle* (University of Toronto Press, 1997).

Fulton, H. (ed.), *A Companion to Arthurian Literature* (Wiley, 2012).

Gandolfi, C. and J. Gershman, *Tales & Songs of Ireland* (Peter Pauper Press, 2002).

Gantz, J., *Early Irish Myths and Sagas* (Penguin Classics, 1981).

Green, M. J., *The Gods of the Celts* (Allan Sutton, 1986).

— —, *Symbol and Image in Celtic Religious Art* (Routledge, 1989).

— —, *Dictionary of Celtic Myth and Legend* (Thames & Hudson, 1992).

— —, *Celtic World* (Routledge, 1995).

— —, *The Gods of Roman Britain* (Osprey, 2008).

Grimal, P. (ed.), *Larousse World Mythology* (Hamlyn, 1971).

Halsall, G., *Worlds of Arthur* (Oxford University Press, 2013).

Harding, D. W., *The Archaeology of Celtic Art* (Routledge, 2007).

Haywood, J., *The Historical Atlas of the Celtic World* (Thames & Hudson, 2001).

Heaney, M. (ed.), *Over Nine Waves: A Book of Irish Legends* (Macmillan, 1995).

Henig, M., *Religion in Roman Britain* (Batsford, 1984).

Higham, N. J., *King Arthur: Myth-Making and History* (Routledge, 2002).

Hunt, R., *Popular Romances of the West of England: The Drolls, Traditions and Superstitions of Old Cornwall* (Felinfach, 1865, vol. II, repr. Chatto & Windus, 1923, and Forgotten Books, 2008).

Hutton, R., *The Pagan Religions of the Ancient British Isles* (Basil Blackwell, 1991).

——, *The Stations of the Sun* (Oxford University Press, 1996).

Jackson, K., *A Celtic Miscellany* (rev. edn, Penguin, 1971).

James, S., *The Atlantic Celts: Ancient People or Modern Invention?* (British Museum Press, 1999).

Jestice, P. G. (ed.), *Holy People of the World: A Cross-Cultural Encyclopedia* (ABC-CLIO, 2004).

Kinsella, T., *The Táin: From the Irish Epic Táin Bó Cúailnge* (Oxford University Press, 1969).

Koch, J. T., *Celtic Culture: A Historical Encyclopedia*, 5 vols (ABC-CLIO, 2006).

Korrel, P., *An Arthurian Triangle: A Study of the Origin, Development, and Characterization of Arthur, Guinevere, and Modred* (Brill, 1984).

Lacy, N. J., *A History of Arthurian Scholarship* (Boydell & Brewer, 2006).

—— (ed.), *The Arthurian Encyclopedia* (Boydell Press, 1988).

Leeming, D., *From Olympus to Camelot: The World of European Mythology* (Oxford University Press, 2003).

——, *The Oxford Companion to World Mythology* (Oxford University Press, 2005).

Lennon, J., *Irish Orientalism: A Literary and Intellectual History* (Syracuse University Press, 2004).

MacBain, A., *Celtic Mythology and Religion* (Cosimo, 2005).

MacCana, P., *Celtic Mythology* (Hamlyn, 1970).

MacCulloch, J. A., *Celtic Mythology* (Dover, 2004).

MacKillop, J., *Myths and Legends of the Celts* (Penguin, 2005).

Maier, B., *Dictionary of Celtic Religion and Culture* (trans. from German) (Boydell Press, 1997).

Matson, G. and J. Roberts, *Celtic Mythology A to Z* (Infobase, 2010).

Monaghan, P., *The Encyclopedia of Celtic Mythology and Folklore* (Facts On File, 2004).

Moorman, C. and R. Moorman, *An Arthurian Dictionary* (University Press of Mississippi, 1978).

Ó Hógáin, D., *The Sacred Isle: Belief and Religion in Pre-Christian Ireland* (Boydell Press, 1999).

Padel, O. J., *Arthur in Medieval Welsh Literature* (University of Wales Press, 2000).

Paice MacLeod, S., *Celtic Myth and Religion* (McFarland, 2012).

Pu, M., *Rethinking Ghosts in World Religions* (Brill, 2009).

Snyder, C. A., *The Britons* (Wiley, 2003).

Trevelyan, M., *Folk-Lore and Folk-Stories of Wales* (Kessinger, 1909).

Whitelock, D. (ed.), *English Historical Documents, Volume I, c.500–1042* (Eyre Methuen, 1979).

Whitlock, R., *In Search of Lost Gods: A Guide to British Folklore* (Phaidon, 1979).

Woodard, R. D., *Indo-European Sacred Space: Vedic and Roman Cult* (University of Illinois, 2006).

INDEX